D0325926

WEALTHY
&
WISE

WEALTHY

&

WISE

(secrets about money)

HEIDI L. STEIGER
NEUBERGER BERMAN

JOHN WILEY & SONS, INC.

Copyright © 2003 by Neuberger Berman. All rights reserved.

Published by John Wiley & Sons, Inc., Hoboken, New Jersey.
Published simultaneously in Canada.

No part of this publication may be reproduced, stored in a retrieval system or transmitted in any form or by any means, electronic, mechanical, photocopying, recording, scanning or otherwise, except as permitted under Sections 107 or 108 of the 1976 United States Copyright Act, without either the prior written permission of the Publisher, or authorization through payment of the appropriate per-copy fee to the Copyright Clearance Center, 222 Rosewood Drive, Danvers, MA 01923, (978) 750-8400, fax (978) 750-4470 or on the web at www.copyright.com. Requests to the Publisher for permission should be addressed to the Permissions Department, John Wiley & Sons, Inc., 111 River Street, Hoboken, NJ, 07030, (201) 748-6011, fax (201) 748-6008. e-mail: permcoordinator@wiley.com.

Limit of Liability/Disclaimer of Warranty: While the publisher and author have used their best efforts in preparing this book, they make no representations or warranties with respect to the accuracy or completeness of the contents of this book and specifically disclaim any implied warranties of merchantability or fitness for a particular purpose. No warranty may be created or extended by sales representatives or written sales materials. The advice and strategies contained herein may not be suitable for your situation. You should consult with a professional where appropriate. Neither the publisher nor author shall be liable for any loss of profit or any other commercial damages, including but not limited to special, incidental, consequential, or other damages.

For general information on our other products and services, or technical support, please contact our Customer Care Department within the United States at (800) 762-2974, outside the United States at (317) 572-3993 or fax (317) 572-4002.

Wiley also publishes its books in a variety of electronic formats. Some content that appears in print may not be available in electronic books.

Library of Congress Cataloging-in-Publication Data:

Wealthy & wise (secrets about money) / by Neuberger Berman.
      p.   cm.
   Includes index.
     ISBN 0-471-22141-4 (cloth : alk. paper)
     1. Finance, Personal.   I. Steiger, Heidi L.
   HG179 .W364 2002
   332.024'01—dc21

                                 2002009961

Printed in the United States of America.

10 9 8 7 6 5 4 3 2 1

To my parents, Lucille and Wilhelm Schwarzbauer,
who taught me so well.

PREFACE

Recently, a woman asked our firm to try to resolve a tangled situation that had started with the best of intentions. Eileen had launched a technology company a few years before, using seed money from her father. To minimize the tax implications of the seeding, Eileen and her father had established an intermediary trust vehicle. Included was a substantial number of shares in the new company. Eileen had placed the shares in trust for her young children.

The company grew faster than anyone had expected, and Eileen was able to sell the business at an astronomical profit. Suddenly she realized that her children were likely to have assets in the tens of millions of dollars by the time they graduated from high school. She worried that her children would lose all incentive to construct purposeful lives.

Eileen's tangled web had another worrisome complication: Her share of the proceeds from the sale of the business was mostly tied up in the new company's stock. Diversification of those assets needed careful and sensitive handling. Timing, taxes, where to invest, how to invest and with whom—the questions hit Eileen like an avalanche.

She was always capable and responsible in her business life, but in this new realm of serious personal wealth, she feared making mistakes. She recognized, as many wealthy people do, that the events that gave her this good fortune would probably never happen again. This wealth had to be preserved.

Through the years, I've noticed how fear and frustration often surround the subject of money—especially new money. Many wealthy individuals have a history of expending all their energy on their work. One day, they wake up and realize that they have become wealthy.

Their situation is enviable, but most people are completely unprepared for dealing with wealth. The interplay of money and emotions takes them on a roller coaster ride, and managing all that money raises their doubts and fears.

This phenomenon of "sudden wealth" has proliferated tremendously in the past decade. For the first time in our history, the landed gentry—those who inherit wealth—no longer dominate the upper echelons of money. As recently as the 1980s, 60 percent of the wealthy had inherited the majority of their fortune. Now, inheritors account for only about 20 percent.*

Despite the shock waves of recent years, the technology revolution and its related entrepreneurial fields have expanded the ranks of the newly wealthy. Given the economic wealth of a decade-long boom economy, monetary rewards at the top levels of many fields rose rapidly. At the same time, taxation was at its lowest rate in over 50 years.

These conditions have consequently created whole new images of wealthy persons.

Few people begin their adult years with a knack for how to handle wealth. The new clients who come to our offices usually have lots and *lots* of questions! Whether they have $1 million or $100 million, there's no correlation between the size of their fortune and their level of financial sophistication. They all need help because, for most people, investing their income and expanding their holdings wisely have not been the leading passions in their life.

If you have become a wealthy individual, you need to know how to make your wealth work *for* you. Without a degree of comfort with your wealth, your fear of making a mistake might easily progress to hesitation, doubt, and unhappiness.

This book will help you to avoid snags that might turn the boon of your wealth into the bane of your existence.

Each chapter offers wisdom and advice from an authority on wealth and its issues. In writing about their areas of expertise, the contributors explain the dos and don'ts in a way we can all understand. The chapters are independent essays, so you can browse through the book and concentrate on the topics that are pertinent to your situation.

The book is organized to tackle three primary aspects of monetary wealth. Part One focuses on the psychological issues that may arise: the interplay of emotions and objectivity. Part Two delves into the functional management of wealth: the workable medium between risk and

---

* *Source:* "Is the U.S. Income Gap Really a Big Problem?" by Sylvia Nasar, *New York Times,* April 4, 1999.

trust. Part Three explores how wealth can enrich your life as well as your portfolio: the combination of enjoyment and purpose.

The practical advice given here is supported by many real-life examples that illustrate how various concepts can be applied. You may not become an instant expert, but this book can help give you the confidence and comfort you need to achieve your life's dreams and perhaps to serve a higher purpose.

In closing, I am proud to say that all royalties and other proceeds from *Wealthy & Wise* received by Neuberger Berman are being donated to the National Foundation for Teaching Entrepreneurship (NFTE, pronounced "nifty"). NFTE's mission is to teach entrepreneurship to low-income young people, ages 11 through 18, so they can become economically productive members of society by improving their academic, business, technology, and life skills. To learn more about NFTE, visit them at http://www.nfte.com.

HEIDI L. STEIGER

New York, New York
September 2002

ACKNOWLEDGMENTS

The production of *Wealthy & Wise* has been a highly collaborative process, and I am pleased to acknowledge the assistance and input I have received from so many sources.

First, I thank my boss, Jeffrey Lane, and the Executive Committee of Neuberger Berman for believing in me and in the idea for this book. Second, I thank all of my investment colleagues and client consultants. Their experiences, over the years, helped me to decide what subjects to include herein. I owe special gratitude to the loyal and constructive clients of Neuberger Berman who have freely shared their experiences and insights.

I am grateful to the many friends and business associates who, for years, have been sources of advice, encouragement, and candor. Among those especially close to this project were: Janice Ellig, Paul Steiger, Marilyn Puder York, Jewelle Bickford, Nancy Amiel, Beverly Aisenbrey, Lynn and Nick Nicholas, Peter Levin, Alan Ronson, Steven Massarsky, Diana Murray, Steven Baldas, Kenny Slutsky, Pamela Sicher Cantor, Christina Seix, Robert Dow, and Gene Silverman.

When they look back on their career, most people say they were lucky to have one boss who, more than any other, guided them successfully and helped them achieve their career goals. My good fortune was to have five such bosses. Besides Jeff Lane, I owe thanks to Ron Ziemba, Roger Servison, Bud Fuhrman, and Dick Cantor. All of them made me wiser and made my long career enjoyable.

To me, the chapter authors in this book represent the height of professionalism and expertise in their respective areas of concentration. I appreciate their work and dedication. A number of people have been ongoing sources of assistance since the beginning of this project:

Andrea Trachtenberg, Margaret Towers, Jacqueline Strobel, Philip Maher, Peter Collins, and Frank Mangan. I also extend my thanks to Debra Englander at John Wiley & Sons.

Most of all, I want to thank my children, Isabelle and William. They give me simply the most joy I have ever known and a reason to spend every waking moment trying to be the best I can be.

H.L.S.

CONTENTS

PART ONE   THE DYNAMICS OF WEALTH   1

1. Clearing the Emotional Hurdles   5
   How to Turn Wealth's Conflicts into Opportunities
       Susan Remmer Ryzewic

2. Money and the Modern Family   17
   The Challenges of Parenting in a Wealthy Family
       Judith Stern Peck

3. The Business of Marriage   29
   Love Conquers All, But Assets Need Protection
       Robert Stephan Cohen

4. The Value of Work, Part I   42
   When You Love What You Do, Why Retire?
       Roy R. Neuberger

5. The Value of Work, Part II   50
   A Better Career the Second Time Around
       Janice Reals Ellig

6. When Giving Is Gaining   56
   A Strategic Approach to Philanthropy
       Ellen E. Remmer

7. Resolving Conflicts in a Family Enterprise   69
   Preserving Wealth and Relationships
       Fredda Herz Brown

8. Family Meetings That Work   80
   *Conducting Successful Discussions About Money and
   Other Sensitive Subjects*
       Dennis T. Jaffe, Stephen Goldbart, and Joan Indursky DiFuria

PART TWO   MANAGING YOUR WEALTH   95

9. Working with Professional Money Managers   99
   Balancing Control and Delegation
   Charlotte B. Beyer

10. How to Build a Winning Team of Financial Advisors   111
    A Collaborative Approach Yields the Best Results
    Charles A. Lowenhaupt

11. Balancing Act   122
    The Art of Asset Allocation
    Jonathan Spencer

12. Adding Real Estate to Your Investment Mix   140
    A Complement to Your Stock and Bond Portfolio
    Richard J. Adler

13. Wealth Management and Trusts   152
    Building a Legacy for the Ages
    Albert C. Bellas and Diane E. Lederman

14. Prudent Investing for Private Family Foundations   164
    Keeping an Even Keel in Stormy Markets
    Ralph D. Sinsheimer

15. Family Offices   179
    Why, When, and How
    Ellen M. Perry

16. Finding an Outstanding Trustee   191
    *What Wealthy Families Look for in a Trustee and
    How They Get It*
    John P. C. Duncan

PART THREE   PRIVATE LIVES   209

17. The Joy of Collecting   213
    From Simple Pleasures to Rare Treasures
    Kathleen M. Doyle

18. Collecting Contemporary Art   223
    Traditional Values, New Meaning
    I. Michael Danoff

19. Enjoying the Good Life   235
     Money and Time Well Spent
          Milton M. Ferrell, Jr.

20. Safe and Sound   248
     Developing a Sensible Strategy for Your Personal Security
          Milton M. Ferrell, Jr.

About the Editor   259
Index   261

PART ONE

The Dynamics of Wealth

If you are fortunate enough to have wealth, it should be just one among the many elements that constitute your life. Often, however, the "meaning" of wealth may get tangled up with your emotions and the emotions of the people around you. Everyone harbors vague assumptions about wealthy persons. Those assumptions have an odd way of becoming self-fulfilling prophecies unless a balance is established between the objective benefits of wealth and the emotional presumptions that can sour everything.

Emotions and objectivity: Almost everyone has a difficult time keeping these polar opposites in balance. When wealth enters the picture, finding and maintaining that balance can be overwhelming.

The road to wealth clearly allows only one-way passage. Once you've embarked on that road, going back to how you lived before—or, sometimes, even to who you were—can be very difficult. Once wealth enters the picture, individuals and families confront unfamiliar territory every step of the way.

Each stage of your journey has its own tug-of-war between emotions and objectivity. Part One of this book details the most important encounters.

Whether you're wrestling with how wealth is affecting you, your children, your marriage, your outlook on working, your philanthropic role in the world, or the preservation of a family legacy, the emotional impact of wealth must be openly, frankly, and objectively scrutinized.

When psychologists talk about the stages of adjustment to wealth, they use terms similar to those that describe traumatic events like divorce or a death in the family—events that are followed by stages of denial, anxiety, and euphoria before a healthy acceptance can begin. You might like to think of wealth as the "happily ever after" part of your personal story, but that won't be the case unless you're prepared.

Essentially, harnessing wealth requires establishing boundaries for yourself and others, and setting limits on requests and expectations. You must define your own rules of good conduct, leadership, and stewardship. By keeping these guidelines in mind, you can steer confidently through countless different situations.

With the first appearance of wealth in your life, people may treat you differently. Outsiders' presumptions about you and your wealth will often have no bearing on who you are. You will be confronted with requests for contributions, loans, and donations, many of which will put you in an awkward position. For example, given all the initial public offerings (IPOs) during the past 15 years, newly wealthy corporate executives frequently experience sudden inundations of requests. Word travels fast when a company goes public. Long before your stock options become reality, people will begin seeking you out—sometimes in extraordinarily bold and abrasive ways. They will pressure you to pledge contributions to myriad causes to which you had no previous connection. Their approach may take you by surprise; the wealth *they* see when they look at you may be part of the future, not necessarily the present. You may also begin to realize that, far too often, they aren't seeing *you;* they are seeing *money.*

Wealth can also chip away at longstanding friendships. Little things such as gift giving between you and your friends may become monumental stumbling blocks. Now that you're rich, they decide that nothing they could get you could possibly impress you. Now that you're rich, you wonder whether giving a simple gift (no matter how thoughtful) might be interpreted as your being cheap. Even after many years of friendship, newly acquired wealth can raise psychological barriers that need to be dispelled—possibly in words, but, more certainly, in actions. Invariably, you will need to initiate the dismantling process, and that role may annoy you. You may feel "put upon." Why should you be expected to fill a diplomat and peacemaker role when the effort to reaffirm friendship should be a celebratory transition?

Wealth will test everyone's integrity, patience, and understanding. It requires rebalancing emotions with objectivity.

Objectivity and rules of good conduct are especially needed to raise balanced, happy, productive children—children with purpose and without affectations. Every generation has its issues, regardless of money. The changes in society and in the way we live are contributing factors, but many people see this generation's children, particularly children of wealthy parents, growing up with less sturdy personal foundations. They hesitate to make attachments because various caregivers come and go while their parents work. They may tend to be physically inactive and easily distracted, and they may suffer when guidance and discipline are lacking.

Children learn by example; it's your responsibility to set an appropriate tone. If you regard your wealth as a functional, practical, *objective* part of your life, you will be giving your children the best possible chance to integrate that wealth productively into their own lives.

The person most directly and intimately affected by your wealth is your spouse or life partner. Compromise, common ground, respect, and love are heavily tested when a couple's financial status is unequal. Money shouldn't be used as an emotional weapon but, frequently, that's exactly what happens when substantial wealth is involved. Unless your marriage or relationship is built on a firmly balanced foundation of emotions and objectivity, you will be inviting immense and unnecessary strife in the event of a divorce or breakup.

Perhaps the most visible and telling evidence of your wealth—as seen by your children and others—is how you use your time. Has your productive involvement in life increased or decreased because of your wealth? Children, especially, will notice.

The essays in Part One offer two interesting views on the value of work. When you are wealthy, work may no longer be a compelling necessity, but your need for purpose and fulfillment should not change. Some newly wealthy individuals continue working just as they did before. (Roy Neuberger's chapter is a delightful and inspirational argument for this choice.) Others start new careers or pursue activities that were only avocations before. Wealth can also free you to devote your time and attention to philanthropic activities. That choice can greatly enhance and deepen a sense of stewardship that will ennoble you and inspire those around you.

The emotional challenges of wealth are probably most difficult for newly wealthy individuals, but those challenges never stop. What legacy do you want to leave the world? What legacy do you want to leave your children? Choosing your bequests presents a new set of challenges; however, the balancing of emotions and objectivity remains at the core. Perhaps the most difficult achievement is building and maintaining a family legacy. It requires ongoing, open communication; respect for the capabilities and talents of each family member; and a commitment to finding an emotional/objective balance among multiple individuals when it's difficult enough to find that balance within yourself! This section contains two illuminating and useful chapters on the related concepts of conflict resolution and conducting family meetings.

As you read the chapters in Part One, you will be considering several questions: How can you protect good friendships? How do you maintain a healthy alliance and respect with your spouse or partner? Are you guiding your children so that they will grow up with purpose and without affectations? Are you using your wealth to imbue your life with greater purpose and fulfillment?

If you want to be wealthy *and happy,* you need to guide your emotions with objectivity and soften your objectivity with the emotions that make you most content.

1

CLEARING THE EMOTIONAL HURDLES

How to Turn Wealth's Conflicts into Opportunities

SUSAN REMMER RYZEWIC

My teenage son refused to invite his community baseball team to our house for the end-of-the-season party last year. He was embarrassed, but not because our home is too small or too remote. We live in an exclusive part of an affluent suburb. Most of my son's teammates attend the local public schools; he goes to a private school. Our wealth makes him feel uncomfortable in his peer group. When developers began building a group of more opulent houses nearby, he commented, "Now my friends can see where rich people really live."

I sometimes experience a similar discomfort. As a manager of family assets, I dread being asked what I do for a living. One of the service providers I deal with calls me "the princess." Outsiders perceive my role as a "nonjob" job; I can coast along under a relaxed set of standards. I can see or hear people's surprise when I describe my education and business background or answer the work phone in the evening. Did they really presume that I was lazy, spoiled, and incompetent just because I inherited money? On the contrary, the heavy responsibility I feel for managing my family's assets makes me even more diligent and scrupulous than I would be if I were working for a corporate employer.

Without question, money solves more life problems than it causes. Wealth brings with it the opportunities and privileges of freedom and power, and the capacity for experience and accomplishments. The practical and intellectual issues involved in deciding how to spend, invest, donate, or save a fortune are readily embraced.

5

We've long been told that wealth is not automatically synonymous with happiness. People who are born to wealth—or who acquire it during their lifetime—are often surprised by unforeseen emotional conflicts related to their good fortune.

A lyric in an old Cyndi Lauper song warns: "Money changes everything." Wealth magnifies certain aspects of life to an unreal proportion. Where you might expect money to simplify matters, it often complicates ordinary decisions and day-to-day existence. Although money attracts people and facilitates new connections, it can often make you feel very much alone. The resolution of these apparent contradictions might lie in more open and direct communication, but, for a variety of social and personal reasons, money remains a very difficult subject to discuss. The emotional conflicts of wealth are seldom (if ever) completely eliminated, but a constructive confrontation of the issues—and of oneself—can help ensure that money *facilitates* happiness rather than undermining it.

THE LESSONS OF EXPERIENCE

The conclusions I present here are based largely on my personal experience and my conversations with others. In the 1950s, my father started a contract engineering business that built synthetic fiber plants at various international locations. Through good years and bad years, the business was an integral part of my family's life. It affected the ways we functioned and defined ourselves, regardless of whether we actually worked there. The value of the business grew, and we enjoyed a comfortable upper-middle-class existence. As children, we did not have immediate access to cash, but we were engrained with the reasonable expectation that money would not be a worry and, one day, we would inherit more than we could earn or save. As it turned out, we gained access to liquidity when we sold my father's business a year and a half after his death.

We welcomed the wealth, but we were jarred by some of the unexpected emotions that emerged. Depending on their connection to the business, the family members felt varying degrees of loss after the sale. My father had made all financial decisions on our behalf; we now had to forge new methods of making decisions together. Each of us had to deal with the impact of the wealth on our life. The process has provided ongoing life lessons in pleasure and pain. Following are a few of the things I have learned.

MINIMIZING THE DISTORTIONS

Money has the potential to magnify some of life's opportunities and challenges; it can make positive experiences better and negative experiences worse. Like a lack of money, an abundance of wealth can dominate other aspects of life. Money makes it easy to subordinate or postpone decisions about more central issues such as career, personal satisfaction, health, and relationships. To reach a balanced response, you first have to recognize the extremes.

When a person reaches the age at which a career would normally begin, money can accelerate or delay professional development. On the fast track, he or she can afford to take a low-paying job or an internship to develop contacts and skills, or can perhaps gain easier access to professional opportunities through personal connections. But because a wealthy young person is likely to have less work experience, the process of conforming to imposed rules and adjusting to day-to-day workplace routines can take longer than it would for someone who depended on earned income for pocket money or educational expenses during adolescence.

At any age, independent income creates the freedom to pursue a true vocation and make a positive difference in a field such as art, education, or public service. I know someone who was brought up in a business track and recently ended a 15-year stint as a real estate developer to pursue a new career in teaching. He is proving to be much better at teaching than at developing, he says, because this time he loves what he's doing. When parental or self-imposed expectations get in the way, the result can be paralysis rather than progress.

Even after career choices are made, it may be difficult to invest the time and energy needed for training and practice; the financial return from the work is likely to be dwarfed by income from other sources. A friend's son—a young man who had no financial need to commit to a career—chose to be a professional athlete, then a stockbroker, and then a sports agent, within a short period of time. In the end, he gave in to what he perceived as the easy way and joined the family business.

Wealth, particularly in one's initial encounter with it, can turn the pleasure of acquisition into an obsession. When cost need not be a consideration, wardrobes, real estate holdings, required garage spaces, and travel budgets tend to grow. Purchases are made and possessions are replaced not out of necessity, but out of a preference for newer, bigger, or better choices. Superficial appearances may take on new importance as a person confronts a prevalent social attitude—for example, people with money should never be overweight, unkempt, or looking any less than their personal best.

In the other extreme, some wealthy people go overboard to keep their wealth concealed. I know of a young attorney who had significant independent means but insisted that his family had to live in a house that was consistent with the earnings of a first-year associate at a law firm. He deliberately denied himself and his family a level of comfort he could easily afford. He was concerned that a more obvious display of his means might influence his firm's view of his dedication to his career and his compensation requirements.

The challenges of instilling good values about money in children escalate with wealth. Private-school peers may share experiences of toys, cars, and vacations that create unrealistic expectations in your child. Striking a healthy balance between indulgence and beneficial deprivation is not easy. Given their perceived safety net of family wealth, some professionals might be motivated to take some productive risks as possible professional choices. One acquaintance worked first as an investment banker and then decided to follow his true passion: working as a public policy analyst (unpaid) for a think tank. My sister, whose early career was in management consulting, was able to pursue her first interest, philanthropy counseling, once our family wealth became more liquid.

Other professionals might be less impelled toward a career and more tempted by risks that are ultimately dangerous or destructive. A friend who has a large trust fund earned two master's degrees but has never committed to a full-time job, choosing instead to bounce between part-time jobs and to pursue meaning in the adrenalin rush generated by somewhat risky activities such as bungee jumping and skydiving. Be aware that the way you use and talk about money, as well as your decision on whether to work, will also shape your children's views.

Money magnifies vulnerability and suspicion. If you are by nature a trusting person, you may be prey to people who are unworthy of your faith in them. They may pretend to care about you when they only want to get something from you. More skeptical types can approach paranoia in thinking that their money is the only thing that attracts people to them.

Minimizing money's tendency to distort other life issues requires a strong sense of self, a clear set of goals, and an articulated path for using your wealth to get you where you want to be. A first step is your ac-knowledgment that you control whether wealth will be a positive or neg-ative life force. Identify at least three things you value most—family, health, spirituality, friendships, the environment, human rights, animal rights, art, or whatever else you are closest to—and make these things your primary focus. Defined priorities should impose a discipline that puts true desires and dreams ahead of hastily acquired material posses-sions. Trite though it may sound, you need to find your passion and then direct your actions and your resources toward pursuing it.

SIMPLIFYING THE COMPLICATIONS

Money makes life easier but not necessarily simpler. The perceived freedom of wealth often conflicts with the reality of increased de-mands and pressures to choose from a nearly unlimited range of op-tions. Empowerment is accompanied by high expectations—your own and other people's. When you are rich, people find you and want to talk to you—about joining boards, making donations, sponsoring causes, managing your affairs, hosting events, introducing them to other people. In addition, you have your own interests to pursue: fam-ily, career, friends, travel, education, self-improvement. Day-to-day life has more dimensions—and details—with multiple homes, cars, boats, planes, investments, trusts, taxes, social obligations, and philanthropy. The natural tendency to embrace opportunities can lead to overcom-mitment. Don't diffuse your time and energy to the point where you are doing too much and accomplishing nothing.

Defining priorities, and developing the discipline to refuse offers that fall beyond them, will keep you focused and help you to complete the things you want and need to do. Your priorities and passions should also direct your decisions on where to live, where to travel, and whom to see. The most critical questions, however, are: How will you spend your time? and Will you work?

We commonly define ourselves and others in terms of occupation. When your daily routine does not depend on having a job, however, the definition of *occupation* and its relationship to worth becomes very complicated. In our capitalist structure, a person's worth is measured by a salary. But money is a commodity; human beings also need to be valued for something unique to their individual minds and hearts. If you do not have to work for food or rent, and you have not yet discov-ered a passion that drives you to work, you still need a direction for your life. There is a limit to the amount of time anyone can spend exercising or socializing.

This is one of the main reasons wealthy people become involved in philanthropy; they are not just distributing their wealth, they are validating their existence by focusing their energies and making an impact in some realm. If your focus leads to full-time volunteering or caregiving, you have to be sure that the value of the emotional satisfaction or social validation you derive compensates adequately for the absence of a worth assigned objectively by the marketplace. Choosing to work for pay, on the other hand, requires you to discover how you will define motivation and success.

Money makes relationships more complicated, too. It can shift the balance of power between mates and create conflicts over who controls it, who benefits from it, and who is entitled to it. The traditional "breadwinner" role may be diminished by inherited wealth, thereby undermining the working partner's sense of contribution and self-worth. Friends at different levels of wealth also face challenges to their relationships. Those with more may fear offending those with less. Those with less may fear appearing to expect assistance.

Money as power is a paradox. In the macro social sense, the power can effect positive social and political change; in the micro interpersonal sense, this power is easily misused and potentially destructive, especially when actions are not aligned with words. Wealthy people may claim they are just like everyone else but then act as if they expect to be exempt from common standards, thereby fueling resentment and rancor in those around them.

These complications, combined with the absence of a need to work, can bury a person and may lead to a passive and unsatisfactory use of resources. To steer clear of a quagmire, you need to develop both passions and priorities.

AVOIDING ISOLATION AND ALIENATION

Remember Richie Rich, the "poor little rich boy" of long-ago comics? Like all caricatures, the exaggeration had a foundation in truth. Wealth can alienate you from others, within your family and outside of it, and even from yourself. Wealth attracts people like a magnet, but it can leave you feeling very much alone. Nurturing of the connections you want to maintain requires a concerted effort, along with an understanding of mutual terms and expectations.

To some extent, money's tendency to isolate is grounded in practical realities. The more land you have, the farther you are from your neighbor. Informal encounters that typically bring middle-class people together—"stopping by," borrowing a cup of sugar, contributing to potluck suppers, and carpooling kids—are not in the gestalt of most affluent communities. Country clubs and tennis courts have an ambiance of expectation and competition that often sabotages true connections. Isolating patterns also emerge within wealthy families. The more services you can pay for around your house or property, the fewer opportunities family members have to share chores or child care responsibilities. With more time to pursue outside interests, less time is spent together at home. Family business relationships can preclude loved ones as sources of support. If your husband is having a hard time working for your brother, you risk escalating the problem by asking a parent or sibling for advice. Divisions can also emerge over the relative investment and return of those who are employed by the business versus those who are not.

If you work for the family business, you're never really "one of the gang" and you may feel alienated from your colleagues. While employed by my father's business one summer, my brother did not immediately understand why his manager just laughed when he asked to take an unplanned day off. It never occurred to him that others would perceive him as being above the rules. The wife of a former employee of my father's company—a woman I had long considered a real friend—shocked and hurt me by telling me she would have been nice to me even if I were not the owner's daughter. I had never considered that factor as affecting our relationship.

Among friends, you may not feel comfortable discussing pressing problems or reporting recent activities. How can you describe the difficult politics of making grants from your foundation to a friend who's looking for a job to support himself or herself? How will a person who took a vacation at a beach cottage react to your photos of a luxurious African safari? Should you invite a friend to do something expensive when you know he or she cannot afford it? How often should you offer to pick up the tab? Even if these worries exist only in your head and are not shared by your friends, the feelings of isolation they cause are real.

Having money can alienate you from yourself by causing you to question your own abilities. Other people's belief that you never would have gotten as far on your talent and personality alone can creep into your consciousness, making it hard to develop and maintain self-confidence. Many people go through phases of disdaining their wealth, or feeling guilty about it, because they cannot successfully integrate it with their identity.

On the plus side, wealth takes you to new places and introduces you to new people. It's also easier to maintain faraway friendships when you can afford to call and visit. With a sharpened radar for sincerity and an investment of time in the relationships you want to keep and nurture, money need not be an impediment to vital human connections. As more people vie for your attention, you need to identify and strengthen your key relationships. Examine your behavior to see whether you have created discomfort or invited jealousy in any ways that you can change. Broaden your idea of *community* to a national and international level.

MAKING MONEY EASIER TO TALK ABOUT

Money magnifies, complicates, and isolates—largely because conflicting social attitudes about wealth make it difficult to discuss. Americans tend to champion the underdog and admire those who achieve greatness after starting from nothing. There is honor in the struggle, but the perception is reversed at the pinnacle when wealth is achieved. Bias against concentrated wealth and an ascendant aristocracy is inherent in our democratic values and manifest in the nation's onerous estate tax structure.

At the family level, some parents do not discuss their wealth with their children because they have not fully articulated their own feelings about it or they don't want an assumption of an inheritance to adversely affect their offspring's ambition. Senior members of a family may also keep quiet about finances as a way of maintaining control. Their reluctance to address financial matters openly only passes the money taboo to the next generation.

When money is seldom discussed, wealthy people often are not aware of their own sense of the meaning and purpose of their wealth. We carry vague attitudes around in our own heads, alluding to beliefs we dangerously assume are shared. In a family wealth situation, for example, a group of siblings can agree conceptually that money means freedom. For one member, that freedom might be associated with maximum discretionary income. For another member, that freedom might be to take risks and create new enterprises. On the surface, they think they agree, but when it comes time to establish an investment policy for the family's assets, they will be totally at odds.

If money seems to be creating a problem in a friendship, you might think that *not* talking about it will save the relationship. Instead, silence risks destroying it. Unspoken discomfort and jealousy are manifested in many different types of negative behavior. Admissions or accusations are not easily made; if left to fester, however, envy will eventually explode in a manner that may well be irreparable. If you care about a relationship, it's best to get the issues on the table, no matter how painful the discussion.

Talking about money can help you understand your own attitudes toward it, as well as other people's attitudes toward your wealth. Before initiating a conversation, it may help to acknowledge the difficulty. It also pays to keep an open mind and to invite responses that will enable you to see whether your actions match your professed attitudes and beliefs.

THE ROLE OF THE PERSONAL MISSION STATEMENT

Preparing for and constructively confronting the emotional hurdles of wealth requires an evolving self-awareness as well as an awareness of the hurdles themselves. For many people, the development of a personal mission statement provides a useful framework for decisions about allocating money, time, and energy.

According to my colleague Jacqueline Merrill—founder of Center-Point, a company and retreat in Aspen, Colorado, where people develop personal mission statements during leadership and hiking stints—a personal mission statement addresses three questions: "What is my life about? What do I stand for? and What action am I taking to live what my life is about and what I stand for? A useful mission statement includes two pieces: what you wish to accomplish and contribute, and who you want to be—the character strengths and qualities you wish to develop."

These statements can be short or long, simple or complex. Here are a few examples borrowed from people I know:

- My personal mission is to live a highly principled life, full of achievement and success, while being of service to my family, my friends, and my community.
- My life is about exploring many facets of my potential: as a leader who empowers others; as a mentor, lifelong learner, mother and grandmother, devoted friend, romantic partner,

and activist philanthropist. I honor my creativity, spirituality, and sensuality. I stand for pushing away my limits and past my self-doubts and fears.

As a recovering perfectionist, I stand for being gentle with myself and for learning to nurture myself. I seek balance between time for contemplation and time for being productive.

- My mission: To achieve happiness in this lifetime by growing the spirit to the maximum capacity it can encompass.
- My goals:

    To wake every morning with a beginner's mind and to be awake.

    To express compassion to all, especially to myself.

    To mentor all who ask, and to learn as much from them as they may learn from me.

    To be a caring grandfather to my grandchildren and a friend to my children.

    To continue a committed relationship in which I can learn to feel and express emotion and to grow old in love.

    To be a good steward of financial capital.

    To be careful of my body by engaging in healthy habits so as to be as little as possible a burden physically to those who care about me.

The process of developing a personal mission statement requires you to examine the various aspects of your identity, to consider the way you are perceived by others, and to inventory your values, talents, accomplishments, and goals. You can develop a personal mission statement through a number of sources: self-help books; values clarification or self-actualization workshops or instruments; writing retreats; New Year's resolutions; or even some of the tools developed for corporate mission statements. Exercises such as writing your own obituary, imagining yourself in old age, or comparing your declared priorities with your day-to-day activities may help you get started. There's no single "right" way to do it; you have to find the way that feels genuine to you.

Just as a corporate mission statement keeps a company focused on its essential purpose and away from businesses where it does not belong, a personal mission statement gives you the criteria for accepting or declining opportunities. If you are a project-oriented person who likes to finish what you start, you might refuse an opportunity to be part of a long-term research team. If you believe local community activism is the way to make a difference, you can focus your energy there rather than on global initiatives. If music is your passion, you can politely decline a solicitation for a donation to an art museum. Your statement should be specific enough to be useful, but open enough to inspire you and to accommodate the inevitable changes in circumstance that life will bring. It should also be subject to revision periodically, so as to benefit from your additional experience and wisdom.

Using the conflicts created by wealth as a means to learn about yourself and the world in a continuous process should help you maintain a healthy and productive attitude toward your status in society, in your family, in your profession, and in your individual life. The worthwhile result should be an existence enhanced but not dominated by money.

Words to the Wise

- Wealth is a two-edged sword. It provides the freedom to pursue your dreams, but it can also take over your life if you let it.

- Money need not be an impediment to vital human connections. You can learn to distinguish between true friends and those who are interested only in your wealth.

- The challenges of instilling good values in children escalate with wealth. The primary challenge is to strike a healthy balance between providing them with a "safety net," while still giving them incentive to seek and achieve their goals.

- If money seems to be causing a problem in a relationship, it's best to put the issues on the table, no matter how painful the discussion may be.

- A personal mission statement helps you to focus on what you wish to accomplish and contribute—and who you want to be.

- In your mission statement, identify the three things you want most and make those your primary focus.

———————————— **Susan Remmer Ryzewic, Ph.D.** ————————————

Susan Remmer Ryzewic is president and CEO of EHR Investments, Inc., a family business. She is responsible for the management and investment of the company's finances. She is also director of The Remmer Family Foundation, a charitable foundation that helps empower disadvantaged girls in an attempt to break the cycle of the feminization of poverty. Ms. Ryzewic is an advisory faculty emeritus to the Institute of Private Investors, and she participates on the Investment Committee of Asset Management Advisors. She sits on the board of directors of Endless Pools Incorporated and William Smith Enterprises, Inc.

2

MONEY AND THE MODERN FAMILY

The Challenges of Parenting in a Wealthy Family

JUDITH STERN PECK

Writing this chapter prompted me to ask my three children—who are now adults—about their own experience of growing up with wealth. We gathered shortly after the Thanksgiving holiday and talked about their memories: the good and the bad. To my great relief, they had mostly good things to say about their upbringing. They believe their father and I passed on a strong work ethic to them, with an understanding that money does not buy happiness. Most importantly, they grew up with a strong value system and a set of beliefs that helped them keep an even keel in their lives.

Their most negative memory about growing up with wealth had nothing to do with their parents; it came from people outside the family. My daughter recalled how friends at school began to treat her differently when they learned she had a wealthy family. We had not prepared her for the ways others would relate to her. She did not have the tools to counter the playground taunts. These encounters left her, as well as her brothers, frustrated and confused.

If I could go back in time, I would want to prepare her for these incidents by talking more openly about our family's wealth: what it meant to us, and what it did not mean. Like many young parents, her father and I were reluctant to talk about money issues directly with our children. But in my 20 years as both a family therapist and a family business consultant, I have found that conversation is the best medicine. In family conversations, we can come to define the belief systems and values that make us unique and strong. This awareness, along with kindness and sensitivity, can enable young people to handle wealth with maturity and responsibility.

Wealth and family: Of all the words in our rich English language, few are as fraught with meaning as these two. They can suggest intense emotions, from joy to sadness. When they are combined, wealth and family form a powerful dynamic that can work positively or negatively.

As an example, let's visualize the positive image of family wealth: a loving, extended family, full of healthy individuals who work hard, are good citizens, contribute to the community, and have a genuine appreciation for life.

Now picture the negative scenario used as a premise for countless movies and books: the siblings are fighting bitterly over inheritance money; the young adults are lost in their life journey; and the children are unaware of the meaning and implications of their family's wealth.

Every wealthy parent I have ever met worried about the influence of money on their children. How can we raise our children to have a sense of responsibility toward work and society? How can we transmit a value system that both informs and transcends the amount of wealth? How can we build a family in which money is a resource for our children, rather than a corrupting force? We all know the pitfalls of wealth, but few of us were given a map for avoiding them.

Worrying about the effect of wealth on your family is actually a good first step. It shows that you care. It indicates that you are ready to take responsibility for helping to define your family's values. Meeting the challenges of family wealth requires effort on your part: conscious thought, collaboration, consistency, and a willingness to be flexible as life unfolds. Most of all, it requires the one thing that money can't buy: your loving attention.

THE CHALLENGES OF WEALTH

The great Leo Tolstoy was wrong when he wrote that "all happy families are alike." The truth is that every family, happy or unhappy, is completely unique, especially in our multicultural society. From the single parent to the "traditional" nuclear family with 2.3 children, or the blended family created by second and third marriages, or the extended multigenerational family, each family has its own values, needs, goals, and priorities. The dynamics of even the smallest family are complex. The dynamics of a larger family are *very* complex!

Although every family is different, the challenges of wealth are generally the same: inheritance issues; money's impact on family values; and the issues that arise with divorce, remarriages, and extended families. Let's take a brief look at each of these and sample some "case histories."

Inheritance Issues

After 15 years of working for a highly successful software company, Anne and Michael find themselves wealthier than they ever imagined they would be. They are thinking about estate planning, and Michael wants to create trust funds for their two young children. But Anne vehemently disagrees. She went to school with rich kids who burned through their trust funds and wasted their college years on partying. "Leave your money to charity," she urges Michael. "Our children will be stronger individuals if they have to make their own way in life, the way we did."

Anne and Michael are facing the same dilemma that every parent with wealth faces. Even Warren Buffett, the famous investor and billionaire, has said he intends to leave his children "enough money so that they would feel they could do anything, but not so much that they could do nothing." Buffett, like many wealthy parents, is trying to find the middle ground between two opposing emotions. On the one hand, he wants to help his children reach their full potential, but at the same time he fears that too much money will sap their will to achieve. His quotation is clever, but it doesn't really answer the riddle of achieving this goal.

How do Anne and Michael find a solution? In their first meetings with advisors, they receive many recommendations, but none of them resolves their basic conflict. Finally, they meet with someone who does not try to tell them *what* to do but is trained to facilitate *conversations* of this kind. By sharing their feelings and formative experiences regarding money, Anne and Michael become aware of the psychological "baggage" that arrived with their new wealth. They are able to sort through their differences. They spend some time talking about the possible remedies and finally are able to make decisions based on the "here and now," not the past. They set up educational trust funds for each of their children because they place a high value on education. In addition, Anne and Michael agree that they have a much better understanding of their decision and the underlying motivation for both of them. They know that, in the future, they will be able to make financial planning decisions for their children that reflect their own joint values.

Divorce

Jan and Richard have experienced lots of tension in their marriage. After 10 years of struggling to "keep the family together," they finally decide to separate. As a result, there will likely be a major discrepancy in their lifestyles. Jan came to the marriage as

a wealthy woman, and, upon her parents' urging, she arranged an airtight prenup-
tial agreement. Richard, in contrast, was raised by his mother alone, under very dif-
ficult financial circumstances. An academic, he has chosen a profession that will never
allow him the quality of life that Jan enjoys.

Because Jan and Richard have been able to separate the emotional
aspects of divorce from the "business" of divorce, they are able to have
a conversation about the challenge they will face in coparenting their
children. Although they will no longer be husband and wife together,
they will be parents together forever. But many difficult issues remain.
Richard's big worry is the challenge he will face in being a father to his
children when they experience the discrepancy between his modest
lifestyle and Jan's lavish surroundings. Jan worries about the same
issue, but from the opposite side. She fears that, given their material
comforts, her children may find her materialistic. Jan realizes that the
issues involved go beyond money. What does she "owe" Richard? How
should she arrange for her children's future welfare, in case something
happens to her? What criteria should she use to inform her decision
making in the financial aspect of the divorce?

Jan confronts these issues by having the same conversation with
many different people. She collects diverse views on this issue and finally recognizes that she needs to differentiate herself and her life experience from her family's opinions. She presents her ideas, listens
very carefully to her family's responses, and ultimately decides on a financial settlement that she believes will be respectful for the father of
her children. Her value of respect for Richard overrides her own family's obsession with money and power.

Second Marriages and Blended Families

Rhonda and Fred, two successful professionals, were both divorced parents when they
married each other two years ago. Rhonda had three children from her previous mar-
riage, and Fred had two. The children range in age from 3 to 30 years. Now Rhonda
and Fred have a new baby girl. Rhonda would like to establish a family foundation
that would benefit all their children. But Fred keeps balking at visiting the estate plan-
ner and offers increasingly weak excuses to postpone the appointment. When Rhonda
finally confronts him, she learns that Fred is simmering with issues. He is not sure he
wants to leave his wealth to Rhonda's children from her former marriage. He feels that
he barely knows them, and at least one of them seems hostile to him. As for his own
children, frankly, he's not sure they can handle the responsibility of wealth.

Families are deep wells of love and emotion, and money issues can't be separated from emotional issues. This is why arguments over money can tear a family apart, and unspoken emotional issues can make estate planning a profoundly difficult exercise. The good news about Rhonda and Fred is that they were able to have an open conversation and discuss what was troubling them. Too often, people experience an impasse, the conversation stays at the money level, and the issues that are blocking the financial decision making are never addressed.

Fred's acknowledgment of his ambivalence led to a deeper discussion about the partners' feelings toward their stepchildren. The nature of any adult's relationship toward stepchildren differs, depending on when the connection begins and how the relationship develops over time. Rhonda realized that she was pushing Fred into a financial action plan that fulfilled *her* dream, not his. Eventually, after sorting out their issues, they decided to set up several philanthropic trust funds. One will be an organizing force for bringing all of their children together around a value that Fred and Rhonda hold dear: giving to one's community. The other trusts will reflect and acknowledge the differing nature of parent-child relationships.

In blended families, the emotional dynamics are especially complex. When you "inherit" children in a second marriage, should you feel as much love for them as you do for your "blood" children? When a family includes "yours, mine, and ours," what premises can be used for financial planning? Where do your children's spouses' children fit it in? The permutations are endless. The definition of "family" has become so complicated that flexibility in thinking is required by all! You may be surprised one day to find your own beliefs challenged.

Impact on Family Values

Karl and Ilse recently moved from Switzerland to New York City. Their teenage daughter is having a difficult transition socially. One afternoon, she tells her mother that she wants a "sweet sixteen" party—the kind arranged for the other girls at her private school. Ilse enthusiastically agrees, but Karl learns that these parties are elaborate affairs that cost more than $100,000. He can afford to spend the money, but he feels strongly that this expense would contradict the family's entire value system. Ilse seems hell-bent on it, and, as they argue, their daughter's problems seem to become an afterthought.

Karl and Ilse need to have a talk about money and its role in their belief system. Unfortunately, it's a little late to be having this talk, but, for many people, this type of conflict often sparks the beginning of the talking process. Better to be dealing with a sweet sixteen party than with a bigger event, such as their daughter's marriage. Karl and Ilse begin to resolve their conflict when Karl attends a family wealth seminar and describes his dilemma during a group discussion about money and children. Participants who have faced similar issues give Karl some compromise options to consider—for instance, having a smaller party but donating a sum of money, in their daughter's name, to a charity of her choice. Karl feels good and looks forward to bringing the information back to Ilse.

Too often, families with wealth don't begin to resolve their differences about money and values until late in life, if ever. Your family values are the most important legacy you will bequeath to your children. The values they inherit from you will determine their ability to handle their wealth and its effects. You may have done a great job of putting your finances in order by creating a will, trusts, and an estate plan, but have you taken the time to talk with your family about your values? It's probably time you did.

DEFINING YOUR FAMILY VALUES

The above scenarios described how issues of wealth can create conflicts in families. The conflicts arise because, when we come to a marriage or union, our perspective about money has been shaped by our own family experience. Money means different things to different people. To some, it is a way of keeping score or measuring success. To others, it is simply a means to an end. To a few others, it may be the root of all evil.

When two individuals form a union, they have an opportunity to start anew. They can consider the belief set and values they bring to the union and, through discussion, form their own family values. Unfortunately, in our society, talking about money is virtually the last taboo. Friends are more likely to talk about their sex lives than their finances. To develop a healthy family attitude toward wealth, you should talk about money and finances with your future spouse or partner at the very earliest stage.

You can start a conversation about finances by asking some very basic questions and insisting that your family members give you their opinions or answers.

▪ What does money mean to you?

That is generally one of the first questions I ask my clients. Most people can't answer it outright. They have never really thought about it. So I begin by asking them how finances were handled in their original family. Did their parents argue about money? If so, how has that experience informed their own view of money? Do they use money as a measurement of their success in life, or is it a means to an end? The answers tend to emerge only through discussion.

Start to define what money means to you and you will begin to understand why you make certain financial decisions. Someone who sees money as power may be reluctant to give wealth to children. I know a 97-year-old man who has substantial wealth and has transferred little of it during his lifetime.

Ultimately, money is simply a commodity, a tool for effecting transactions. Its meaning to you is whatever you make it.

▪ Does your family have a coherent view about money?

Couples come together with different premises about money, and inevitably, as we all know, couples argue about money. Often, when they argue, they are speaking different languages. It's important to understand each other's views about money before talking about its uses. If a husband has grown up thinking that money is power, and his spouse believes money is simply a means to an end, they will probably have very different attitudes.

The key to resolving a conflict is to understand it. Remember that money is a great taboo in our society. The first step toward achieving a mutual ground for discussion is understanding each other's thoughts and feelings about money. Only then can you begin to reconcile them. Some reflective thinking may be required on everyone's part. I have found that case exercises—discussing hypothetical families' challenges, for instance—often trigger some important realizations.

▪ Who "owns" the wealth—the person who earned it or the family?

This is such a delicate issue! If you started a business, and you have spent 20 years putting in 12-hour days and seven-day weeks to build it, you darn well consider yourself the owner of the wealth. For these very good reasons, you may believe that the decisions as to how the wealth is allocated are yours alone.

But have you forgotten that your spouse was raising your children and creating and running your home while you put in the hours needed for your business? Families don't raise themselves. In business jargon, your spouse paid "the opportunity cost" to raise your family. Again, this highlights the primary issue of being able to talk to your spouse about money.

What about your children? They should not dictate what you do with your wealth, but you bear much of the responsibility of its effect on them. If you abdicate that responsibility, you will be relinquishing your parental responsibility and letting the outside world shape their attitudes toward wealth.

COMMUNICATING YOUR FAMILY VALUES

"Know thyself," said the Greek philosopher Thales. This is wise advice for meeting the challenge of family wealth. Before you take action, reflect on what's truly important to you and your family, and how you might best act on it.

First, what values do you want to instill? Do you want your children to believe that hard work is its own best reward? Or do you want them to believe that material rewards are the reason for work? Will your children believe that contributing to society is more important than making lots of money? There are no right or wrong answers. Know yourself, so that you can be clear in transmitting these ideas to your children.

Remember that you will transfer your attitudes about money to your children whether you intend to or not. You exhibit your beliefs, consciously or unconsciously, through your actions and words. Your children will internalize the messages you send. The more consistent your words and your actions, the more successfully you will communicate.

It's important to discuss money with your children at age-appropriate levels. A child in grade school is too young to hear about trusts but can understand that money is earned by work. I don't endorse the common wisdom that young children should be paid an allowance for doing household chores. I fully believe children should help with the chores, but not solely as a means to make money. An allowance is a means for teaching them financial responsibility, the beginnings of money management, and budgeting.

Philanthropy can be an excellent way for your children to learn about the responsibilities of wealth. Becoming personally involved with a philanthropic endeavor, and getting your children involved with you, shows where your values lie. As your children grow older, include them in the financial decision making of charitable endeavors or family foundations. This will give them an excellent introduction to wealth management.

Anticipate potential conflicts when a major life transition, such as a child's marriage, occurs. When your children are old enough to consider marriage, talk to them about the importance of prenuptial agreements. Don't wait until the last minute. (I knew some parents who drew aside their daughter some weeks before her planned wedding and demanded that she present her fiancé with a prenuptial agreement. Although it was a perfectly reasonable request, it took the groom completely by surprise. The bride wasn't prepared for his reaction, the whole affair turned into an ugly row between the families, and a shadow was cast on what should have been a joyous event.)

As your children grow and look toward having children of their own, your discussions of wealth and values should also enter a mature stage. Be ready to discuss generational wealth planning; introduce your children to your financial advisors, and discuss the estate planning techniques the advisors have recommended.

Finally, face and deal with the most difficult issue: inheritance. Personally, I regard the dollar amount as less important than the way in which you transfer your wealth. If you have done a good job in fostering open communication with your children, they will understand your decisions. If you have refused to talk about your wealth, your children may see their legacy as a yardstick of your love.

At what age should children receive inheritances? That's up to you and your family situation, but, in my experience, children can best handle wealth *after* their early adult years—namely, when they are past their twenties. By age 30, they will have learned the real meaning and value of work. This doesn't mean you should not help them in their twenties, but beware of the dangers of simply handing over large sums of cash with no strings attached.

Should children receive equal amounts of money even if they clearly have different capacities for managing it? Here, it is important to understand the difference between equity and equality. An equal distribution of money may not be equitable (fair). Suppose a family has two sons: one is a promising artist and the other is a promising entrepreneur. The artist needs living expenses to support himself and his art, and the entrepreneur needs substantial cash to fund a new business venture. The best solution may be to give each son the resources needed to fulfill his dreams—and that will mean giving unequal sums.

Be prepared to fine-tune and adjust your plans as your life unfolds. The only sure thing in life is change. Many of your best-laid plans may need to be rewritten as your family's circumstances change. Make it a habit to review your estate planning regularly.

Are you having trouble discussing money issues in your family? A growing number of consultants and family business advisors specialize in wealth/family issues. Like all professionals, they run the gamut of quality and style. Find a qualified professional whom you trust. Contact organizations such as the Family Firm Institute (www.ffi.org), or the American Association for Marriage and Family Therapy (www.aamft.org), or ask friends for personal referrals. But remember: Discussing your family's wealth is ultimately your responsibility. Parenting is not a role you can delegate, but you can call upon the available resources for support.

Parenting in a wealthy family has few easy steps. Talking about your beliefs and sharing them with your family are essential remedies.

■ Have the conversations.

Start with reflective thinking, and then talk about money and its meaning with all members of your family. You don't have to take a formal tack, but a formal conversation is better than no conversation. Ideally, talking with your spouse and your children about money and wealth should be a comfortable and informal practice. (If your children are young, remember to keep the conversations age appropriate.)

■ When appropriate, be transparent.

If your children ask "Are we wealthy?" give them a truthful age-appropriate answer. Money is nothing to be ashamed of. Giving your children a firm understanding of money issues, including the limitations and responsibilities, is far better than having them grow up experiencing the contradictions.

■ Be conscious and deliberate about wealth issues.

Don't assume that "things will take care of themselves." Wealth is a powerful force, and you can help to make it a force for good. Understand that instilling values in your children is as important a part of parenting as education.

■ Avoid mixed messages.

Remember that actions really do speak louder than words. If you say that wealth is a responsibility, then you should demonstrate it. For example, if community and family are important values to you, reflect this belief in your behavior. Get involved with charitable or philanthropic organizations and share the activities with your children. Your involvement will give them a lasting lesson.

■ Help your children "shape their own reality."

Understand that no matter how well you prepare your children, you can't control the world they live in. Help them build a strong sense of self-awareness and self-confidence so that other people's opinions or attitudes do not unduly sway them.

■ Promote decision-making skills as a family.

Learning decision-making skills improves your family's ability to reach agreement on complex issues. Developing these skills together as a family can lay a strong foundation for the future.

■ Appreciate the differences.

Every individual is unique. Learn to appreciate your children's differences, and find a way, together, to support them in their chosen life endeavors. If you have an extended family, follow the same philosophy on a larger scale.

■ Create your own family rituals.

One of my most cherished memories of raising my children is centered on our Shabbat dinner and our weekly synagogue attendance. When we couldn't go to synagogue, we devoted Saturday to family visits. These rituals had nothing to do with wealth, and everything to do with building our family's legacy. I hope you can enjoy the same.

Words to the Wise

- Money issues can't be separated from emotional issues.
- Arguments over money can tear a family apart, and unspoken emotional issues can make estate planning a profoundly difficult exercise.
- To develop a healthy family attitude about wealth, you must learn to talk about money and finances with your spouse or partner at a very early stage.
- Help your children build a strong sense of self, so that they are not unduly swayed by other people's opinions or attitudes.
- Learn to appreciate your children's differences, and find a way to support them in their chosen life endeavors.
- Create your own family rituals as regular religious, social, or recreational events that bring—and keep—the family together.

Judith Stern Peck, M.S.W.

Judith Stern Peck is Director of the Family Wealth, Family Life project at the Ackerman Institute for the Family, a not-for-profit agency devoted to research and study of the family. The project seeks to respond to the needs of families with wealth by "exploring the human side of wealth." In addition, she has had extensive experience as both a family therapist and a consultant to family businesses, foundations, and offices. She participates in the consultant referral service of the Family Foundation Services department of the Council on Foundations and is very active in the philanthropic sector, having served in many leadership roles.

3

THE BUSINESS OF MARRIAGE

Love Conquers All, But Assets Need Protection

ROBERT STEPHAN COHEN

Daniel, the fourth-generation scion of a textile manufacturing family, was in his late twenties and planned to marry a young model he had met in the company's New York showroom. His father was insisting on a prenuptial agreement to make sure the family business stayed in the family. Although embarrassed, and fearful that his soon-to-be wife, Jana, a recent arrival from the Czech Republic, would not understand their mutual need to protect their interests, Daniel finally agreed to hire an attorney to draft an agreement that safeguarded the family's wealth. Jana hired her own attorney to make sure the document would provide her with "reasonable security" in the event of a divorce.

Ten years later, Daniel and Jana decided to end their marriage. The family business, which had gone public since the time of the wedding, now had a substantial market value. Without the prenuptial agreement, Daniel's significant ownership interest in the family business might have been considered marital property. Jana would have been entitled to an equal share, creating the risk of a battle for control if Daniel could not afford or arrange a buyout of the marital property at the market price. Under the terms of the agreement, the business stayed with Daniel. Jana retained the security of a home and an adequate lump sum of money, which Daniel could afford because the agreement provided for a payout over time. The prenuptial agreement allowed the two to move on without excessive rancor or remorse.

Y ou've fallen in love and set the wedding date. The big day is fast approaching, and your heart skips a beat with every wedding arrangement you make: choosing the florist, interviewing the caterer, and picking the music that will accompany your romantic stroll

Note: Daniel, Jana, and all the people described in this chapter are composites drawn from years of experience and do not reflect actual persons or cases.

down the aisle. With so much love in the air, it's easy to understand why happy couples might be reluctant to sit down with lawyers and consider the possibility of a divorce.

Nevertheless, the significant discomfort of proper divorce planning is far outweighed by the potential emotional and financial gains. In fact, by talking about what's "mine, yours, and ours" before you get married, you endow your partnership with a much better chance of surviving the long haul. Although many people view prenuptial and postnuptial agreements as anti-marriage, they can, in fact, often be anti-divorce. When spouses know they do not have a claim to their partners' significant assets, they may make more effort to seek counseling and improve marital satisfaction. A prenuptial agreement may keep them working at their marriage rather than thinking, "I'm not happy in this marriage. I could be happier and wealthier if I got out of it. Why not get a divorce and start over?" When there's nothing to gain and no easy way out, many people are not so quick to dissolve their union.

Prenuptial and postnuptial agreements are not part of the storybook romance we envisioned in our youth, but they are becoming as much a fact of life as the ever-climbing divorce rate (about 50 percent) in the United States. With the terms of celebrity divorces getting wide media play, people have gained a growing awareness of the challenges in dismantling economic assets when a marriage does not last. Young people getting married for the first time may seek these agreements to avoid the acrimony they've observed in their parents' divorce. The agreements are also common in second marriages, where one spouse has had the experience of divorce. If the bride and groom have worked for a while, they may want a formal accounting of the assets they are bringing into the marriage. When significant family assets are at stake, as in the example of Daniel and Jana, and the bride or groom is particularly young, the parents on the wealthier side of the union often insist on the agreement.

Nuptial agreements may seem cold and businesslike in contrast to the feelings that inspire the decision to marry, but in reality they can minimize the negative emotions that commonly accompany divorce. Most people would probably never put their assets at risk in a business partnership without consulting a lawyer and delineating how the assets would be distributed in the event the business was later dissolved. From a purely financial perspective, a marriage warrants the same type of "better-safe-than-sorry" insurance. The alternative is that the state courts will dictate property division and spousal support, often without regard to important detail.

In 30 years of practicing matrimonial law, I have represented everyone from teachers to supermodels to real estate moguls. I have learned that keeping the lines of communication open and maintaining realistic expectations of your union is the best way to get a marriage started. I can't tell you how many people come into my office with financial problems that could have been easily remedied with a little time and effort before marriage. And I've long since lost track of how many times I've sat and listened to clients rue their failure to secure their assets.

Through my clients' experiences, I have discovered the art of damage control. Whenever I meet a new client, I ask myself what can be done to rid the divorce process of as much emotion as possible, find a mutually satisfying resolution, and get it done in a way that limits the psychological and financial burdens to the couple. No matter how many cases I've won or how many settlements I've negotiated, nothing is as satisfying to me as helping two people settle their financial affairs and get on with the business of living.

This chapter will take you through the steps needed to safeguard your assets before getting married, throughout your marriage, and during a divorce. Keep in mind that this information should only be used as a primer. The variations in state laws and procedures, which are substantial, make divorce a very complex matter and affect what needs to be included in a marital agreement. Just as you wouldn't think of performing surgery after reading a medical procedure manual, you shouldn't attempt to draw up a prenuptial or postnuptial agreement without the aid of a qualified attorney. Reading this chapter, however, will certainly give you a start.

BEFORE MARRIAGE

Prenuptial Agreements

A prenuptial agreement is a contract between two people outlining the method of distributing assets. It may deal with such eventualities as death or divorce. These agreements have grown in popularity since the 1980s, but they have existed for centuries, in one form or another, for the protection of family wealth.

A prenuptial agreement can significantly minimize the financial and emotional damage of a divorce. The agreement doesn't have to take a toll on the happiness of the engaged couple, provided it is done well in advance of the marriage ceremony. Because it streamlines any future divorce proceedings, it can save time, money, and risks to reputation.

Do I Need a Prenuptial Agreement?

Most couples still don't sign a prenuptial agreement, but my experience tells me you should seriously consider one if any of the following situations match yours:

- You own assets such as a home, stocks, options, art, retirement funds.
- You own part or all of a business.
- One person will be the primary child-care provider.
- You anticipate receiving an inheritance.
- You have children and/or grandchildren from a previous marriage.
- One partner is much wealthier than the other.
- One of you will be supporting the other through college, graduate school, or both.
- You have elderly parents who require financial support.
- You are forgoing a career or rejecting a lucrative job offer and being married instead.
- You are concerned about being left to settle your spouse's debts.
- You are pursuing a degree in a potentially lucrative profession.
- You foresee a big increase in your business income.

Is It Valid?

States recognize prenuptial agreements in varying degrees. The parties to the agreement generally should obtain counsel in the state they expect will pass on the validity of the document.

When weighing the validity of a prenuptial agreement, there are many issues to consider. If the agreement is too one-sided or unfair, it can be declared unconscionable—defined as "no person of sound mind would sign that agreement." In such a case, two things may happen:

- The state may declare the agreement invalid, ignore it, and divide the marital assets according to the distribution laws of that state. These laws include community property states (e.g., California) that view all assets acquired during marriage as property of the marriage community and subject to a 50–50 split.
- The courts may rewrite the agreement to make it fairer.

Each state views these agreements differently, but the following basic steps will help make an agreement enforceable.

1. The agreement must be put in writing and executed before the marriage, in accordance with the requirements of the laws of the state in which you live.
2. The agreement cannot be signed under duress. If your spouse-to-be offers you the contract and asks you to sign it 20 minutes before the ceremony, it may not be valid. It's preferable to have it signed months before the marriage.
3. The agreement must be reasonable, and it is helpful if it is based on a full disclosure of assets by both parties. In some jurisdictions, full disclosure may be required by statute. You need to have a clear understanding of all the financial data provided. You must also carefully consider the value placed on hard-to-value property such as unmarketable shares in a newly formed business venture.
4. Each party should have independent counsel. The same lawyer should not represent both parties.

Family Matters

For centuries, families of great wealth and status have grappled with the issues of keeping their wealth within the family. Long ago, producing a male heir was enough to ensure the preservation of assets. Today, with equitable distribution and community property laws governing divorce, families wishing to ensure the passage of wealth from generation to generation within their own families need to do some very careful planning.

The level of a family's involvement in their child's marriage varies with every couple. In one case, a family with tremendous wealth throughout the United States and abroad came to my firm to identify the best place for their child to be married and establish a home where their family holdings would be protected. The parents handled everything; in fact, I didn't even meet the ultimate client until the decision had been made to settle the newlyweds in France, a country known for protecting the wealth holder.

Of course, there is some room for compromise. One family, which had significant real estate holdings all over the United States, brought me a list of 10 states where the couple would consent to live. We then figured out the best jurisdiction for residency. The family was secure in the knowledge that their assets would be protected, and the newlyweds felt comfortable with their role in the decision—a truly win–win situation.

Some families ensure that their assets will stay within the family by placing them in a trust or a similar arrangement with provisions that prevent the child from distributing assets to the spouse in case of a divorce. Trusts can also outline how much money can be used for family expenses, such as homes, household help, cars, and the like. And if the family wishes to avoid issues of title and marital property division after these items are acquired, the trust instructions can specify that the titles are to be left under the trust rather than in the name of the child.

Although some readers may regard it as too restrictive, a trust can actually take a lot of pressure off the soon-to-be-married progeny who must discuss asset division with his or her spouse. It's much easier for the son or daughter to discuss finances when he or she doesn't have to be the "bad guy."

Still, this arrangement has one drawback. The transfer of assets to a trust carries substantial gift tax considerations. Early planning is the key here, as evidenced by the following example.

John and Glenda had been married for well over 30 years. They were tremendously wealthy, having developed land and bought considerable property throughout the country. When their youngest daughter, Julia, announced her engagement to a man considerably less well-to-do, her parents were concerned that their wealth might go to him in case of a divorce. They planned to create a trust to tie up some of Julia's holdings, but were disturbed by the exorbitant gift taxes built into the plan.

I worked with them and determined that the best course of action would be to fund the trust only with options to purchase real estate just acquired. Because the options would be worth very little until they were exercised and the underlying real estate appreciated in value, there would be little or no tax to pay. After the project was completed, the real estate would likely have significant value, but, for now, the asset existed only in the form of options with little value, thus avoiding any significant gift tax. Julia could not get interests in the significant real estate already owned, but the family adjusted that inequity by giving her more than her siblings received from future real estate acquisitions.

We were still very concerned about the possibility that those real estate options might appreciate in value if the properties were developed. In that case, the appreciated real estate value of those options could become subject to an equitable division between the parties, and Julia would lose considerable assets if she chose to divorce. Finally, after a lot of deliberation, the family decided to place the options within a trust with very strict provisions. We believed this approach would keep the property out of the marital estate.

In every marital contract, along with other financial impacts, it is important to consider and address tax issues.

DURING MARRIAGE

Postnuptial Agreements

A postnuptial agreement is similar to a prenuptial agreement, but it is drawn up after the marriage takes place. Working with estate and family lawyers, couples wishing to draft postnuptial agreements should do so with the intention of gaining a clear understanding of their financial roles in the marriage. And while it is not always comfortable to discuss divorce and the division of assets, especially in the middle of a marriage, these types of conversations can actually strengthen the marital union by opening channels of communication and person-to-person trust. It's never too late to outline and secure your assets.

Being prepared is what solid planning is all about. Trying to tie up your assets when divorce seems imminent can actually lead to more troubles—and, sometimes, to a divorce court. The key to drawing up a post-nuptial agreement is: Act when things are going well and the marriage is stable, and draw up a plan as part of a general estate protection strategy.

Estate planning can also play a significant role in asset management; it can funnel money from the realm of marital assets to the next generation. But you have to be careful. If you give assets to children in a trust without various protective measures (e.g., putting limits on how much of the trust they can use to acquire property and other household purchases during the marriage), those assets may lose their separate nature, be declared "marital property" by the courts, and be divided according to the family laws of that state.

Sarah, the owner of a successful PR firm, had the opportunity, as part of a general estate plan, to make large conveyances into a trust for her children while incurring very low tax costs. She ultimately got divorced, and her husband ended up suing her and challenging those conveyances, claiming that they took too much wealth out of the marriage. The children were the beneficial owners of the trust, and they got involved in litigation against their father. Sarah and the children were successful because they proved that the intent of the transfer was not to deplete the marital pot, but to protect assets from significant taxation.

Negotiating a postnuptial agreement is not easy. I've found that the best way to start the conversation about postnuptial agreements is to ask your lawyer to raise the issue during a routine meeting. Or, you can ask your spouse directly how he or she would feel about creating a personalized agreement that reflects your mutual views on the marital partnership. For postnuptial agreements, timing is critical. You have to be careful. The agreement must be completed before anyone thinks about divorce. At that time, all bets are off.

Most importantly, don't put off drawing up an agreement. Even if you're lucky enough to never have the need to use it, the peace of mind it can bring is invaluable.

Do You Need a Postnuptial Agreement?

Following are some circumstances that might make you consider a post-nuptial agreement:

- You did not create a prenuptial agreement, and you want to define your financial relationship with your spouse in case of divorce or death.
- Your financial situation has changed considerably through inheritance, increases in stock, or business fluctuations.
- You're not satisfied with your prenuptial agreement.
- You have experienced a change of circumstance in your career. For example, you stopped working to become a full-time mom, or you enrolled in school to pursue a higher degree.

AT THE END OF THE MARRIAGE

Protecting Yourself

Various costs are associated with divorce: the financial costs, the emotional costs to the former spouses, and the significant psychological costs to the family. The key to protecting your assets during a divorce proceeding—without the aid of pre- or postnuptial agreements—is damage control. Protect yourself from an emotional battle, avoid common financial traps, and find a good matrimonial attorney who will vigorously defend your rights.

You may want to keep the proceedings all business, but there's no telling how the emotional issues of your marriage will play out in a divorce proceeding. In one case that comes to mind, James, a young investment banker, was divorcing his wife of four years. He came into my office and said, "I thought about the divorce, I know what I'm worth, and I'm prepared to give my wife half of the estate. I brought all my records and I don't see any reason why we couldn't wrap this up in 90 days."

Unfortunately, he didn't stop to consider that this wasn't merely another business deal. Divorce always has an emotional component. Both parties may not necessarily be coming in with the same expectations. One spouse may not be ready to end the marriage. James's divorce took far longer than he anticipated. You can't treat your divorce like another business deal, but you can make concerted efforts to minimize the financial damage and protect your emotional well-being.

The problem with keeping the emotional and financial issues separate is that some people view money as their only emotional leverage during a divorce. They make unreasonable demands for the sake of exacting revenge or settling old debts. In many cases, especially where there was abuse of some kind, getting a good financial settlement is much more than just business; it can become a principle. Despite the hardships of keeping the situation strictly business, you can take these steps to keep the lines from blurring:

- Make sure all your actions are guided by reason and practical considerations.
- Try not to react if your spouse or the opposing counsel becomes aggressive.
- Don't be pulled into playing the blame game.
- If you have to meet with your spouse, schedule your meetings, keep them businesslike, and meet in a public place.

Avoiding Common Financial Traps

Here are some of the most common but least constructive actions you should avoid.

■ Excessive spending

During a separation, some people have a tendency to spend compulsively, either to make themselves feel better or because they fear they will not have as much money to spend after the divorce. The insecurity brought about by the impending divorce can create some hoarding tendencies which, if left unchecked, may result in financial problems. A buying frenzy can significantly affect your financial position and leverage during a divorce proceeding.

■ Clouded judgment

When emotions are at an all-time high, it's easy to get sidetracked and begin to doubt your own judgment. Many clients begin to waver; they ask for too little or too much. Some want the divorce to be over quickly, and they end up surrendering too many of their assets. Others get caught up in the greed game and invite conflict by indulging unrealistic expectations of what they stand to gain. It's important to find a balance that clarifies what you want, what your spouse wants, and what both of you are entitled to.

■ Hiding money

When a divorce is pending, one spouse may begin to transfer assets and postpone payments in order to avoid merging new income with marital property. Secretly transferring into a separate account the marital assets that belong to both spouses will clearly be viewed as fraud. All of the transfers will come back and will significantly undermine the secret transferor's claims. To safeguard against this, make a concerted effort to follow the household's cash flow, and keep a careful watch over all joint accounts.

■ Failing to hire a good financial manager

Lawyers are critical to the divorce process, but they are not trained to make investments or maximize income. That's where a qualified financial manager comes in. Often, clients already have these professionals in place, but a matrimonial attorney can often recommend a financial manager.

Hiring a Good Divorce Lawyer

Choosing a capable divorce lawyer to settle your affairs is one of the most important steps toward protecting your assets. Ideally, your lawyer should be part of the solution, not the problem. Having an experienced and assertive counsel working diligently on your behalf will give you the time and energy to cope with your emotional issues, lifestyle changes, and children.

Don't consider only how vigorously your attorney will defend you; assess his or her ability to reach a mutually satisfactory compromise without launching a full-blown legal battle. You'll need someone who: won't let the divorce degenerate into a sideshow, will keep the proceedings dignified and on track even when the lines of communication have all but broken down, will know when to be aggressive and when to retreat, and will understand and successfully help you to balance your emotional conflict and your particular financial circumstances.

You may be impressed by the first lawyer you talk to, especially if you're eager to get your divorce behind you, but you should interview more than one attorney. Your divorce is likely to be the most significant financial event of your lifetime. Here are some of the basic questions you should ask—and the reasons to ask them.

▪ What is your professional background? How many cases have you handled, and how many of those cases have gone to trial?

You want a lawyer who is experienced and has a good track record. Divorces that go to trial may become very public and very expensive. Most divorces are settled out of court; try to find someone who has achieved more settlements than trials. Your preference, however, may be a function of your circumstances and your outlook for your spouse's reaction.

▪ Have you ever contended with the opposing attorney? If so, how did you get along?

In general, the outcome will be better for both parties if their attorneys are not personal adversaries.

▪ How available will you be to me? And how available do you expect me to be to you?

Ask whether the attorney prefers to communicate with clients via personal meetings, telephone calls, or e-mail. Consider how this choice matches your preferences.

▪ Do you use a support staff and outside experts?

A paralegal's time is billed at a lower rate than an attorney's, but you will want to feel that your case is getting the attention it deserves. Be sure you understand who will be your day-to-day point of contact. Outside experts may be needed to determine the value of real estate, art, or private businesses.

■ How much will your services cost?

Matrimonial lawyers commonly ask for a retainer, which serves as a prepayment for time and expenses. The attorney's billable hours (including time spent on the phone, in meetings with you and your spouse's attorney, and in court) are charged against that retainer. If the retainer is used up before the case is settled, there will be additional billings. The amount of time a divorce will take is nearly impossible to calculate at the outset, but you should ask your attorney to estimate typical fees for a variety of scenarios. Make sure the fee agreement is in writing, even if your state doesn't require it to be.

Bottom Line   The complicated process of divorce will have some impact—legal, financial, and emotional—on every part of your life. Prepare for the worst-case scenario via smart divorce planning and asset management, and you may be avoiding significant hardships.

Author's Note: The anecdotes in the chapter do not depict actual clients.

Words to the Wise

- A marriage warrants the same degree of financial protection as a business partnership.
- Your partnership will have a much better chance of survival if you talk about who owns or gets what *before you get married*.
- A prenuptial agreement can significantly minimize the financial and emotional damage of a divorce. It should be discussed and signed well in advance of the wedding.
- A *postnuptial* agreement is similar to a prenuptial but is drawn up after the marriage takes place. This step should be taken when things are going well and the marriage is stable.
- During a divorce, people tend to view money as their only emotional leverage. Make sure your financial judgment isn't clouded by the emotional issues.
- Choosing a capable divorce lawyer and a good financial manager to settle your affairs are two of the most important steps toward protecting your assets.

Robert Stephan Cohen, Esq.

Robert Stephan Cohen is chairman of and partner in Morrison Cohen Singer & Weinstein, LLP, a full-service New York-based law firm. He is the firm's leading matrimonial lawyer and heads the firm's Family Law Practice, one of the preeminent such practices in the country. Mr. Cohen has represented many prominent and high-net-worth individuals in cases involving divorce and the division of complex and substantial marital assets. He is also engaged in matters involving paternity and custody. He is a lecturer and writer for a variety of professional organizations and publications, and is the author of Reconcilable Differences.

4

THE VALUE OF WORK, PART I

When You Love What You Do, Why Retire?

ROY R. NEUBERGER
FOUNDER, NEUBERGER BERMAN

At age 99, I go to work every day. I have been working on Wall Street for 73 years, since March 1929, and I still find it fascinating.

Once I thought about retiring, but the thought passed. When I reached the age of 65, I just continued to do what I did before. Perhaps I was influenced by two friends who made careful retirement plans.

One, a municipal bond expert who worked for a large bank, spent much of his career planning his retirement at 65. He loved golf and was pretty good at it. His plan was to spend a lot of time in Scotland playing golf. He never got there. He died at 65.

The other friend was in retail trade with his wife, the daughter of Lane Bryant. George Paley was a nice-looking guy, an amateur sculptor, who also carefully planned his retirement, which was to include two days a week as a volunteer at the Neuberger Museum of Art. We never had the pleasure of his services at the Museum. He, too, died at 65.

I don't say that these friends died because they retired. Something physical happened. But there is no doubt that their fate had an influence on me.

Generally, I think that you must have some powerful influences to stay alive in the most healthy manner.

I have heard about doctors who become depressed after they retire. They don't fully realize how important their work is to their identity. Seeing patients is a vital part of their social as well as their professional lives.

I think that a person who retires should just substitute other work. In my case, I continued to go to the office, doing what I had been doing for years. I ran the Guardian Mutual Fund, which I had founded in 1950, and handled many individual accounts. After my seventy-fifth birthday, I began thinking that perhaps with a public account like Guardian Mutual Fund, which had thousands of investors, a person over 75 shouldn't be running it. So within a year I stepped down.

But barely had I divested myself of running Guardian when the Eastman Kodak Company asked me to handle its pension fund, which I then ran for a decade.

This meant that at age 76 I was essentially starting a new career. I liked the company and the people who ran it. I loved the relationship that developed with the people at Kodak.

After I celebrated my eighty-fifth birthday, I decided to shift from managing other people's money to focusing on my own portfolio and my family's. If I should ever make a bad call, I knew I wouldn't lose a client. Eventually, I turned my family's holdings over to younger people. Now I only take care of my own account, which keeps my mind plenty busy.

Some time ago, when I sensed that the stock market was close to its peak, I thought seriously about switching my portfolio to Treasury bonds. It would have been the prudent thing to do. I would have had a nice income. I knew I would be risking millions of dollars if I stayed in the market.

But I realized that if I pulled out of the stock market, there would be a big problem: when I woke up in the morning there would be no office, no work colleagues, no trading. I have many interests, particularly in the visual arts, but there is still time to go to work.

HOW WORK BECAME CENTRAL TO MY LIFE

Making money has always had a special purpose for me: to buy the works of living artists. The genesis of that decision came in my earliest jobs.

I lost my mother when I was nine years old, and my father four years later. After their deaths, I lived with my older sister Ruth and her husband, Aaron Potter, my closest friends in the world. In DeWitt Clinton High School, I was captain of the tennis team that won the Greater New York Championship. I was recruited by New York University, mainly to play tennis. But the freshman year in college was frustrating. I felt I could learn much more out in the world. I quit college at

the end of the year and went to work at the B. Altman department store.
I stayed there for three years.

This, my first job, was a tremendously valuable experience. I moved
so fast unloading furniture from trucks that they transferred me up-
stairs to the interior decorating department, where I soon became an
upholstery fabrics buyer. I learned a lot about retailing, customer relations, and trading—inventory for cash, and cash for inventory—and
absorbed a valuable lesson that would apply to my own firm in the years
ahead: You are in business to make a profit, but if you are excessively
greedy, you will lose.

Equally important, I learned about the arts from my colleagues in
decorating. They took me to art galleries, to the theater, and to the
opera (way up in the rafters), and they encouraged me to study painting. I decided that I would never be a good painter, but I did become
an art lover. My eye for painting and sculpture evolved from my days
at Altman's.

I also learned to respect talent, regardless of gender or lifestyle.
Many extremely nice people in the interior decorating department
were not in tune with mainstream sexuality. Long before the advent of
political correctness, I learned that people's private lives were their
own business and should not affect our opinions of their personalities
and skills.

I left Altman's to educate myself by living in Paris. In addition to
visits to the Louvre and classes at the Sorbonne, I worked for Alexan-
dre Dumas, an avant-garde decorating concern and purveyor of modern wallpaper. The company also had a basement full of antiques. I
earned $10 a week plus 10 percent commission on sales. That arrange-
ment gave me $5,000 on $50,000 worth of antiques I sold in the summer of 1926, when the French franc was momentarily cut almost in
half. That job fused two of my budding interests: the art world and the
financial world.

While in Paris, I read a book that changed my life: *Vincent van Gogh*
by Florent Fels. It told the sad story of how the nineteenth-century
French ignored van Gogh's wonderful paintings. He couldn't sell them.
Ultimately, van Gogh took his own life. He died in poverty. I was
shocked by this book, and I determined to see that the same fate did
not befall contemporary artists in America.

This was the impetus for my pledge to myself: Earn enough money
to buy the work of living artists. Little did I know, at that moment of

decision, that one day I would purchase a work called *Number 8,* by a young painter named Jackson Pollock, who, that winter, would use the money to pay the heating bills for the Long Island house he shared with his wife, Lee Krasner.

I returned to New York from Paris with a clear objective. But to buy art, I would need to make a good deal of money. I went to Wall Street because, as Willie Sutton said of banks, "That's where the money is." I was hired by a highly respected brokerage firm, Halle & Stieglitz, as a runner at $15 a week. The date was March 9, 1929. The bull market would continue until Labor Day.

LEARNING FROM THE PANIC

As an investor in 1929, my own portfolio went up 12 percent: from $30,000, which my father had left me, to $35,000. But by the end of September, my $5,000 gain was wiped out. At that time, the most actively traded stock was Radio Corporation of America, which reached a high of 574, split 5 for 1, and declined to 100, which still seemed high to me. I set out to discover why the stock was so high and so active. Nothing seemed to justify the seemingly excessive price. To me, a radio was just another new appliance that didn't work very well. Reception was terrible. The radio seemed to be a far less promising product than the automobile.

I sold 300 Radio shares short—exactly my equity on the long-side stock I was holding onto. This was my first foray into hedging—short $30,000 on Radio and long $30,000 on my portfolio of blue chips. I would use the same technique for the rest of the century, whenever I thought the market was creeping too high.

Unlike many older and wiser investors, I was able to survive the Panic—Black Tuesday, October 29, 1929. I didn't have a margin account. I had paid the full amount for my portfolio when I purchased mostly conservative stocks in the spring of 1929. Of course, I was required to put some money in a margin account when I sold Radio Corporation short.

The market hit bottom on November 13, 1929, and plunged to a new low in October 1930. Within another two years, the market was worth only 11 percent of its September 1929 high. Radio Corporation, which I had sold short at 100, ultimately sank to 2.

I learned that the common sense I had acquired by age 26, even as an entry-level employee on Wall Street, was a commodity in short supply. I also learned that while my goal was to buy art, I enjoyed working on Wall Street. It was a perfect fit for me. I credit that to my early training on the artistic side. I found that success on Wall Street was less a science than an art.

In those days on Wall Street, you were expected to know all aspects of the business: bookkeeping, statistics, research, margins—everything. Working hard at my apprenticeship, I rotated through the company, learning as I went. When I felt I had pretty much conquered the operations of each department, I decided I was ready to become a customer's broker, or money manager. I felt confident about my financial accomplishments, having lost only 15 percent in a year when 100 percent losses were commonplace.

I had received a real education in seeing things as they are, not as one might wish they were. I learned that the market has a rhythm of its own, like the waves of the ocean. I became closely attuned to the changing waves.

An even greater benefit from my years at Halle & Stieglitz resulted from my investigating a stock in the research department. There I encountered a lovely young economist named Marie Salant, who, within a year and a half, became my wife and, later, the mother of our three wonderful children, Ann, Roy, and Jimmy.

While at Halle & Stieglitz, I also met an extremely bright, ambitious, hardworking man seven years my junior. His name was Robert Bennett Berman. He was a Columbia graduate (and coxswain of a famous winning Columbia crew) who earned his law degree at night while working as a floor clerk for a man who had a seat on the Stock Exchange. Berman was also holding down two or three other jobs.

At the close of the 1930s, with my wife Marie and Bob Berman at my side, we launched Neuberger & Berman on start-up capital of $64,000. I was 37 years old. My departure from Halle & Stieglitz was amicable, even though I took 100 percent of my accounts with me. Spending ten years with a large and diversified firm before starting my own business had been enormously helpful in preparing for anything that might come.

Bob Berman died of leukemia at the age of 44. We have kept his name in the firm since his death in 1954. Today, Neuberger Berman manages more than $60 billion. And I am still there.

WORKING AT 99

To be a healthy and happy person, you have to keep your mind engaged, even though age in our society is not accorded the same kind of respect as in China and many other civilizations. Of course, an older body will play tricks on you. At 99, I can't walk as well as I did at 95.

But rather than retire to focus just on leisure activities, I have made a point of integrating walking and exercise into my workday. I do exercises first thing in the morning. For many years, I took a walk along Central Park with good friends before going to work. I also meet with a personal trainer three times a week, after work.

My work continues to provide me with the means for a good life that is shared with my family, and for acquiring the art that overflows from my apartment, country home, and office to the 70 institutions in 24 states to which I have given art, including the Neuberger Museum of Art on the Purchase College campus of the State University of New York.

The Museum came about when Nelson Rockefeller was Governor of New York. In 1965, I received an anonymous offer of several million dollars for my whole collection. I wasn't interested in selling. I later learned that the person who wanted to buy it was Nelson Rockefeller. He then asked me to give my collection to the State University campus at Purchase. "Give me your collection," Governor Rockefeller urged. By "me" he meant the State of New York. I agreed. The brilliant architect Philip Johnson designed the building, and 300 of my paintings and sculptures became the core of the Neuberger Museum permanent collection. By now, I have given more than 800 pieces to the Museum, which also exhibits some of the most exciting artists at work today.

My life now centers around my office, my family and old friends, the Neuberger Museum of Art and the Metropolitan Museum, where I am an honorary life trustee, and the wider world of art, which keeps me in touch with new artists and openings of new shows, to many of which I loan art.

My writings—for this book, for a published memoir (*So Far, So Good—The First 94 Years,* John Wiley & Sons), and for a new book on art— necessarily bring up the past. But when I go to the office in the morning, I am very much in the present and always looking toward the future.

WHY RETIRE?

Should everyone follow my lead and not retire? I wouldn't say that. I have a terrific nephew, of whom I am very fond, who retired from Neuberger Berman at 65 and is enormously happy living in Colorado and traveling everywhere. He loves people; he is surrounded by people. Like his mother (my sister) and his father, he has a wonderful disposition. Retirement works for him.

But, for most people, I think it is better to stick to working. You must do something with your life that has meaning for you and for others. Generally, I believe that people who work are happier than those who don't, at any age. Dr. Freud would back me up on that.

Work is fun. It can be more fun than playing a game. There are always new adventures. In my field, there are constantly new securities to study, new fundamentals to learn in a changing economy.

The main thing is to stay curious. In my one hundredth year, I still have a lot of curiosity. I want to know why things happen. I still greet each day with enthusiasm because I want to see what will happen next. And I know that every day I will learn something new.

Words to the Wise

- To be a happy and healthy person, you need to keep your mind engaged. That is why it often is better to continue working after the so-called normal retirement age.

- A powerful motivation for success at work is an interest in building income for a purpose that goes beyond support of family—such as philanthropy or patronage of the arts.

- If a person retires from business, he or she should substitute other meaningful work.

- At any age, make an effort to integrate exercise into your workday.

- As we grow older, we tend to think about the past, and it is often rewarding to do so. But it's best to focus primarily on the present and the future.

- Stay curious. Greet every morning with enthusiasm, knowing that each day you will learn something new.

Roy R. Neuberger

Roy R. Neuberger is a founder of the investment management firm Neuberger Berman, a renowned professional investor, and a recognized collector of American art of his time. From its founding in 1939, Neuberger Berman has had a focus on managing money for wealthy individuals. Mr. Neuberger expanded the firm's capabilities in 1950, when he launched Guardian Fund, one of the industry's first no-load mutual funds. On the art front, Mr. Neuberger has donated over 1,000 works to colleges and museums throughout the country. His donation of paintings and sculptures to the State University of New York (SUNY) at Purchase forms the core of the school's Neuberger Museum of Art. Currently in his late nineties, Mr. Neuberger continues to stay engaged in active management of his own accounts. He exercises and goes to his office daily.

5

THE VALUE OF WORK, PART II

A Better Career the Second Time Around

JANICE REALS ELLIG

Starting as an executive trainee 15 years ago, Alexander Novak rose rapidly through the ranks at MBS Funds, a Baltimore-based mutual funds organization. Ten years later, at the age of 35, he was named Chief Operating Officer. During his tenure, the company's fortunes increased dramatically, by every conceivable measure. MBS even held its own during the dot-com bust and the subsequent general downturn in the markets.

Alex Novak was on top of the world. But then, in June 2001—to the surprise of practically everyone except his wife—he quit his job. In September, he began a second career as a teacher of third graders in an inner-city school.

Because Alex's first career had been so successful, he had accumulated sufficient wealth to afford this precipitous reduction in earnings. And he had chosen to do what he always wanted to do—teach kids.

(Incidentally, Alex Novak's name and all other personal and company names in this chapter have been changed, with two obvious exceptions—my husband's and mine—but all of the stories about second careers are true.)

Consider this case. For 10 years, Jennifer Millman was a highly successful financial marketing executive. Then, in 1999, she decided that she had earned all the money she'd ever need. Now, she works just as hard and just as effectively as she used to. But she doesn't get paid for her efforts. Instead, she devotes her time to a sociopolitical issue that interests her tremendously. Utilizing her marketing background, Jennifer writes position papers and engages in unpaid lobbying efforts to influence Congress to pass the legislation she favors.

Do Alex Novak and Jennifer Millman represent extreme cases? Of course. Voluntary cuts in annual compensation from $1.3 million to $32,000 and from $450,000 to $0.00 are certainly not everyday events in the world of business. But the decisions of these two successful people—to move on to second careers, offering success of a different sort—are far from unusual.

THE FIRST PREREQUISITE: ACCUMULATING SUFFICIENT WEALTH

What enables these people to make these dramatic, life-changing decisions? The common denominator is *wealth,* defined as what you will need and want when you decide to "live your life." Their financial success in their first careers provides them with the freedom to choose second careers *without regard to the financial consequences of their actions.* No matter what they choose to do—or how little it might pay—their accumulated wealth provides absolute assurance that they and their families will be well provided for.

If you intend to break away from your first career, as Alex, Jennifer, and many others have done, you (or your spouse) need to have enough money to support your lifestyle. You must be able to finance the transition, pay any necessary tuition, or cover the expenses involved in launching an entrepreneurial venture. And if your second career is not intended to be a money maker, you need sufficient funds to provide a comfortable level of support for the rest of your preretirement life.

Wealth is the fuel that launches the second-career rocket. Without a sufficient amount of money, you'll be hard put to realize your dreams. And of course, the definition of sufficiency varies with each individual.

THE SECOND PREREQUISITE: POWERFUL MOTIVATION

Alex Novak and Jennifer Millman, like many other people I've worked with, listened to, or read about, were motivated by a powerful and persistent need to control the course of their own lives. Some of them wanted complete control; they became entrepreneurs. I am probably in that category myself. I moved from a successful and very rewarding 20-year career as a corporate human resources/marketing executive to my current, basically entrepreneurial position as a partner in an executive search firm, as well as a writer and lecturer. My husband, Bruce Ellig, provides another example. After a 36-year career as a corporate executive with Pfizer, Inc., Bruce retired. But now, five years later, he's busier than ever: publishing books, speaking to audiences around the world, teaching, and serving on boards.

Bruce and I have made significant changes in our careers, from the corporate to the entrepreneurial world. Yet we still work in human resources and marketing, the arenas in which we started.

Others have chosen second careers that bear absolutely no relation to their previous work experience. CEOs have become farmers. A social worker I know has become a successful physical therapist. Accountants, lawyers, and doctors have evolved into priests, ministers, and rabbis.

I have even encountered a man who has followed the example of Voltaire's famous character, Candide, who—after traveling the world and accumulating and losing vast fortunes—decided to settle down and "make his garden grow." A highly successful investment banker recently did essentially the same thing. At age 38, he quit his job, opting to stay home with his wife and three young children.

When I called him and started to describe a position that had become available, he cut me off by saying, "I was tending my garden. You interrupted me. I don't want to hear about business again. I'm taking at least a year off and don't want to think about work, so please don't call me."

Again, an extreme case. But like all the rest of us who chose to move on to second careers (or noncareers), he did so in order to achieve some very important personal goals.

Those goals boil down to three basic ideas. We wanted to *control our own lives* or at least gain greater autonomy. We wanted to *integrate all the disparate parts of our lives.* And we wanted to *make a difference.* We wanted to achieve something of which we could be proud.

Consider the case of Margaret Sinclair. She was a marketing executive with a corporate consulting firm. Her specialty was mergers and acquisitions. Last summer, at the age of 50, she quit her job and went back to school. Today, she's enrolled in a graduate program in psychology at an Ivy League university.

Why? "Because," she told me, "I realized that what made me successful in my marketing job was my understanding of people's motivations, and I wanted to use that ability to help those in need. Don't get me wrong. I wasn't ashamed of what I had been doing. I was helping a reputable firm to sell a valuable service to a sophisticated clientele. And for a long time, it was fun. But one day, I said, 'Is that all there is?'

'Can't I find more meaning in life?' And I realized that the answer to that question was a resounding 'Yes!' "

THE THIRD PREREQUISITE: A
LONG-TERM STRATEGY

The best model here is financial. When starting out in the world of business, every young man or woman is well advised to select a retirement vehicle as soon as possible. Over the years, regular contributions and prudent investment management decisions will enable the fund to grow. It will benefit from appreciation in market value and the powerful long-term effects of compound interest.

Similar advice applies to planning for a second career. (In many cases, this too can be thought of as retirement planning because, for the vast majority of people, retirement, beginning at age 50, 55, 65, or even later or earlier, will constitute the beginning of a second career. That career may well be devoted to hobbies, studies, travel, volunteer work, or a combination of these and other activities.)

For people like those whose stories I've been telling in this chapter, a second career will begin much sooner. In fact, at the start of a first career, no one can predict when, and under what circumstances, a second career might begin.

But one needs to be ready for that career. That's where the retirement–financial-planning analogy comes into play. The best time to plan for a second career—the best time to design a strategy—is right at the beginning of a *first* career.

If you enjoy your work, that's fine. But consider what else you enjoy. What gets you really excited? What would you like to learn more about? Yes, your first career may be very demanding, in terms of time and energy. But make an effort to set aside sufficient quantities of those two resources for the purpose of exploring other options.

Become involved in interests and activities that are not directly related to the job. Consider joining professional organizations. They can open up new areas that may prove to be of interest to you; they may offer opportunities to build a second career that makes good use of your professional experience and expertise. Volunteer to speak and write for those organizations. Activities of this kind will enable you to encounter very interesting people and organizations that have nothing whatever to do with your job, and those new influences can set you on an entirely new path.

SOWING THE SEEDS

Some people inadvertently begin developing their second careers in early childhood. A person who has always been interested in arts and crafts, or music, for instance, might pursue that interest in early adult life by signing up for various training programs and courses. In time, that avocation may develop into a second career.

I know a man who had established a first career as a partner in a medium-size accounting firm. The work was mildly interesting, gave him a certain amount of satisfaction, and provided more-than-adequate support for his wife and two young children. But his major passion wasn't his work but his hobby. As a young boy, he had become fascinated by the radio programs of the 1940s: Jack Benny, Charlie McCarthy, the Shadow, the Lone Ranger, and others. These programs—and bigtime network radio itself—eventually fell by the wayside as television took over, but this man never lost his interest in that bygone medium of entertainment.

He began collecting recordings of the old shows. For several years, he traded with other like-minded hobbyists. When he was in his late forties, it occurred to him that there was a far larger market out there than he or his fellow hobbyists had previously believed. This market was just waiting to be tapped.

And tap it he did, using mail order—and, later, the Internet—to sell recordings and other memorabilia of old-time radio. After a few months, his new business was successful enough to enable him to quit his job as an accountant, and he never looked back.

He and his wife worked very hard to build the company. But they loved what they were doing. They were passionately dedicated to it, and their passion led to success. They made—and are still making—millions. And the founder of the company, now in semiretirement, continues to search for those elusive recordings of the programs he loves so well.

Perhaps his example offers the best advice of all. Follow your passion. Pursue your dreams. Expand your horizons. Constantly reinvent yourself. Learn new things—just continue to learn. Ask yourself if you feel fulfilled by what you do during the workday. Ask yourself whether all parts of your life are fully integrated. In simple terms: Are you happy in your work? If not, or if you feel that you've achieved all the success and satisfaction your first career can offer, take a long and hard look at the alternatives.

The opportunities are infinite. If you have accumulated sufficient wealth during your successful first career, you can pursue the opportunity that interests you the most. Your second (or even third) career can provide all the fulfillment you've ever imagined and can continue to do it at any age. Live your dreams and a life you love, always!

Words to the Wise

- If you feel you've achieved all the success and satisfaction your first career can offer, consider the possibilities presented by a second career.

- People seek second careers in order to control their own lives, integrate the disparate parts of those lives, and make a difference. They want something they can call their own, something of which they can be proud.

- Financial success in your first career can provide you with the freedom to choose a second career, without regard to the financial consequences involved.

- The best time to plan for a second career is at the beginning of a first career. Become involved in interests and activities that are not related to your job but will expand your horizons.

- Follow your passion. Pursue your dreams. Feel complete!

Janice Reals Ellig

Janice Reals Ellig is a partner with Gould, McCoy & Chadick, a premier executive search firm. She has over 20 years of corporate and senior-level recruiting experience and has worked extensively with top management and boards of directors on organizational development, executive compensation, succession planning, and branding initiatives. She is on the board of Fountain House, the National Executive Service Corps, and the Wish List. She sits on the advisory council for the College of Business Administration at the University of Iowa, and on the business committee of the Metropolitan Museum of Art in New York. Ms. Ellig is coauthor of the book, What Every Successful Woman Knows: 12 Breakthrough Strategies to Get the Power and Ignite Your Career. *She appears on TV, and the news media frequently quote her on career issues.*

6

WHEN GIVING IS GAINING

A Strategic Approach to Philanthropy

ELLEN E. REMMER

John and Adele Phillip* were frustrated. They gave considerable sums to charity each year, attended fund-raisers, and were involved in a number of institutions. Instead of feeling that their money was making a difference, however, they felt they had become hooked to far too many organizations. A sense of being out of control is not uncommon among wealthy donors whose obligations and commitments multiply over time.

When asked if there was one single area where they wanted to make a mark, John and Adele identified the schools. As John said, "I got a good education in the public schools, but no one is getting a good education now."

After introductions to people working in school reform, the Phillips met a dynamic pair of educators who were running an experimental high school and were full of ideas about improving the system. Impressed, John gave them a grant to develop a business plan on how they would implement their ideas. When their plan pointed to the establishment of a new institution to work on school reform in their city, the Phillips gave a grant to get it started. It was a challenge grant; other funding would be required after the first year. John became chairman of the board.

That was eight years ago. The ideas proved so worthwhile that a major international foundation has since provided a large grant to the institution the Phillips started. John and Adele still support other organizations, but their hearts are here. And they now feel in control of their giving.

Clearly, giving money is good. Giving can help you make sense out of surplus wealth while connecting you to broader social issues. It can make you feel good about yourself because your contributions bring help to those who need it most.

---

* Names used throughout this chapter are fictitious. Examples of charitable giving and the charities/nonprofits are real.

But you may be like many people—like John and Adele Phillip, in fact—in feeling vaguely unsatisfied by writing checks to various religious, civic, and charitable organizations, in response to their appeals. If so, consider going beyond checkbook philanthropy to what we at The Philanthropic Initiative call "strategic giving." Writing checks offers a temporary fix to those you help and a temporary boost to your self-esteem. Strategic giving means bringing your individual and family values to bear in a focused way that produces a long-lasting impact.

Strategic giving can be especially rewarding when it reflects your interests and passions. It can bring families together in shared efforts to help the community. By strategic giving, we mean effective giving based on a knowledgeable examination of social needs and best practices, and executed through carefully planned strategies. It also helps to have good instincts sprinkled with an entrepreneurial spirit.

To be truly effective and rewarding, strategic philanthropy must reflect your core values and concerns. You should first identify those values and concerns, and then choose a charitable focus. Just as the Phillips recognized the contrast between the schools of yesterday and today, another family was spurred to action by its connection to a babysitter who was a victim of domestic violence. A family with a long tradition of supporting local cultural organizations decided to focus on art opportunities for needy teenagers. Still another established a private foundation to meet the specific needs of adolescent girls.

For many people, finding the right charitable focus takes considerable effort.

FIND YOUR FOCUS

The opportunities—and the needs—are virtually endless. The prospect can be overwhelming. To help you move toward strategic giving when you are ready to do so, we outline three key steps:

1. Identify your charitable values.
2. Build a knowledge base.
3. Concentrate your giving for maximum impact.

As a first step, identify your charitable values and your motivation for giving. If you have been supporting the national and local Alzheimer's Associations because a relative was afflicted with this dread disease, you may not have to look further. If you have been making scattershot gifts in response to appeals, it may take more effort to choose a charitable focus.

Start by reviewing the gifts you have made to date. Which ones have been most meaningful? Try to figure out why these gifts have been personally significant. Then do the same exercise in reverse. Which gifts have given you the least satisfaction, and why?

Donors find satisfaction in different ways. One donor may enjoy supporting innovative programs in small grass-roots organizations. Another may find the most satisfaction in gifts to community leadership institutions. Some donors prefer to make gifts such as scholarships. They know their gift will help needy individuals become self-sufficient. Think about your responses to the most satisfying and least satisfying gifts. What do your answers say about your values and preferences?

Step two involves building a solid base of knowledge. Once you make your preliminary decisions about your family's values and charitable focus, you can be ready to build on what others have learned and done. Instead of reinventing the wheel, find a way to improve the wheel that others have built.

You might seek out position papers or academic research on your chosen areas of interest. Consultants or organizations such as community foundations may offer more specifics about community needs and efforts under way to address the issues you care about. Talk to others who are actively working in your areas of interest. Visit existing programs and try to talk to people who are actually affected by the problems you wish to address.

As step three, determine how you will concentrate your charitable giving to have the most impact. Writing one or two sizable checks to carefully chosen organizations can be a greater impetus for change than indiscriminately writing dozens of smaller checks to assorted charitable groups in the course of a year. Moreover, as the Phillips found, by focusing your efforts, you put yourself in charge. This lets you move from responding to a deluge of charitable requests to making considered decisions about what you want your funding to accomplish. Be proactive instead of reactive.

Ask yourself these questions:

- What issues or organizations arouse my passion?
- Do these issues or organizations have a pressing, demonstrated need?

- Do I know enough about the issues to intelligently assess the difference my funding could make?
- Given my time and resources, how many issues can I support?
- What experience is likely to most satisfy me *and* have the greatest impact on the community?

It's important to remain flexible and to be a listener. Instead of trying to fit a square peg into a round issue, ask the intended recipients what will make your grants more effective. View the recipients of your funds as partners, not adversaries who are out to take your money. Treat philanthropy as a business arrangement in which both parties must benefit.

Another set of questions relates to your role as a donor. Will you support the key issues most effectively as a venture capitalist who is creating a new organizational structure? That's what the Phillips did, in funding a new institution.

Or, will you act as what we call a *capacity builder?* Will you strengthen an existing organization? Mack Anderson became involved in an understaffed community chorale and gave an anonymous grant to bring in a consultant who could strengthen the group's organization and governance structure. Some donors might fund a development person to help a small organization reach a manageable scale. Others might provide a renewing sabbatical for the executive director of a large organization.

Besides making you better informed, these can be your first steps toward building your philanthropic due-diligence network.

THINK OUTSIDE THE BOX

Many people make charitable donations by writing checks to some portion of the annual year-end deluge of appeals. Some go further and plan gifts of appreciated property to organizations they care about. But the truly strategic givers bring a creative dimension to philanthropy.

Being creative means understanding complex and challenging social issues and identifying alternative approaches. If your goal is to feed the homeless, consider the possibilities. You could support research into enhancing world agricultural production. You could fund your local food pantry, and/or volunteer to serve meals there on a regular basis. Or you might help to start a farm with the dual purpose of employing the formerly homeless and providing fresh produce to homeless shelters.

The Reston Family Foundation initially discovered, among family members, a common concern for poor women and their families. Further exploration, with the help of a philanthropy consultant, led to the realization that adolescent girls generally receive little help. The foundation began to fund both research and direct-service programs to help the girls take charge of their lives and become leaders in their families and communities. One program offered a computer clubhouse for girls, intended as a national model to encourage girls to become involved in technology.

The foundation's activities were originally based in Boston. Now that an infrastructure for girls' programs is in place in Boston, the foundation no longer funds programs but continues to support an umbrella body called the Girls Coalition. On an entirely new frontier, it has expanded operations to the culturally different milieu of Florida, where some family members now live. Before making the move, family members interviewed many local advocates and service providers and eventually found a champion for a girls' agenda. Under her leadership, the foundation convened a lunch meeting of people who cared about girls in the community. The result: a Girls Initiative was formed. It was modeled, in part, on the Boston Girls Coalition but had its own unique approach and structure.

It took only a little seed money—basically, the cost of the luncheon—to get the ball rolling. More money will go to the specific programs started by the Initiative. Mostly, it took time and effort on the part of family members who identified the local need and the people who could address the need. The funding, the time, and the effort all grew out of the excitement of the family members who put the unique needs of girls on the agenda.

Thinking outside the box can also mean becoming what we call a "venturesome donor." Grant-making is the central tool for donors, but you can support the community in additional proactive ways. This often requires nonfinancial donations—your skill, time, talent, and networks. They will enrich the philanthropic experience for you and increase the impact of the gift.

As an example, in the early 1990s, the Hustons decided that they wanted to support individuals who had limited opportunity but limitless potential. They set up a scholarship program for local high school graduates—not to fund tuition, but to pay for "extras" such as books and computers.

Beyond providing the money, the couple set up a mentoring relationship with the young people they support. Working with about 10 scholarship recipients at a time (all chosen from the high school Tom Huston attended), they meet with them once or twice during the school year and, between meetings, keep in touch by e-mail. They help the students find summer jobs and are available to lend a helping hand when needed.

RETHINK CURRENT GIVING

If you choose to focus your philanthropic efforts, what will happen to the issues and organizations you've supported over the years? Even as you develop a newly strengthened charitable focus for the future, you may not want to abandon the ongoing causes. You may also have obligatory commitments as a business or community leader. Sorting out "personal" and "corporate" giving can be especially confusing if you are engaged in a family-owned business.

Think about how much you give—your philanthropic "budget," if you will—and determine what portion of that amount you're willing to allocate to be a "good citizen" and what portion should be dedicated to causes, issues, or people you care deeply about.

Look at the important personal values and issues that you identified earlier. Jot down a few of the most satisfying gifts you have ever made and the reasons why. Then make a list of your current gifts and see whether there's a match between what you care about and what you do.

One of our clients felt he had been strong-armed into a $300,000 gift to his alma mater, an institution with a handsome endowment, when he had planned to give $25,000. Preparing his charitable budget helped him to "just say no" to later demands from the university. He then allocated larger gifts to a cause he cared deeply about: underwriting new education models for high school students.

Business always has a certain amount of quid pro quo, but you may be on a slippery slope if you're raising money from colleagues and business associates who expect you to donate to their causes. You may want to raise money from friends to introduce them to an issue you care about. But how often will they get involved in your pet cause, and how often have you been involved in theirs? You might be more satisfied if you give more of your own money to the causes you care about.

DIVE IN AND GIVE

Finding your philanthropic focus, as we've seen, entails identifying the causes, issues, and organizations you care most deeply about. But there's more at stake when it comes to making effective gifts and determining how deeply you want to be involved.

Think about how different types of funding may help to achieve distinct objectives. You can provide seed money to enable a remarkable social entrepreneur to start up a new program, or supply matching funds to help an organization diversify its funding base. Perhaps you're willing to make loans or offer guarantees when an organization needs substantial funds in a hurry. Another issue revolves around how much money you will give to any particular organization, and for how long. You could make one-time grants for a special short-term project, or provide multiyear funding to enable a start-up to get on its feet.

How will you identify funding needs? Will you seek out model projects to support, or will you publicize your areas of interest and solicit proposals? And then there is the "$64,000 question": Do you want to start a new organization to meet an extraordinary need, or will you support existing organizations and expand their influence?

In part, the answer depends on whether there are existing organizations in the niche you've identified, and how well they meet or could meet the social or community needs. Ultimately, you could follow the Phillips' lead and launch a new organization.

The Hartunian family leveraged their giving when they decided to set up a revolving loan fund for land trusts. The grants helped land trusts conduct public funding campaigns. They also provided bridge money so that the trusts could buy property quickly when there was a risk of immediate development. The arrangement helped the family recycle its grant money and have a significant impact.

Before you work with an existing organization, be sure that it meets both subjective and objective criteria for success. Grant-making is more an art than a science, but using a framework for evaluating requests will help you refine your goals and choose among many worthwhile causes and organizations.

On the subjective side, beyond fulfilling your personal passion, does the organization offer the ability to connect and be hands-on, or will your role be restricted to providing funds? After meeting with the organization's leaders, do you have faith in their vision and their ability to carry it out? Take time to visit the projects under consideration so that you can develop a "gut feel" for the people and organizations. Site visits are invaluable.

Objective criteria are not limited to financing. Does the organization have a good track record in meeting its philanthropic goals? Does it have credibility with the population it serves as well as with the larger community? Can you ascertain how many people will be served and the impact on their individual lives? A list of board members can provide insight into the governance of the organization. It can also be a good sign if there is little turnover among key staff members.

On the financial side, ask how much of the charity's income goes to its programs and how much is spent on administrative costs. Too little given to programs might indicate unnecessary overhead; too little to administration may mean the organization lacks an effective infrastructure. Review the organization's annual report and financial statements, and the Form 990 it files with the IRS. Find out whether the organization has a diverse and stable funding base.

In some instances, you may not want to work with an organization at all. We've seen donors be really effective by focusing on people rather than issues. In one instance, an entrepreneur started out as an inventor. When he made it big, he decided to lend support to other inventors launching big ideas.

FOLLOW UP

When you've made your decision and initiated support, be sure to track the results. In strategic philanthropy, as in business, outcomes are important. Look at it as due diligence, accountability, and measuring return. Following up and evaluating the results of your philanthropy will help you understand what has worked, what hasn't, and how future giving could be redirected.

At The Philanthropic Initiative (TPI), we define monitoring as an ongoing process of observing and reporting on programs, thereby comparing actual achievement to what was planned. We define evaluation as a periodic process that attempts to measure a program's impact. The following examples may clarify the distinction:

- *Monitoring:* Did the home visiting program make calls on 100 new mothers and provide them with supplies and advice?

■ *Evaluation:* Did the 100 newborns in the home visiting program become healthy, thriving two-year-olds because of nutritionally balanced diets and attentive parenting?

The amount of monitoring and evaluation you do depends in part on the size and scope of the gifts you make. Objective, long-term evaluations can be very expensive, but you can also learn a lot if you spend thoughtful time just listening to your grantees. In deciding on your approach, ask yourself what you want to learn. What outcomes would convince you that the philanthropic investment has been successful? How will you get the information? And how will you use evaluation data to adjust future grants? Be disciplined but realistic in your assessment plans.

If you are working as a family, build time into family foundation meetings to discuss what you've done in the past, what has been successful, and what could be better.

The Woodley family, for example, agreed to devote one meeting a year to their reflections on what they had learned from their grants to support youth and families. They agreed to visit every grantee during the course of the grant to find out what had been learned and what changes were being made. Finally, they decided to explore hiring an outside evaluator to take a look at six of their larger grants supporting youth development and to provide some perspective on what they had accomplished. The family found that these evaluation steps helped them to focus their grantmaking so that it could become more effective.

CHOOSE YOUR VEHICLE

There are many ways to channel strategic giving. Charitable remainder trusts and charitable lead trusts are popular estate planning tools (see Chapter 13). For lifetime giving, many wealthy donors prefer family foundations and donor-advised funds.

Most donors employ more than one charitable vehicle. The Restons use a family foundation to address the unmet needs of adolescent girls. Individual family members also contribute to donor-advised funds run by their local community foundations.

Private foundations have many advantages for wealthy philanthropists. A foundation is a declaration of who you are, a way to achieve credibility and visibility in your community. Linking a foundation name to a significant issue or cause can draw attention to that cause. With a foundation, you can create a legacy, ensuring the continuation of your family name. You can dedicate your foundation to fulfilling a single passionate interest, or use it to distribute grants that will meet a variety of charitable goals. Either way, in addition to the control you gain when you give through your own foundation, there are the psychic rewards of involving your children and leaving a legacy.

Be aware that, in addition to set-up and annual costs, there are legal restrictions on foundations. You must distribute at least 5 percent of the assets each year. The foundation must file tax returns and pay an excise tax on investment income. It's also worth noting that donations to private foundations are deductible only up to 30 percent of adjusted gross income (AGI) for cash and 20 percent for securities. Donations to other charitable entities are deductible up to 50 percent of AGI for cash and 30 percent for securities. In both cases, deductions in excess of these limitations may be carried over for the succeeding five years.

In recent years, donor-advised funds have become increasingly popular as lower-cost, hassle-free alternatives to private foundations. Donor-advised funds are sponsored by community foundations, by specific charities (such as some universities), and by financial service companies. They all raise funds, make grants, and manage investments. Community foundations generally provide their donors with valuable information about community issues and exemplary programs. The best of them also bring donors together to share ideas.

As with a family foundation, you can make a tax-deductible donation and distribute grants in future years. But there is no federal law requiring minimum distributions and there is no excise tax. Better yet, the parent foundation handles the administrative chores and selects and monitors the investments. You generally can choose between placing your family name on your fund or retaining anonymity. Increasingly, donor-advised funds are ensuring perpetuity, so you can leave a legacy as well.

However, you do give up a certain amount of control. The funds are called "donor-advised" for a reason: You can ask to have distributions made to specific charities, but the fund has the final word. Although donors' wishes are almost always granted, the lack of ultimate control disturbs some would-be donors.

INVOLVE THE FAMILY

Many wealthy philanthropists prefer to make most of their charitable grants through their own family foundations. Doing so provides the most control over giving. It also offers a framework for involving the entire family in a structured way. An adult child might serve as a director; teenagers can participate in grant-making decisions; younger children can be exposed to the idea of philanthropy in less formal ways, such as visiting programs funded by the foundation.

Whether or not you employ a foundation, giving together can be a way to share important family values with your children. Philanthropy can be a tool to educate children about wealth—not just giving it away, but managing it in a responsible fashion. When they are young, this education can start via a three-part allowance: one-third for spending, one-third for saving, and one-third for giving. Later, it can include identifying interesting fund opportunities, joining in grant-making decisions, monitoring investment results, and other tasks that are age-appropriate.

Some families provide a sum for high school and college-age children to allocate to charity as they see fit. Some parents—and grandparents—offer matching funds, and ask the children to show their commitment with their own money or volunteer time. In the Robinson family, the grandparents put up all the money but ask their grandchildren to select the charity or charities and report back on results.

In Boston and some other cities, an annual *Catalogue for Philanthropy* is published. International groups such as World Vision also have catalogs that provide a menu of philanthropic investments. Using such catalogs, all family members can scan the list of organizations, see what's exciting, and decide what groups to explore further. Many families encourage their children to become involved with an organization through a volunteer commitment as well as a donation of money. In fact, we don't want kids to think it's all in the money. Really good philanthropy goes well beyond money to a hands-on experience. It involves doing careful due diligence, making connections among people and organizations, and perhaps sitting on the boards of one or more groups.

One caveat: Many youngsters relish joining their parents in charitable endeavors, but its best to keep participation optional. Invite your children to be involved, but don't assume that they want to become involved, and don't force the issue. Giving together should not become an obligation or a burden. And don't presume that creating a family foundation, as an example, will either "fix those greedy kids" or "bring us closer together." A foundation works well only if everyone wants to be there, working together. In some families, every family member who participates is also expected to contribute some funds to the foundation.

When the younger generation does join in, operate on the assumption that you all have something to learn from each other, regardless of differences in your age or philosophy. Many of our clients point out how much they learn when they listen to their children and grandchildren talk about the different pressures on kids today. And, the younger generation frequently comments on the reservoir of experience that their elders provide.

Recognize that you have individual interests, but working well together means working together for the overall good of the family. You can accomplish this by setting aside a percentage of giving for each family member and reserving the bulk of giving for issues on which there is consensus. Most important: the process of family giving should be enjoyable, offer more kick than individual giving agendas alone, and contribute to the creation of a new generation of philanthropists.

FOR MORE INFORMATION

Many organizations evaluate charities and/or lend support to donors. Here are some that you may find useful:

The National Center for Family Philanthropy (www.ncfp.org) conducts research and develops educational materials and programs for families and individuals.

The Council on Foundations (www.cof.org) publishes useful materials for family foundations and conducts an annual Family Foundation Conference and periodic Next Generation Retreats.

The Association of Small Foundations (www.smallfoundations.org) assists foundations that have little or no staff.

Regional Associations of Grantmakers (www.rag.org) are regional, state, or community associations of grant-making members. Many conduct roundtables for family foundations.

Guidestar (www.guidestar.com) is a source of online information about the operations and finances of nonprofit organizations.

The BBB Wise Giving Alliance (www.give.org) has developed standards for charitable solicitations. They are used to rate the financial and management accountability of nonprofit organizations.

The Philanthropic Initiative (www.tpi.org) provides educational programs, materials, and consulting services on strategic giving.

Words to the Wise

- Pursue *strategic* giving. To produce long-lasting impact, bring your individual and family values together in a focused way.
- Build a knowledge base and an ongoing network by consulting those with experience in philanthropy.
- Understand your charitable values and your motives for giving.
- Focus. You can achieve the greatest impact if you devote much of your charitable giving to one or a few areas of interest.
- Be creative. Think about different ways in which your gifts of time, talent, and financial resources can best meet the social needs at hand.
- Take charge and be proactive. Don't let yourself be drained by an ongoing barrage of responsive requests.
- Require your grantees to report back on your gifts. You and the grantees can then learn how well the goals are being accomplished and what changes need to be made.
- Invite your family to build and participate in a philanthropic process that strengthens your connections to each other and to the outside world.

Ellen E. Remmer

Ellen E. Remmer is director of the family philanthropy practice at The Philanthropic Initiative, a not-for-profit organization that works with donors on strategic approaches to philanthropy. She helps families develop effective giving programs and governance structures. Ms. Remmer serves as a managing trustee of her own family's foundation, which supports programs that help disadvantaged girls. She is also director of her family's investment company. She is vice-chair of the Women's Philanthropy Institute and serves as co-chair of Boston Funders Supporting Women and Girls.

7

RESOLVING CONFLICTS IN A FAMILY ENTERPRISE

Preserving Wealth and Relationships

FREDDA HERZ BROWN

In 1946, Michael Colson* founded ColCorp. When he died, in 1984, he left his wife and three children—Margaret, Philip, and Beth—a thriving textile business (four plants were strategically located throughout the South and in the Midwest) and a nationwide customer base. The second-generation owners-managers of this family business—Philip Colson and his younger sister, Beth—proved to be a very successful team. Under their stewardship, ColCorp continued to grow and prosper.

On the surface, at least, it seemed that all four shareholders—Michael Colson's widow, Elizabeth, and the three Colson children—were content with the direction Col-Corp was taking.

In 1999, the company's board of directors, on the recommendation of Philip and Beth, made a decision that brought a long-simmering family conflict to the surface. The managing siblings proposed to purchase a competing company, and the board approved. However, by the time the deal was completed, the purchase price had soared well beyond the original estimates.

Margaret Colson, the eldest sibling and the only one who was not active in the business, was very unhappy with the outcome of this transaction. She felt that it placed the company in a difficult financial position. Her unhappiness was reinforced when her next quarterly dividend check gave her less than half the amount she was accustomed to. Margaret contended that the actions of her siblings had subverted their deceased father's intention to provide the nonworking family members with ample dividends. She also contended that the decision to buy the company at a higher price should have come back to the board for review.

---

* All the names in this chapter are fictional. All situations are composites. They have been drawn from years of experience with many different families and family enterprises and simplified for purposes of this chapter.

When she made her unhappiness known to Philip and Beth, they told her that the purchase, even at the much higher price, had been absolutely necessary. Without it, they said, the company might not be able to survive.

Margaret was so unhappy with both the tone and the substance of this response that she retained a lawyer and was getting ready to sue Philip and Beth for their actions. Her siblings retained a lawyer themselves. Elizabeth became extremely upset; she feared disaster for both the business and the family.

Margaret's lawyer shared the mother's fears. A lawsuit, the attorney warned, would lead inevitably to a family breakup and to the destruction of the business—the very thing her client wanted to preserve. Her discussion with the opposing attorney revealed that he shared her apprehensions. He too felt that the legal system would only exacerbate the family's problems. The two lawyers agreed that some alternative approach had to be found.

W as an "out-of-court" settlement possible? Was it pursued? Did it succeed? And does it provide a useful model for other family enterprises, including family foundations, mutually managed financial holdings, or family-owned businesses?

The answers to those questions are what this chapter is all about. There are well-established, proven techniques for resolving conflicts in family enterprises that are ostensibly about money. Our firm specializes in this type of conflict resolution. We try to determine the "drivers" of the conflict by clarifying the position of each individual, determining the nature of the relationships between them (historically and currently), and examining the potential resolutions. We also bring into focus a number of issues that go well beyond the boundaries of the current situation. In many cases, issues rooted in the past are the underlying causes of the conflict.

FAMILY CONFLICTS: A DEFINITION

It's important to make a distinction between issues and conflicts. Everyone has issues with other people—in family enterprises and in virtually every other aspect of life. Differences in viewpoints, interests, and lifestyles are inevitable, even among siblings who grew up together. Most of these issues can be resolved with a certain amount of time, effort, and mutual goodwill. When they cannot be resolved, they become, by our definition, "conflicts."

The term "conflict" applies to situations that cause tensions among people. There may or may not be an outright, observable struggle between them; or an issue may take on an emotional focus; or their opinions may escalate into unmovable positions.

Conflicts can seem interminable; some are transferred from one generation to the next. People take sides. They argue. Or they refuse to speak to each other. Their family relationships suffer. And if they are engaged together in a business or other family enterprise, *that* can suffer as well.

In some family situations, there is no way to prevent conflicts from developing. Each party becomes increasingly caught up in his or her own viewpoint. Often, the conflict simmers internally and surfaces only occasionally; when that happens, the manifestations are surprisingly intense. Generally speaking, the greater the intensity surrounding an issue, the more important it has become emotionally.

THE ISSUE OF MONEY IN FAMILY DYNAMICS

Our focus in this chapter is on family conflicts that seem to revolve about money. An issue that is truly about money can probably be satisfied in a purely financial way. However, money is almost always symbolic of other issues, and when a money issue develops into a conflict, money is rarely the *underlying* cause. In many wealthy families, money tends to get connected to power, control, and love.

For all families, irrespective of their financial situations, money is an emotionally charged issue. When family members work together—with people whom they might not otherwise have chosen to work with—the family enterprise becomes a fertile pasture on which these issues can take root and grow.

Lifelong emotional connections tend to call up old issues, patterns, and alliances in a new context—one in which the family members are dependent on each other for their professional and financial success. Family members who manage their money together, or work together, must deal with the intensity of these shared activities and decisions. Old issues—who should be in charge and who was/is the parental favorite—may become central. Structures set up for handling relationships that worked during an earlier stage in the family's development may have become obsolete. They may need revisiting and revision as the family and its needs change.

Despite these negative aspects, a family enterprise can provide immense opportunities. Relatives who work together can build strong lifelong relationships. A family enterprise also provides a very effective means to help the next generation understand the importance of family relationships, of philanthropy, of human and financial capital, and of working with others toward a mutually beneficial objective.

But all these benefits can come to naught if the inherent conflicts in family enterprises rise to the surface and are not dealt with quickly and effectively.

FAMILY ENTERPRISES IN CONFLICT

Let's move beyond the Colson family and look at some of the so-called "money" conflicts that surfaced in my work with wealthy families.

Conflict

The Lewis Family Foundation   Barbara, Sandra, and Constance Lewis were the trustees of the foundation, which was funded by the operating profits of the family business. At one of the earliest meetings following the establishment of the foundation, Sandra proposed that they award a sizable grant—encompassing most of the foundation's available funds for the current year—to establish a college scholarship program for underprivileged children. Her older sister, Barbara, offered a counterproposal: funding a shelter for battered wives and children. Her younger sister, Constance, did not formally take sides but appeared to be leaning toward Barbara's position.

To an outside observer, it would appear that both projects were worthy causes. But neither Sandra nor Barbara could see any merit in the other's position. Each of the two sisters was adamant that her proposed project should receive the funds. By the next meeting, the funding issue showed signs of developing into a full-fledged conflict. Sandra, the middle sister, regarded it as just one more example of the lifelong tendency of her two siblings to "gang up" against her.

The Kazinsky Corporation   In 1949, Marvin Kazinsky founded a company that manufactured work uniforms for nurses, hotel and restaurant workers, security personnel, and people in a variety of other jobs and professions. By the time his son, Ralph, came into the company in 1981, the business had become a sizable enterprise: 10 manufacturing and distribution facilities were established in the United States and Mexico. After a long apprenticeship during which he became familiar with every aspect of the business, Ralph proposed to his father that they upgrade their computer system. They could then receive daily reports on production, income, and profitability from every facility.

Marvin vetoed Ralph's proposal, claiming that this major capital expenditure would be a waste of money. "If it ain't broke," he said, "why fix it?" Marvin had another motive. He didn't want anyone at the company to keep close tabs on the income he was personally taking from the business. Ralph was aware of Marvin's profit-dipping, but his business sense warned that his father's response was shortsighted and would limit the company's long-term growth. Both men took this matter very seriously, and it began to affect their business and personal relationships. It had all the earmarks of an emerging conflict.

The Monahan Family Office   The office had been established by three brothers in the 1930s. It now serves the needs of their grandchildren and great grandchildren—a total of 18 households. Some of these households avail themselves of all the services offered by the Family Office, including paying household bills and balancing personal checkbooks. Other households utilize fewer of the available services. The Patrick Monahan family chose to confine its relationship with the Family Office to investment management.

As Patrick became aware of the extent to which his cousins were benefiting from the office's personal financial services, he asked, at a family meeting, "Since our branch of the family doesn't want or need those services, why should we pay for them?" The answer came from virtually all the other branches: "Because that's the way we've always done it." Patrick and his wife were very dissatisfied with this response. Once the issue was brought out into the open, other branches that utilized some but not all of the available services also began to feel that their contributions were unfair. A full-fledged money conflict was in the offing, and waiting to reappear were some emotional conflicts that dated to childhood rivalries among the three founding brothers!

RESOLVING THE CONFLICTS

Each of these conflicts was capable of resolution, without damaging or destroying the families' enterprises or the relationships among family members.

Resolution

The Lewis Family Foundation   The feuding siblings turned to the third sister, Constance, and asked her to provide the "swing vote" for one proposal or the other. To mediate between her sisters, Constance sought the advice of a professional facilitator. The mediator recommended that, before they considered any proposal, the sisters should focus on their own values and how the foundation could reflect those values. They did so and came to a surprisingly unanimous conclusion. Their values had been shaped by their common experience with respect to the family business. Each of them, in turn, had been welcomed into that business, but career advancement had been blocked on the basis of their gender. "Sure, you girls are all very talented," said their father. "You're doing a great job here. But what about my grandchildren? Shouldn't you be focusing on *them?*"

In time, they all withdrew from active participation in the business, after insisting that their parents set up the foundation and allow them to run it. Their common experience led them to conclude that the foundation should focus on women's issues. And because Barbara's proposal—to fund a shelter for battered women and their children—fell into that category, the sisters voted unanimously to proceed in that direction. They also agreed that Sandra should modify her scholarship proposal, focusing it more narrowly on educating underprivileged women for careers in business. This project was to be seriously considered for the next year's funding.

The Kazinsky Corporation   Ralph continued to feel that his father's decision had been wrong. And he continued to seethe inwardly. But he decided to remain with the company, and, over the years, he was able to accomplish his goal. He used an existing mechanism, the Kazinsky Corporation's executive committee, as his instrument of change. He periodically made incremental suggestions with respect to expanding and upgrading the corporation's management information systems.

None of these suggestions was, in itself, considered a major capital expenditure. In fact, Ralph never characterized them as expenditures at all. The upgraded system presented his father with numbers, of course, but they were numbers of uniforms—production totals and sales quotas met or not met—rather than numbers of dollars. Eventually, his "stealth" strategy enabled Ralph to accomplish everything he wanted. By the time Marvin retired, his son had reconfigured the company's information systems to meet his own standards for growth. And because the conflict had been settled to Ralph's satisfaction—and without Marvin's awareness—relations between the father and son became much warmer.

The Monahan Family Office   Until the current generation reached maturity, the office had served a limited number of families, and all of them were interested in receiving essentially the same services. But as the family expanded, it inevitably grew apart. Patrick and his wife had no wish to reveal their personal finances to the employees of the family office and, by extension, to his siblings and cousins. Other family branches expressed similar views.

Unfortunately, there was no mechanism in place—no system of governance—to handle such departures from family tradition. At Patrick's insistence, such mechanisms were established, under the guidance of experienced professionals in the family office field. Their solution was a logical one. Branches of the family that availed themselves of fewer services would receive proportionate "rebates" from the funds they contributed to the family office. Thanks to third-party intervention, an incipient family conflict was reduced to a simple issue of money, for which there was, of course, an obvious financial solution.

RECOGNIZING THE SIGNS OF POTENTIAL CONFLICT

It's useful to consider some telltale signs that money is becoming a problem, *before an issue escalates into a conflict.*

- Money is too central to the family members' sense of themselves; they focus more on their net worth than their self worth.
- Money is seen as a way to make up for the lack of connection between generations.
- There is a sense of inequity in how family members are treated.
- The next generation's lack of productivity and ambition is being tolerated.

NIPPING CONFLICTS IN THE BUD

Let's consider how a family can deal with these conditions effectively. The outcomes described above all required the use of interpersonal conflict-resolution techniques.

- **Develop a mutual understanding of family members' attitudes and values about money.** How do they use it, save it, and give it? In what ways do financial capital, human capital, and emotional capital interact with one another? How would family members like them to interact? How should the family's wealth be handled in relationships with the extended family, friends, and the community?

- **Discuss the vision and mission of the family enterprise.** Family members can then examine their differences about money and develop a common understanding about the conduct of the enterprise's resources. More and more, wealthy families are instituting policies that prevent the next generation from steering money away from its original intended use. When families make such decisions, they are asserting that family relationships are more important than money.

- **Always seek to fully understand the other persons' viewpoint and their relationship with the issue.** In most conflicts, each person wants the other to hear and understand—and, ideally, accept—his or her viewpoint. Most people will listen better when they feel they are being heard.

- **Figure out what is driving the conflict.** What are the issues that need to be resolved? If money is being used to represent some other issue, perhaps it would be beneficial to understand how money might help to resolve it. What will happen if the issue remains?

- **Establish a structure, a system of governance for the family enterprise.** This more impersonal system—possibly utilizing third parties who are not family members nor beholden to any particular branch—may provide a generally acceptable solution to an emerging conflict before the emotions of family members can come into play.

- **Focus on self-examination.** The more you work toward changing another person's viewpoint, the more tightly that person will cling to it. To achieve any kind of resolution, you must understand the basis for his or her point of view. Very often, the reasons are deeply imbedded in family history.

It is very important—but also very difficult—to ask oneself whether an issue can be resolved by money, or whether something else is at work. Try to shift the focus away from a response to the other person. Instead, look closely at your own position and motivations. If even one individual is able to accomplish this, the differences may not escalate into conflict. Your next step would then be to think seriously about what would resolve that issue.

Back to the Colson Conflict

Let's return to the story of the Colson family, whose conflict was discussed at the beginning of this chapter. Our firm was called in, at the suggestion of Margaret's attorney and with the concurrence of opposing counsel. After separate interviews with all four family members, we concluded that a major part of the conflict was centered around Margaret's feeling that her father had discouraged her from entering the company when she finished college. Later, when Margaret was already married and had two children, her younger sister Beth entered the firm. By then, society's attitudes about women in the workforce had changed, and Beth joined the company with their father's approval.

Margaret resented the fact that her father had never offered her an opportunity to become involved in the business, which her sister and brother now managed for her. Her father had not listened to and respected her wishes, and now her siblings, in her view, were treating her in exactly the same hurtful manner.

For Mrs. Colson, this situation was extraordinarily difficult. She felt that, to a considerable extent, each of her children was right, but she was afraid that, if the situation worsened, she would end up with little means of support.

Independently, each family member was able to articulate that a resolution might lie in acknowledging Margaret's reason for feeling left out, and her right to be included in the current situation, while at the same time agreeing to move ahead with the purchase. They all concurred that the shareholders needed to agree on: (a) a method of making up for the temporary reductions in dividends, and (b) a policy for handling future capital decisions. The nonworking shareholders could then be heard without disrupting the responsibility of the managers in their operation of the company.

Each of the Colson siblings was angry with the others, but they and their mother clearly wanted the conflict to come to an end. When each was asked to suggest a resolution and describe how he or she might play a part in it, each sibling was able to volunteer how his or her own behavior might need to change.

The Colsons finally reached a solution to their current conflict. In addition, they began to establish a framework—a mechanism, a system of governance—that would prevent or minimize future disputes.

THE BOTTOM LINE: PRESERVING THE FAMILY'S WEALTH AND ITS RELATIONSHIPS

The stories in this chapter all had happy endings. The conflicts were resolved, the enterprises continued to prosper, and the families remained intact. But some conflicts cannot be settled so harmlessly.

That's why a feuding family and its facilitators should be open to all possibilities. Perhaps the only solution is to close down or sell the family enterprise, or arrange for one or more family members to sell their interests to other members.

But suppose a conflict results in the termination not just of business relationships but of family relationships as well? That outcome would be truly disastrous and should be avoided at all costs. Having to cut off all contacts *because* of an emotional conflict is just as bad as staying together *despite* that issue. No matter how difficult it may be, parents and children—and siblings—must maintain their family relationships for the rest of their lives. The alternative is almost unthinkable. Even the death of one party to the dispute will not end the anguish and regret.

In the words of playwright Robert Anderson (in *I Never Sang for My Father*), "Death ends a life but not a relationship, which struggles on in the minds of the survivor toward an end which it may never find."

Words to the Wise

- Recognize the source of conflict. When families manage assets together, old issues will very likely reassert themselves in the form of new conflicts, ostensibly revolving around money.

- Conflict develops when an issue is so intense that the current structures and mechanisms cannot hold it safely in place. This dilemma offers a built-in opportunity: it enables everyone to work out old issues in new ways and with new skills.

- Establish structures and mechanisms that will help objectify the family's relationships around the assets. This helps to keep family issues out of the operations of the enterprise.

- Establish a governance structure that defines responsibilities for decision making.

- Set up a procedure for hearing the voices of *all* family members. This will help them to stay on track in managing their common assets.

- If conflict comes to the fore, utilize a methodology that focuses on understanding other persons' viewpoints and puts family relationships ahead of money.

Words to the Wise (Continued)

■ If the family members can keep in mind that money conflicts are never really about money, they are far more likely to come to a workable and equitable resolution. They might even develop a valuable precedent for the resolution (or even the avoidance) of future conflicts.

Fredda Herz Brown, Ph.D.

Fredda Herz Brown is the founder, managing partner, and senior consultant of the Metropolitan Group, an international organization offering consulting and educational services to family and closely-held enterprises. She is experienced in governance and board development, wealth psychology, philanthropy, shareholder education, and transitions in family businesses. Dr. Brown is a founding board member of the Family Firm Institute, a professional organization dedicated to assisting family firms, where she helped to initiate the development of the study of family business dynamics as a field. She is author of Reweaving the Family Tapestry, *and is working on her second book about family enterprises. She has published articles in* The Family Business Review *and serves on the publication's editorial board.*

8

FAMILY MEETINGS THAT WORK

Conducting Successful Discussions About
Money and Other Sensitive Subjects

DENNIS T. JAFFE, STEPHEN GOLDBART, AND JOAN INDURSKY DIFURIA

Max Curwin had spent the first 40 years of his adult life building his business. Three years ago, his company was acquired by a larger firm, and its previously quiet stock suddenly skyrocketed. Without much warning, the Curwins, in their early sixties, had become multimillionaires.

Recently, Max and his wife, Evelyn, planned a day-long family meeting to discuss the sensitive subject of annual financial distributions to their sons, who reluctantly agreed to participate.

Alan, the elder son, is a 35-year-old businessman who runs a dot-com company. He is married, has two young children, and lives out of state. His younger brother, Michael, a 31-year-old single student, has never fully achieved independence. He moves from job to job and comes home when he is in financial trouble. For the past six years, he has been working sporadically to earn his master's degree in art history.

The parents had called in professional facilitators to keep the meeting on track. Each family member was given ample time to say what he or she wanted from, feared, and dreaded about the family meeting.

The facilitators asked Evelyn and Max to explain why annual distributions were so important to them and why they wanted their children to take part in the planning process. They challenged the family's taboos about "money communication." Everyone was encouraged to express his or her individual attitudes toward and beliefs about money.

Alan said, "While appreciating my parents' generosity, I don't want the strings attached to taking this money. I value my independence, and I don't want my career motivations to be undermined. I'd like them to keep all their money for the rest of their lives. I just don't want any part of this."

Michael said, "My parents help me out already. I've really appreciated the financial support and certainly don't mind having more of it. With the distributions,

I won't need to keep asking for money for every little thing, and then I can avoid my mother's questions and comments about my life."

At their family meeting, the Curwins were attempting to deal with the most combustible mixture we know of: money and family. In every family, and particularly in wealthy ones, money becomes linked to all sorts of meanings: who is loved more; who deserves more; and how people feel about each other. Inevitably, the more money there is, the more potential there is for conflict.

To add to the difficulty, families often deal with money in very self-defeating ways. People make assumptions, blame others, and are not open to the idea that other people see the world differently. The possibility of misunderstanding is high. If family members have unrealistic expectations about each other that they don't explore, the stage is set for major difficulties and even potential disaster.

Midway through their family meeting, the Curwins were on the brink of major difficulties. But by the end of day, they managed to resolve most of them, as we'll show you later in this chapter.

THE REASONS FOR A FAMILY MEETING

To deal with the unique challenges that face wealthy families, we propose that all family members get together periodically for intergenerational family meetings. These gatherings could cover such topics as wealth, personal matters, allocation, inheritance, values, philanthropy, and the future. The meetings can also provide a neutral setting for discussion of that most difficult of all subjects: a family conflict or crisis.

A family meeting is a gathering of all family members in a quiet and comfortable place—for instance, a vacation home—with the specific aim of talking openly and honestly to each other about their feelings, issues and desires.

The meetings need not lead to votes or decisions. But they provide opportunities to unearth and explore differences and discover ways to be fair to everyone. Thus, better decisions can be made—in such areas as inheritance and generational transition—and family members will better understand the intentions behind those decisions.

The highest value of such conversations comes from sharing and passing on a **legacy**—the values that one generation honors and lives by and wants to transmit to future generations. These values concern the importance of family connection and the family's ways of doing business, giving back to the community, and raising children. Legacy is an implicit contract and responsibility that goes along with inheritance.

The Major Purposes of a Family Meeting

- To foster healthy communication among all family members.
- To pass on family values, such as work, education, community, integrity, respect, and loyalty.
- To communicate core money values and their relationship to wealth management.
- To communicate with the younger generation by opening up a dialogue about their ideas and intentions, and assessing their developmental readiness to handle money.
- To deal with a change or transition in family circumstances, such as the sale or acquisition of a business or the death of a family member.
- To achieve an emotionally healthy transfer of wealth.
- To overcome a conflict.

HOLDING A FAMILY MEETING

There are many formats for a family meeting, but they have some elements in common. They should be held in *comfortable* places, where there is no disruption. Phones and other intrusions should be kept out. There should be sufficient time to keep the meeting somewhat open-ended. It should be as *inclusive* as possible, with all invited family members present.

A meeting sets up a *process* of communication. Many families open up issues that offer no clear and easy resolution, or raise more issues than can possibly be covered in one evening. Sometimes a meeting is extended into a one- or two-day event. Some families have regular meetings, once or several times a year. Continuity is important.

Each meeting should have a *facilitator*—a person who agrees to keep the proceedings on track, and makes sure that everyone participates. In some families, this role is rotated.

At the first meeting, the family should agree on a set of guidelines for how to listen to each other, how to maintain order, and what sort of behavior is expected during the meeting.

The meeting needs careful and clear preparation and follow-up. It will benefit from some sort of agenda of issues and concerns, preferably communicated in advance. If the meeting leads to decisions or other outcomes, these should be recorded and distributed to family members. If someone agrees to do something in preparation for the next meeting, that also should be recorded.

Retaining a Professional Facilitator

There are two major categories in which a facilitator can help:

1. Fostering a proactive dialogue about money issues and values and their role in preserving family unity.
2. Helping families when they are confronted with a difficult choice or conflict about money.

A facilitator can structure and monitor family communication to help achieve a positive outcome. The facilitator also acts as a mentor, offering guidance and insight into how the family members can create a money plan that is aligned with their core values and goals.

Professional facilitation is also useful during times of stress and strain. The general rule is: An outside advisor is helpful if some family members are very upset or concerned, if the family feels that members will have difficulty talking to each other, or if there is a lot of pressure or conflict. The choice of whether to have a professional present should be made by the majority of the family, in advance of the meeting.

Ground Rules

If your role is to facilitate a family meeting, here are some ideas for achieving success.

1. *Create an environment in which people feel respected.* The family can't just call people together. Family members need to feel that they can talk about emotionally charged and difficult issues without recrimination. The convener needs to make clear what will happen and how it will take place. A good way to create a firm foundation is to pledge that confidences will be respected,

and that everyone will try to maintain a positive perspective. Another form of respect requires avoiding nonessential discussions that create discomfort among some family members. In one family meeting, for example, it was agreed that an issue would be dropped if even one hand was raised.

2. *Turn your mind-set dial to "Open" when you begin.* If you enter a conversation with the primary intention of making your points and persuading others that you are right, you won't get far. One of the treasures of a family conversation is discovering something that you didn't know or, more likely, didn't hear about someone you have known and loved for many years. In one family gathering, the discussion of career and family dreams helped the patriarch see that his children's ideas for their future were very different from those he envisioned for them.

3. *Use conversations for discovery, not for making decisions.* Perhaps a decision must be made, but a conversation is not a debate, and there will be plenty of time to come to a decision later on. The purpose is to explore what people think and to devise ways to turn those thoughts into reality. In one situation, parents were setting up a complex estate plan. They were open to listening to the fears and concerns of their children only after it was established that the purpose of the exchange was to share ideas, not talk the parents out of any choice they wanted to make.

4. *Talk about the family history.* Initiate a conversation about legacy. For a business founder, this meeting would offer an opportunity to talk about how the firm was created, what it means, and what makes him or her proud and satisfied. The founder might talk about struggles, choices, and what he or she knows and how it was learned. Legacy conversations are important. They are a living will and should be recorded or even videotaped. The family's jobs are: appreciate and listen. Ask questions, request more details, but under no circumstances disagree or add your own ideas. Understand where you have come from and what you are heir or heiress to. When they begin to share stories about their history, many families will have talks that last late into the evening.

5. *Begin with what you agree on.* When family members see how many important things they agree on, it may be easier to place their differences in context. For example, a family with divided opinions about the future fate of its business began a discussion

by articulating the many values they shared and discussing how much they had in common. This exchange enabled them to have more flexibility toward their difficult decision.

6. *Allow enough time, and decree that everyone must stay in the room.* Avoid expectations that people will change, that conflict will end, or that one conversation will do the trick. These hopes are unrealistic. Agree to meet for at least a set amount of time. Get people to pledge that they won't walk out—or, if they do, that they will come back when they cool down. We have seen several families overcome major differences when upset family members rejoined the group and voiced their feelings in a constructive manner.

7. *Don't interrupt.* Some families love to interrupt each other. This is a sign that they are not listening; they only *think* they know what the other person is saying. There needs to be a ground rule that a person can talk until he or she is finished, and that the listeners will hold their comments until then. We have used a "talking stick" effectively in family meetings. Only the person holding the stick can speak. This stick is passed from speaker to speaker. This technique almost always slows down conversation and gives many voices a chance to be heard without interruption.

8. *Don't hesitate to order a slowdown.* Sometimes, a single phrase can upset a large number of participants. When tempers begin to boil, the coolest person in the room should step up and say, "Let's slow down." Ask each person to take a break, sit quietly, and then discuss slowly, without interruption, why he or she is upset. Silence can give people a chance to reflect and reconsider. Agree to disagree, and listen to what the others have to say, even when you find this very painful. ·

9. *Put the toughest issues aside.* If this is your first family meeting, don't discuss how the inheritance should be allocated. Talk about simpler issues before you tackle the tough ones. The feelings of a generation can't be resolved in one meeting. We have found that after working on some less contentious issues, a family develops some ways to move into the more difficult ones and is more committed to doing that.

10. *Speak for yourself, not others.* Use the word "I," not "we." Take responsibility for what you feel, and share your feelings. Don't presume to speak for others; don't attempt to express what they feel

or want. They are there to tell you themselves. One family matriarch, who routinely talked about how "we" feel, was guided to see that these were her own preferences and she should not impose them on others. She was finally able to hear that some of her children had very different ideas and feelings.

11. *Encourage everyone to talk.* It is helpful to start a meeting by asking all family members, one by one, to say what is on their minds. If someone is silent, or if one or two people are dominating the discussion, the facilitator should ask the other attendees to speak up.

12. *Avoid or dilute criticism or blame.* There may be strong feelings about past events. People who are angry and hurt may want to blame others. This response may be inevitable, but it is not productive. Try instead to focus on what they want to do *now.* One family repeats this instruction whenever one family member begins to use past behavior to blame others: "Let's not look at who is responsible; let's solve the problem."

13. *Get to the concrete level.* Family conflict builds up over many small events and misunderstandings. Over time, these misunderstandings develop into huge and hurtful areas of disagreement. When you unearth such a problem, allow time for each involved person to talk about what happened to make him or her feel that way. Resist the tendency to interrupt and say what you really intended, or what you think you meant.

14. *Write down what is important.* Some things that are said—reminiscences, stories, values, or understandings—are important enough to record. As a useful aid, have large sheets of paper available for people to note what they want to remember. If you don't write down minutes, decisions, and understandings from a meeting, you will lose valuable information and sources to refer to when, inevitably, family members' memories are less than reliable.

15. *Follow up with individual conversations.* You can't always say everything you want when you're part of a group. Sometimes, you need to have one-to-one talks. Agree, at the meeting, to schedule some of these talks for people who have the most difficulty talking to each other. One family uses the following plan: When two people say they will have lunch together or arrange for another joint activity, one family member writes down that agreement, and a third party makes a phone call to make sure

the meeting has happened. At first, some of the family members felt that this was too intrusive; later, they began to see the value. One family member said: "Sometimes it's hard to pick up the phone even though you agreed to do it at a meeting."

Common Hurdles at Family Meetings

Family members must remember that they spent many years avoiding issues and will need some time to unlearn that harmful practice. Here are some common challenges that come up repeatedly when a family tries to set up meetings.

People Who Don't Want to Participate   Family members should be encouraged to come to the meeting, but they should be informed that the meeting will be held even if some members are not willing to participate. We have found that when a family forges ahead, the reluctant member sees the cost of not participating and may then decide that the family is really willing to listen to long-held grievances or concerns.

Deep-seated attitudes that inhibit communication about money need to be challenged. Any fear of retaliation for expressing one's point of view must be neutralized. Family members who are more comfortable with disclosure can demonstrate the benefits of communication, if the conditions are safe and the outcome will not be disastrous. Those who hold both emotional and financial power need to be heard by the family, recognized for their authority, and then contained in the overall process.

People Who Can't Get Beyond Their Own Opinions   Some family members may seem to feel that they hold a monopoly on morality. If conditions are safe, a facilitator can challenge some of the assumptions that underscore a person's rigid point of view. This can lead to a more constructive dialogue that opens the door either to conflict resolution or to a recognition that further communication would be fruitless. The worst cases involve people who are so self-centered that they are psychologically unable to empathize with or understand the validity of the ideas and opinions of other family members. This degree of narcissistic self-involvement creates a dead end for family communication.

People Who Are Highly Impaired   Some family members may be too disruptive. Their personal problems may be too great, or their views may be so upsetting, angry, or rigid that they cannot follow the ground rules for participation in a family discussion. They often erupt, or storm out, or make impossible demands. If this happens, the family leaders should have individual conversations with these members and engage professional help if needed. Emotional issues can be deep, difficult, and painful.

People Who Do Not Want to Upset Others   Because money is a difficult and conflict-laden topic for most Americans, some family members may passively drift toward the view that they do not want to "make waves." The facilitator should directly address their concerns, identify them as normal responses, and remind the group that taboos about money communication are obsolete. Greater involvement should be encouraged.

Keeping People to Their Agreements via a Follow-Up   During a meeting, everybody has good intentions and lots of energy. But after they go home, nothing happens. The family should not disband the meeting until someone is appointed to keep things moving ahead. Scheduling a next meeting, to make certain progress is being made, can also be helpful. However, the various family units need to be gentle with each other when things don't happen as quickly and easily as expected.

THE RESULTS OF THE CURWIN FAMILY MEETING

This chapter opened with a description of the Curwin family's meeting, which was held to discuss the possibility that the two adult sons might receive regular money distributions from their newly wealthy parents. Here's how the meeting turned out.

After the sons expressed their very different feelings about the subject, the parents clarified the reasons for introducing this possibility. They made it clear that they didn't want either son to see the distributions as a form of parental control. They had no wish to undermine Michael's education, nor did they want to harm Alan's self-esteem and work motivation. Michael expressed both his pleasure in getting the money and his guilt about not having earned it. Alan voiced his concern that Michael's needs could result in his receiving an unfairly large portion of the parents' estate. Alan didn't want the money at this stage in his life, but needed assurance that he would not be financially punished for his success.

These points of view were stated and restated throughout the afternoon. Although certain differences could not be resolved—notably, Alan's and Michael's views about receiving financial assistance from their parents—the family, with the assistance of the facilitators, was able to arrive at a workable consensus on core money values:

- *Money distributions will empower, not disempower, each recipient.*
- *We will separate money matters from emotional matters.*
- *We expect family members to learn money management skills.*
- *We value a work ethic, so distributions will be given only when family members demonstrate that they are serious and responsible about work.*
- *We will commit time and money to starting and running a family foundation.*
- *The parents will not interfere, so long as Michael and Alan follow the above guidelines.*

The family agreed that the open discussion had helped them to cool down issues that had been simmering for many years. They felt they had developed a new understanding about dealing with their sudden acquisition of wealth and its relationship to long-standing family values.

HOW YOU CAN GET STARTED

The first step is to call on your family members individually and ask them to consider the value of a meeting. Your approach may be most difficult if you are an heir and want to initiate the discussion with your parents, who, of course, have financial control. But we find that if the proposal is tactfully worded and acknowledges the real source of power, the patriarch and/or matriarch is often willing to consider a discussion.

You may want to ask a professional advisor to act as a sounding board before you approach other family members. Next, get a commitment from each person, and set up a date and time for a first meeting. A few conversations regarding the guidelines and agenda may be helpful.

Setting up regular family conversations will open the door to a better way to deal with money. When children grow up and move away, a meeting provides a forum for dealing with all sorts of issues. A meeting can also be a wonderful way to share as a family and to develop a lasting legacy for future generations.

STEPS FOR FACILITATING A FAMILY MEETING

Table 8.1 outlines guidelines for a facilitator, who can be an outside advisor or a member of the family, to help run a family meeting. This table includes suggestions for what to do and say at various points in the meeting.

Table 8.1 Facilitating a Family Meeting

Task	What to Do	What to Say
Define purpose of meeting.	Advisor leads the meeting by defining the main agenda (you may or may not elect to go around the room).	We are here to talk about X and later I will be asking you to talk about your understanding.
Set the tone.	Create safety, respect, honesty. People talk one at a time. Engaged listening.	It is important that this be a process that feels safe for every member. Everyone will agree that what is said here will be kept in this room and that we agree to no later reprisals. Please hear each other out without interrupting. If you start to feel too uncomfortable, as in the dentist's office, raise your hand and say "Ouch." Stay open minded about what others say.
Gain agreement on the purpose and agenda of the meeting.	Leader again states what he or she believes the purpose to be and then asks each member for his or her viewpoint and buy-in.	I'd like to hear why each of you is here today. Can we all agree that this meeting will focus on X?
Deal with reluctant or resistant family members.	Get resistant members to clarify their positions. Empathize with their concerns. Reframe if possible and get a limited buy-in.	I hear that you don't want to be here. Please tell me more about that. I can see how what you feel makes sense. I think, given your feelings, it is great you are here and I will keep your concerns in mind as we move forward today.

Table 8.1   Facilitating a Family Meeting (Continued)

Task	What to Do	What to Say
Raise issues and encourage participation.	Encourage family members to speak openly. Ask them to take responsibility for what they say, feel, and want. Take the time to really hear each other.	Let's hear from everyone about this issue. You've been quiet; I wonder what you are thinking. This is difficult. Why don't we slow things down so we can hear from everyone?
Facilitate dialogue.	Encourage clarity. Keep discussion focused. Monitor safety. Enforce ground rules. Encourage people to build on others' ideas.	I'd like to clarify: Could you repeat in a different way? Let's return to your main point. Is everyone okay so far? Are there any concerns or questions? Sally said "X" and Joe said "Y" perhaps we can see how these fit together.
Deal with conflict and obstacles.	Attend to the obstacle/ conflict. Use communication skills for conflict resolution. Set limits to ensure safety and constructive outcomes. Compromise and collaborate.	I see that your tone changed. Is something troubling you? I need to interrupt for a moment and ask you to take a time out and quiet down. You are stuck in all-or-nothing thinking. Can we find the middle ground?
Concluding the meeting.	Summarize what has occurred. Talk about what has or has not been agreed on. Set action steps for the future.	Let's conclude today by reviewing what we have discussed. Let me summarize what we have agreed on and what remains undecided. Let's come to an agreement on the next steps we will take together: when, how, and with whom.

Words to the Wise

- A family meeting is a gathering of all family members, in a quiet and comfortable place, to talk openly about their feelings, issues, and desires.
- A family meeting offers a way to pass your family values on to the next generation.
- A family meeting should be a discussion, not an argument. The atmosphere should be friendly and open, and each person should have ample opportunities to express his or her opinions.
- A family meeting provides an excellent opportunity to discuss *legacy:* where the family has come from and the values that each member is heir to.
- A family meeting may be the best way to overcome a serious conflict or to deal with a difficult subject such as inheritance or a change in family leadership.
- A professional facilitator can help a family to foster a proactive dialogue, make difficult choices, and deal with reluctant or resistant members.
- The decisions made at each meeting should be implemented and followed up.

Dennis T. Jaffe, Ph.D.

Dennis T. Jaffe, a licensed psychologist and family business consultant, is an associate at the Money, Meaning and Choices Institute, where he helps family businesses deal with transition and create effective management teams. He is also a professor of organizational systems at Saybrook Graduate School in San Francisco, a founding member of the Aspen Family Business Group, and a fellow of the Family Firm Institute. Dr. Jaffe is coauthor of Working With the Ones You Love: Building a Successful Family Business, *and* Working With Family Business: A Guide for Professional Advisors.

——————— Stephen Goldbart, Ph.D. ———————

Stephen Goldbart is cofounder and director of the Money, Meaning and Choices Institute, which instructs private clients and financial professionals on the psychological role of money in people's lives. Dr. Goldbart is a licensed clinical psychologist with over 25 years' experience as a clinician, professor, author, public speaker, and organizational consultant. He consults with individuals, families, and organizations to help them find balance in personal, professional, and philanthropic interests. He also conducts seminars and workshops at the Marin Psychotherapy Institute. He has coauthored a book— Mapping the Terrain of the Heart: Passion, Tenderness and the Capacity to Love—*and has contributed to many articles on psychology and money.*

——————— Joan Indursky DiFuria, M.F.T. ———————

Joan Indursky DiFuria is cofounder and director of the Money, Meaning and Choices Institute. Prior to her role in forming the Institute, she worked for 18 years in corporate marketing and strategic operations positions. Her business background, combined with her Marriage and Family Therapist designation and experience, provide Ms. DiFuria with a unique perspective and expertise in working with corporate leaders, financial professionals, venture philanthropist groups, and family businesses. Her focus includes the emotional issues that accompany wealth: stewardship; raising children of affluence; philanthropy; family and business values; and legacy planning. Ms. DiFuria's articles on wealth and relationships have appeared in California Lawyer *and* New Jersey Life.

PART TWO

Managing Your Wealth

A ll wealth is not the same. Within the broad category of wealthy individuals and families, four subsets of investable assets can be distinguished: $1–$5 million, $5–$25 million, $25–$100 million, and over $100 million. These subgroups indicate approximate threshold levels which, once attained, place your assets within new and increasingly complex frameworks. As your wealth rises past each threshold, the opportunities for sophisticated investment vehicles and services increase. The focus of most clients also changes as their affluence increases. They lean more and more toward preservation of their wealth and will take fewer excessive investment risks.

Just as the individualized tailoring and complexity of financial management increase at each level, the need for professional expertise and advice also grows. The balance between risk and trust requires some recalibrating at each level. For example, estate planning can benefit all wealth subgroups. But trust vehicles and the services of trust company professionals offer many other important functions for the more affluent subgroups. Trust companies can help to restructure a business to fit its changing needs—for example, by structuring family limited partnerships or assisting with the complex process of diversifying concentrated private business holdings into an Employee Stock Ownership Plan (ESOP).

I repeatedly encounter clients who are experiencing a wealth category transition because their previous methods for managing their assets have become outdated or constricting. The greater financial management horizons newly opened to them are greeted with hesitation and doubt.

One interesting example took place at an early stage of one client's road to wealth. It demonstrates the problems that arise when you limit your horizons. In a way, it's an allegory for us all:

Years ago, I had a successful talent agent as one of my clients. He and his wife inherited $1 million from his mother, and immediately earmarked that money for their retirement. They put it "to the side" and consequently crossed off "retirement" on the mandatory list of the events they had to plan for. They then concentrated on their children's college education and similar expected outlays.

About two years later, the agent called to tell me he had parted from his firm. I asked him, "Do you want us to make any changes to your portfolio?" His answer—both then and throughout the ensuing months—was "No." He explained that he was taking a few of his major clients with him and needed only one or two other big clients to maintain his level of income. When he couldn't land those two new clients, the agent went from being very difficult to contact to calling me almost daily to check on his account balance. His nervous anxiety rose with each call. I always asked the question: "Do you want us to make any changes to your account?" And, always, the answer was "No."

Finally, I asked him to come into my office for an in-person meeting. When we began talking, the disconnect became apparent. He still didn't have one or two new big-name talents, and money was becoming a problem. I suggested that he should alter the asset allocation of the account so that he could derive some income from it. He said he couldn't do that because the account was his retirement nest egg and he couldn't touch it.

"Who said you couldn't touch it?"

My question confused him. "Well, you're just not supposed to."

In the best of all possible worlds, that would be the right answer. But his world at that moment needed a solution that fit him, not some rigid notion of financial planning. I explained to him some of the creative ways we could approach the present. The income he needed was only part of his overall income, and his present situation might be resolved favorably within the next few years. I worked up some comparative tables to show him the possible levels of bond allocations and the current income levels they could provide. I also showed him the potential effect on his "retirement" portfolio. The end amount would not be the same, but it would not represent a drastic reduction.

This simple example illustrates a message that is important at all levels of affluence: There are no rigid rules. All financial planning decisions must be appropriate for your temperament and your individual situation.

The chapters in Part Two discuss wealth management approaches and vehicles for various high-net-worth levels. You will learn when to stop "going it alone" and how complex estate plans and family foundations can be structured to preserve your wealth for present and future generations.

Each chapter will provide you with wealth management *fundamentals* to explore, but be aware that extensive fine points come into play when the basic precepts are adjusted to fit each individual's situation.

Individualized service is a central key to wealth management. The chapter on trusts explains that trusts are highly flexible and can be precisely structured and worded to fit your needs. Asset allocation also has wide-ranging possibilities that are always created and structured specifically for each individual.

As your assets increase, so will your need for specialized services and multiple advisors. Normally, the central wealth advisor is an accountant or an attorney—not an investment specialist. This central position of the advisor resembles the role of a conductor of a symphony orchestra. The conductor makes sure all the instruments (your investment choices) are playing in harmony and not deviating from the musical score (your investment plan). The conductor/advisor analogy supports several other similarities. For example, only the conductor looks at the full score of a symphony: each member of the orchestra sees only the notes that he or she must play. Multiple advisors are specialists: they concentrate on their responsibilities and usually have only a passing understanding of the roles of your other advisors. Your central advisor coordinates all the specialists' activities.

The chapters in this part of the book will help you to understand that the success of your wealth management will greatly depend on your relationship with your central wealth advisor. Even the most intelligent and experienced investors should not go this route alone. Advice and breadth of experience are crucial to making balanced decisions. Whether you work with three, five, or 15 specialists, the rapport and the level of trust you experience with your central advisor may well be the most significant factor in realizing your wealth management success.

9

WORKING WITH PROFESSIONAL MONEY MANAGERS

Balancing Control and Delegation

Charlotte B. Beyer

After finding himself suddenly liquid following the sale of his business, a member of the Institute for Private Investors (IPI)—an educational and networking resource for high-net-worth families and their advisors—described a feeling akin to vertigo. He had focused on finding one "right" advisor but soon discovered that the volume of possibilities made the search dizzying. (The United States is home to more than 20,000 registered investment advisors and 60,000 stockbrokers, virtually all of whom are willing to provide discretionary money management.) After a few seminars and one-on-one interviews, the promised capabilities of the various advisors all began to blur. The IPI member eventually concluded that before he could make a good decision about hiring an advisor, he had to learn something about investing.

For many people, the challenges of managing wealth are more daunting than the challenges of creating it. "What kind of help do I need?" and "Where do I find it?" may seem like simple questions, but, when applied to personal finance, they can quickly become complex. Help is available from a variety of professionals: attorneys, accountants, stockbrokers, financial planners, and registered investment advisors. Look for them to be in home offices, suburban office parks, and urban financial districts. (The term "advisor" in this chapter includes the whole range of people who are in a position to say, "Give me your money and I will manage it for you.") People who come into wealth without a framework for the way the world of investing works are likely to become confused and may choose an unsuitable advisor.

Wealthy people represent a spectrum of attitudes toward money management. At one extreme are those who think they can do it on their own and need a broker only to execute their trades. At the other extreme are those who want no part of the details and are eager to hand over the responsibility. Those who start at one end may, after some time and perhaps some painful experiences, gravitate toward the other. Success and satisfaction are most commonly found in the middle, by people who achieve a proper balance of control and delegation. They set goals and monitor results, but execution is left to a well-chosen group of professional investment advisors.

MORE CHALLENGING THAN IT APPEARS

Like any professional discipline—law, engineering, medicine, social work, design, and so on—money management has its own combination of science and art. Its history, vocabulary, and set of guiding principles are best learned through a combination of education and experience.

In the late 1990s, the simultaneous phenomena of Internet trading, 24-hour business news, and the longest bull market in history convinced many people that investing is easy and fun. A portfolio manager from Neuberger Berman commented, at the time, that investing had now become "America's favorite hobby." When the dot-com bubble burst, however, the fun stopped. Everyone realized that, despite appearances to the contrary, the principles of investing success had not really changed. Investing should be regarded as a disciplined process that requires continuing attention and analysis. Few people have what it takes—analytical training and talent, and a deep understanding of the nature and history of the securities markets—to achieve consistently good results over time.

To become a smart investor, you don't need to learn everything there is to know about the markets. You should, however, develop a basic understanding of risk and return, asset class distinctions (large-, medium-, and small-cap stocks; short-term and long-term government bonds; corporate bonds; distressed debt; hedge funds; private equity; cash equivalents), and investment styles (value, growth, opportunistic) so that you can evaluate the professionals whose services you may be considering.

ABDICATION IS NO ANSWER

Some people misguidedly look for one financial advisor who will address all their needs and remove all their anxieties about their money.

Certain advisors may make such promises, but their fantasies will never be realized. Giving the total responsibility for your financial affairs to a single individual, no matter how apparently brilliant or trustworthy he or she is, invites a tremendous risk. Investors need to devote some of their own time, sweat, and energy to learning enough to perform the necessary due diligence at the outset, and monitoring the advisor's performance over time. This learning can be relatively painless if taken in small doses via the interactive seminars or educational meetings offered by many investment firms and private banks. If you fail to acquire this knowledge, you are abdicating an important responsibility of wealth. You would do better to give all of your money outright to your favorite charity instead of watching it evaporate through mismanagement. Your attention to learning how to properly screen potential advisors is vital to your fiscal health.

BEGIN WITH YOURSELF

In the early days of her liquidity, a member of the IPI network aimed to find a "best-in-breed" financial advisor by conducting thorough research and consulting with her friends. As she began to interview prospective candidates, she learned that the "best" advisor for one individual might be the worst for another, and vice versa. The first step toward knowing who is right for you involves examining your own biases and feelings about your money. What do you want it to do for you? As a start, I suggest formulating your own answers to key questions and using these answers to inform and narrow your search. Four basic tactics can serve as first steps toward a strategy:

1. Define your risk precisely. How much of a loss will you tolerate from any manager in one quarter? One year? Five years? Will the loss cutoff point be an absolute amount or a percentage of the market?
2. Define an expected rate of return. Will you measure it versus inflation? The S&P 500? The five-year average of the S&P 500? Before the year 2000, investors had become conditioned to expect double-digit returns from stocks. Are your expectations realistic, given the current environment?
3. Specify your time frame for the preceding two tactics.
4. Diversify by manager, by asset class, and by style of investing.

Your comfort level with these four tactics depends on the amount of your investment knowledge and experience. If the advice in the first three tactics is not clear, do some more reading and talk to more people until you develop a better understanding of your own goals and risk tolerance. An ability to articulate investment goals and risk tolerance—and to evaluate any prospective manager's response—is the foundation of successful investing.

GLEANING THE RIGHT INFORMATION

Growth in the amount of money managed (the assets under management) is the measure of success for an investment advisor; the more assets under management, the more fees (usually based on account size) generated. Growth occurs via the addition of new clients and the selection of investments that appreciate in value. In short, competition for your assets begins with marketing pitches that are designed to put an advisor's best foot forward. It is your responsibility to do the due diligence, break through the sales hype, and get the information you need to make a good decision. Which managers will best *get you where you want to go?*

Too often, investors hire advisors on the basis of a short-term track record, which is rather like driving a car by looking only in the rearview mirror. Performance, like markets, tends to move in cycles. Clients who sign on with a manager who posted a 60 percent return in the previous year may be getting in just in time to ride the downtrend from the crest. Performance is one of several factors you should consider. Analyze a potential manager's performance across market ups and downs, preferably over at least five years. Since the market break in 2000, investors have been in a better position to assess performance because advisors no longer have the benefit of a consistently upward trend.

When institutional investors such as pension funds, endowments, and foundations are looking for money managers, they typically put out a "request for proposal" (RFP), which requires detailed answers to a host of questions. Only firms that complete their screens on the RFP are invited to make personal presentations.

The process for individual investors need not be equally rigid, but it ought to be thorough and disciplined. Having some background information before hearing the "pitch" will leave you less vulnerable to the beauty-contest aspects of the process. Here are some of the points you should explore prior to a personal meeting:

- *What is the history and/or ownership of the advisor's firm?* The investment management business is constantly consolidating. You may not want your professionals' energies diverted from your account by a need to work out the "synergy" with a new parent company.
- *What is the tenure of the principal professionals?* If you have found a firm with a good track record, make sure the people who created that performance are still there.
- *What are the credentials of the principal professionals?* Chartered Financial Analyst (CFA) and Certified Investment Management Analyst (CIMA) designations are among the most rigorous and highly regarded.
- *Are all portfolios managed the same?* Whether you want a "Yes" or a "No" depends on your preferences. You probably want equal access to the advisor's best talent and ideas, but you may have unique issues that require special consideration.
- *How is risk measured and controlled?* Look at standard risk measures such as standard deviation and Sharpe ratio. Standard deviation is a statistical measure. In terms of portfolio performance, a high standard deviation indicates high volatility and therefore high risk. Sharpe ratio is commonly used to measure risk-adjusted return. It is calculated by subtracting the "risk-free" return (usually, the three-month Treasury Bill) from the portfolio return and dividing the resulting "excess return" by the portfolio's risk level (standard deviation). The result is a measure of return gained per unit of risk taken.
- *What is the investment approach? Has it been consistently applied across portfolios?* Insist on seeing concrete evidence of the advisor's stated investment philosophy in action. If you are hiring an investor with a value style, for example, you want to be sure that he or she does not deviate from the defined standards during periods when the market favors stocks with potential for accelerated earnings growth. Ask for real-life examples of a successful pick and of one that did not work out equally well.
- *Are taxable and tax-exempt accounts managed the same way?* If they are, you may get an unpleasant surprise at tax time. Because of their tax-exempt status, endowments and pension funds do not have to worry about generating taxable income and capital gains. Individuals do. Your advisor should not make investment decisions solely on the basis of tax consequences, but you may

want your tax status to be a consideration in the timing of sales. Be sure to ask about the after-tax performance of your taxable portfolios. Advisors should be happy to provide this information.

■ *How is the performance track record presented? Is it compliant with the industry standards set by the Association of Investment Management Research (AIMR) or the Investment Management Consultants Association (IMCA)?* These voluntary standards for performance reporting were developed to promote consistency among advisors. When investors look at the performance of different advisors, they can be confident they are comparing apples to apples. Compliance makes sure that published track records are not distorted by the method of calculation or picked from only the best accounts. Indications of compliance can be found in footnotes or disclosure statements. Some advisors have their compliance verified by an independent accounting firm.

■ *Ask for references—people who have a similar portfolio size and similar objectives.* A refusal to provide references is a red flag. "Client confidentiality" is not an acceptable excuse.

■ *How often can you expect the portfolio manager and/or client service representative to meet with you?* An annual face-to-face meeting is the minimum standard for appropriate monitoring. An advisor should be willing to meet with you more frequently if you wish, but once a year is usually enough if the quarterly reports are thorough.

Many institutional investors employ the services of a consultant during the search process, and a parallel trend is emerging among wealthy individuals. For the institution, the consultant provides a level of scrutiny and objectivity that helps to fulfill the fiduciary responsibility. For the individual, the consultant helps to minimize the confusion among so many available alternatives. Some of the larger institutional consultants, such as Callan and Cambridge, also offer services for private investors. Other national firms, such as CTC Consultants, Windermere and Greycourt, emphasize the individual market. Accountants or brokers who have earned the CIMA designation can also play the role of consultant.

Hiring a consultant does not relieve you of your ultimate responsibilities. Even when a consultant agrees to monitor your advisors for a fee, you still have to monitor the consultant.

QUALITATIVE ISSUES

After listening to a very smart consultant's asset allocation presentation, which was filled with formulas and charts, an IPI member commented to me, "This task of allocating assets and selecting managers for my family is not just about charts and dots. I need to have more of my own intellect and intuition involved in the process." He was absolutely right. Successful investing requires both qualitative and quantitative decisions, as well as constructive dialogues between the investor and the advisor.

Finding a financial advisor is a bit like finding a mate; compatibility is important. If you don't like the person, you are less likely to listen to his or her strategy or advice. If you do not feel comfortable, you may not solicit the answers needed to maintain an adequate level of control. If the manager fails to engage you or neglects to solicit your expectations of risk and return, the relationship is not likely to succeed. At a qualitative level, these are the questions to ask:

- Do I like this person?
- Is the presentation focused on his or her skills or my needs?
- Do I believe this person?
- Will he or she be responsive to my needs?

Consider whether the representative you are speaking to is the "relationship manager" or the person who will actually be making the investment decisions. Good portfolio managers sometimes make bad presenters; they would rather be in their offices—watching their screens and reading their research reports. Smart clients have figured this out and understand that the amount of time a portfolio manager spends on marketing and relationship management is time that might be better spent attending to the portfolios. Whether you want or need to meet the person who is actually managing your portfolio is a matter of personal preference.

ONE IS NOT ENOUGH

One of the basic tenets of sensible investing is diversification—not putting all your proverbial eggs in one basket. All investors should examine how and when they might diversify. Why? If you listen to a financial news channel for three hours a day for three straight weeks, you will discover an alarming and repetitive cycle of language and a disturbing absence of continuity from one day's analysis to the next. Few (if any) advisors get it right all the time. If you don't have enough money to meet the minimum account size at more than one firm, you should, at the least, have your assets diversified among asset classes.

Surveys of the IPI's network show that most member families employ four traditional (i.e., long-only) managers and eight "alternative" managers for hedge funds, private equity, or venture capital funds. Almost half of the members use a consultant to assist their search.

ESTABLISHING EXPECTATIONS

I view the relationship between investor and advisor as something like a marriage, and I always advise a prenuptial agreement. Reaching such an agreement requires you to be brutally honest with yourself. It means first getting your own house in order and developing, to the following questions, specific answers that you all can live with:

- What are my spoken and unspoken expectations?
- What are the components of a successful client/advisor relationship? Am I looking for a financial counselor or strictly a money manager?
- Are my income and investment needs clear?
- Does my past investment experience rightly or wrongly influence my current thinking?
- How will I evaluate my choice of an advisor? What proof will I have that I made the correct choice?
- When should this evaluation begin? At the first year-end? First quarter? What will I do if I lose money in the first six months?
- What role will the market's performance (up and down!) play in my evaluation?

If you are investing your family's wealth, the family members have to answer these questions individually and then reach a consensus as a group. The answers to these questions will inform the investment policy with which your advisors will be expected to comply.

Clear benchmarks should also be established and documented with the advisor, to cover common expectations such as:

- Timing and formats of reports.
- Response time to written, e-mailed, or telephone inquiries.
- Frequency and format of personal meetings.

Another issue to consider is the type of communication you expect from your advisor during crises. One private investor/member was stunned when his money manager opted not to give any opinion on the market impact of the September 11, 2001, terrorist attacks. As a "bottom-up" manager focused only on company fundamentals, he said, he would not invest based on his opinion of world events. Making matters worse, when the investor asked about the already dismal year (his portfolio was down 12 percent through August 2001), the manager quipped, "Don't forget, we had our biggest up quarter after the Persian Gulf War." The callous glibness of the remark offended the investor, and he fired the manager. With the benefit of hindsight, we can see that this investor unfortunately sold at the market's bottom and missed out on the subsequent 20 percent rebound from the mid-September lows. Firing a manager solely for emotional reasons is dangerous.

Among IPI members, phone calls from their advisors are the most personal connection and the most appreciated form of communication. Not valued were standardized "Don't worry; be happy" conference calls and "long, rambling" reports. If you are considering an advisor, ask for an example of a crisis communication.

AWAKE IN THE DRIVER'S SEAT

Once the hard work of setting the goals, selecting the advisors, and allocating the assets has been completed, you may be tempted to envision the rest as a self-sustaining process, particularly if you tend toward the abdication side of the control-delegation spectrum. Phone calls to and from the advisor might taper off, meetings may become less frequent, and account statements may go unread. Failing to monitor the managers on an ongoing basis may put you at risk for some unpleasant surprises.

At the outset, compile a list of the aspects you need to monitor. Ask for a quarterly one-page summary of key points such as:

- Since inception, what is the absolute net return of the portfolio, and how does it relate to the agreed-on benchmarks?

- To what does the advisor attribute the performance during the previous quarter?
- How has the asset mix changed (if at all) in the previous quarter?
- What purchases/sales in the portfolio were most significant?
- What personnel changes have occurred in the advisory firm?
- Have the market dynamics or the advisor's outlook changed since the previous quarter?

You have the opportunity to take charge of the annual meetings by setting the standards for the advisor to meet. Every personal meeting should be an educational opportunity that adds value for you, not merely a stage where the advisor can wax eloquent on the market.

Remember, too, that the relationship is not necessarily permanent. I remember hearing a respected investment professional say that it takes 99 years to determine whether a manager's performance is a function of luck or skill. As a rule of thumb, an advisor should be allowed between three and five years to prove his or her skills. Still, you should reevaluate a relationship immediately if there is a change in ownership, if the returns start to fall consistently short of the benchmark, or if some other event occurs that gives you cause for concern. For example, I serve on the investment committee for an endowment that hired an international money manager in mid-2000, or at about the worst possible time in the market. We expected our portfolio to go down, but not to decline more steeply than the benchmark. In general, ask your advisor for an explanation of unusual performance or events. If the answer is satisfactory to you, there is no reason to change; if it's not, you may want to start a new search.

In the fourth quarter of 2001, as it became clear that the economy was in recession, almost half the IPI members doubted their managers' ability to deliver good results, given the difficult environment. They planned to change their roster of managers for the coming year. The reasons cited included:

- Underperformance (particularly after taxes).
- Too much concentration with one manager.
- Below-index results at managed-money prices.
- A lower rate of return for equities in the immediate future.

Their answers indicated that this group of investors was taking an appropriate and active interest in the management of their wealth.

THE REWARDS ARE YOURS

One IPI member initially found the process of selecting and monitoring advisors intimidating. She confided to me, "When I first started, I thought that to be a really smart investor I needed to get from here to there in my knowledge." (She drew a steep upward slope.) "Once I got into it, I decided that perhaps I needed to learn only half of that. By the time I gained some experience and studied a bit, I came to realize that most of the issues are common sense, and I really did not need to learn so much after all. What a relief!"

You do not need to understand derivatives and duration to be a smart investor, nor will knowing what those terms mean necessarily increase your chances for success. You need enough perspective to be able to listen to an investment professional and know whether he or she is making sense, and to determine the level of partnering in the money management process that works best for you.

Words to the Wise

- Wealthy individuals tend to over- or underestimate their ability to manage their wealth.
- You don't need to make each investment decision yourself. A far more effective approach is to select a team of professional financial advisors and then monitor their decisions.
- An important first step to a successful money manager relationship is the articulation of your goals and your tolerance for risk.
- Many investment issues are matters of common sense. If you gain a basic knowledge of investment fundamentals, you should be able to know whether your advisors are making sense for your situation.
- Investors who function as partners in the process tend to get more attention and better results from their advisors.
- Well-informed investors usually enjoy more rewarding relationships with their money managers.

Charlotte B. Beyer

Charlotte B. Beyer is founder and CEO of the Institute for Private Investors (IPI), a membership organization that provides educational and networking resources for wealthy individuals and their advisors. Prior to founding the organization in 1990, Ms. Beyer spent 20 years in various financial service firms, including a New York bank's trust department and two money management companies. She is President of the Board of Trustees of Westover School, an all-girls school in Middlebury, Connecticut, and also serves on the advisory board of Institutional Investor's Journal of Wealth Management.

10

HOW TO BUILD A WINNING TEAM OF FINANCIAL ADVISORS

A Collaborative Approach Yields the Best Results

CHARLES A. LOWENHAUPT

Conrad Overton was the founder and driving force behind Overton Worldwide Industries, a major manufacturing company with substantial value. He retained a broker, who purchased tax shelters for his account, and an accountant, who prepared his corporate and personal tax returns. Approximately one year before he died, Conrad asked our law firm to help with his estate planning. After several meetings, we designed a charitable lead trust and marital and nonmarital trusts to take effect on his death. He died in 1979, survived by his widow, his four children, his broker, his accountant, us, and several trusts. Virtually all of his wealth was in Overton Worldwide stock.

We spent three years resolving his estate and designing postmortem tax savings for the family, none of whom had been involved in building the company or in Conrad's management of his assets. As part of that planning, we decided to participate with other Overton Worldwide shareholders in a secondary stock offering that enabled each family member to sell 30 percent of his or her stock. The result of that secondary offering was a more diversified family investment portfolio that required the services of a more extensive team of financial advisors. The Overtons decided to have multiple investment managers.

Individually and together, the Overton family developed a strategy of encouraging contests among those advisors. The investment managers were to be seen as "competing" with each other for return. The broker was asked to evaluate the performance of the investment manager; the broker's investment recommendations were presented to the investment manager; our planning advice was presented to the accountant; and the tax returns he prepared were sent to us to "find mistakes." This approach could best be described as the financial equivalent of an armed joust. Each advisor was pitted against the others. The family apparently felt that these contests would keep their advisors honest and on their toes.

The gladiatorial approach to managing $30 million of diversified assets and another $100 million of Overton Worldwide stock seemed to us unproductive and harmful to the development of the family's wealth management strategy. We noted the likelihood that policies and strategies would conflict, the possibility that "wash sale" rules would interfere with tax planning, and the fact that we had not seen advisors work harder on account of a competitive overlay.

We recommended instead that the Overtons should change their thinking and structure entirely, to utilize their advisors on a fully collaborative basis. There would be no competition among the members of the team, and no manager or advisor was to feel threatened by another. Everyone would focus on the financial and general well-being of the Overton family.

Today, with four money managers (each representing a different investment approach), a bank custodian, an accountant, a lawyer, and several other advisors, the Overton family and their advisors agree that this collaborative process has succeeded far beyond the expectations of those of us who were involved in its design. All information relating to portfolios, tax planning, and similar matters is shared, so that all participants have a sense of the overall portfolio and strategies. The advisory team works collaboratively to design reporting standards, facilitate communication, resolve problems, and build value.

The team has worked together to create a process to sell more of Overton Worldwide stock; to design portfolios of different investment classes (in each case, selecting one of the managers to create the portfolio for each different class); to raise cash as needed for various purposes; and to build emergency support for family members when needed. When value investing is down, the growth managers on the team encourage patience and point out the cyclical nature of style predominance. When growth investing is down, the value managers help explain that situation. All managers recommended a portfolio of small-cap stocks, managed by an advisor chosen by all. Together, they all consider the strengths of performance, even when the portfolio of one lags behind the other portfolios.

Each family member feels comfortable discussing matters with one of the advisors, because he or she knows that each advisor will communicate with the others as appropriate. Family members feel free to miss the quarterly meetings. They rely on the team of advisors to raise and resolve issues on their behalf and to report all discussions in extensive minutes of meetings. The team members have become friends as well as colleagues. Their friendship and sense of shared purpose have successfully guided the Overton family through the development and maturation of its wealth management.

THE WORLD OF FINANCIAL ADVISORS

A wealth management team requires a number of skills but not necessarily a large number of advisors. Some wealth possessors have two or three; others have 15 or 20. The functions of advisors differ; individual advisors often serve a number of functions. It is helpful to analyze some of the core functions available to facilitate wealth management in terms of specific types of entities performing those functions, but it is always necessary to remember that each can perform the functions of another.

Family Offices

These are discussed at length in Chapter 15. However, it is worth noting that if there is a family office, it is almost always part of the team. In many cases, it performs some of the services allocated to various team members, as described in the discussion below.

Investment Managers

Nearly every wealth management team includes one or more investment counselors, money managers, or asset managers. Often, families have more than one manager, to provide diversified investment management and expertise in the various investment classes. As an example, a family may have several managers of equities (covering, for instance, such areas as large-cap growth, large-cap value, small-cap management, and international management), as well as several managers of fixed-income securities, hedge funds, commodities, currency real estate, and private deals. Alternatively, a family might have funds of managers.

Investment managers generally make the day-to-day decisions concerning the purchase and sale of assets, and they often advise on asset classes and allocation. As illustrated by the story of the Overtons, when the investment managers are collaborating, they can add great strategic value. When they are not collaborating, they can add confusion by operating at cross purposes to buy and sell stocks, bonds, and other assets.

Consultants (Managers of Managers)

Many wealth management programs utilize a consultant to manage the managers. This consultant does not buy and sell specific securities. Instead, he or she helps the client select and evaluate the managers. In effect, the consultant offers another layer of investment expertise to help deal with investment counselors and money managers. If a wealth possessor has a strong family office, a consultant is rarely retained, except in transitional situations or cases where the consultant has particular skills not possessed by the family office. Recently, we saw a consultant who was being used by a family office to move management of portfolios from an elderly family member to professional managers; as a complete outsider, the consultant could risk the wrath of the elderly family member as the "modern" investment approach was being applied.

Brokers

A broker is often used to execute trades, and a good broker provides support for the investment managers. The broker is often a family member who is gathering the commissions to keep revenue within the family; a child or in-law has employment in a brokerage house so that, as commissions are paid, that family member secures a proportion of them. Sometimes, the broker is actually one of the investment counselors or money managers; many investment counselors and money managers execute their own trades as brokers. Most trades of publicly traded stocks and bonds are executed at steep discounts from the old schedules, but a good independent broker can still add value to the team.

Banks

Banks almost always play some role in wealth management. Banks are frequently involved in loans, transactions, and other traditional banking relationships with the wealth possessor or his business. A bank may serve as the trustee of substantial portions of the managed wealth. In that capacity, whether as sole trustee or cotrustee, the bank becomes an integral member of the management team because its portfolio is central to the wealth. Sometimes, a bank will serve as a family office.

Banks are often custodians of families' assets. A preference for bank custodians generally derives from a perception that the bank's role as custodian is more protective than that of a broker. Some lawyers will say that a bank's trust accounts (where custody usually resides) are free of the claims of the bank's creditors. In fact, many wealth possessors continue to use brokerage accounts (in "street name") with full comfort. Special asset classes may require bank or specialized custodians.

Many banks have developed technology to facilitate the supervision of wealth and the evaluation of investment managers. This option is usually offered as an adjunct to trustee or custody services, but, in many cases, the technology is desired as a stand-alone service.

Technologists

Increasingly, technologists are participating in wealth management, organizing information, developing strategy, evaluating performance, and enhancing communication. Although banks and some investment managers are offering good technology for some of these purposes—and many investment managers and consultants are offering technology relating to their own responsibilities—complete integrated solutions are hard to find. Some technologists specifically focus on private wealth, and we might expect the development of more technology designed for that purpose.

Accountants

Wealth management requires substantial accounting and bookkeeping services. Preparation of tax returns, auditing of providers and employees, and, from time to time, special services are appropriately provided by accountants. Analysis of income and transfer tax consequences should often precede design of an investment strategy, an investment decision, or a decision to make charitable gifts. The accountant can "crunch the numbers" before important decisions are made. We frequently see situations where the "black-letter rules" are proven wrong by the numbers for a particular transaction. For example, with some frequency, we find that once pro-forma returns and calculations are prepared, a client can conclude that raising and making a charitable contribution of cash is preferable to contributing appreciated securities.

Lawyers

Lawyers create the documents that govern and facilitate the transmission of family wealth: wills, trusts, corporations, partnerships, other business entities, and agreements relating to them. A good lawyer can also be a counselor who helps the family develop its wealth objectives and some of its strategies. A lawyer skilled in expression can articulate those objectives and strategies. Frequently, the lawyer is the expert on tax strategies, particularly those that minimize estate, gift, and generation-skipping transfer taxes.

Equally important is the lawyer's ability to monitor a strategy or entity and ensure its "clean" operation. The Internal Revenue Service is authorized to assert that the terms of a trust or partnership are not being adhered to and should therefore be disregarded. To forestall such an adverse finding, a good tax lawyer will emphasize that the wealth management team must honor the terms of the instrument and that participants must hold and document regular meetings, in which the appropriate roles are played.

We recently met with a 45-year-old grandson, a new client, who repeatedly referred to the $20 million trust established by his grandfather for his benefit as "my own money." He said that he and his brothers, the cotrustees, had decided that he could "do whatever" he wanted with the trust and he was planning to do "exactly that." The terms of that trust provided that the grandson could access the corpus for his "health and support," and that the trust would pass, as he directed, among his children and grandchildren at his death. If the trust assets were really the grandson's "own," they would be reduced by something like $10 million in estate taxes at the grandson's death. We will be helping the grandson to understand the trust, and will develop procedures that respect the integrity of the trust.

Tax lawyers might well assert that the greatest value of a good lawyer is in his or her role of monitoring and preserving the character of the wealth vehicles.

Life Insurance Consultants

Life insurance can offer tax-favored benefits for those who hold investment portfolios. However, life insurance products are complex and require analyses related to pricing, terms, and designs of policies. That's why many clients use the services of experts in this field (either commission-based agents or fee-based consultants). The expertise of a life insurance consultant may simply reside in the placement, design, and pricing of policies, or may more broadly include the use of policies and the details of their taxation.

Concierge Services

These specialists offer the personal services often desired by wealthy individuals and families: vacation arrangements, automobiles, planes and boats, residential and leisure real estate, theater tickets, personal shopping, and other services. Concierge services are not always easy to find and are rarely aggregated in one company or place. Such services are often considered unnecessary "fluff," but they can be valuable for the wealth possessor because they allow him or her to utilize the wealth more easily.

Other Consultants

The world of financial services is full of consultants. Some specialize in the design of wealth management structures around family values. Others focus on helping families deal with their internal dynamics from a psychological standpoint. There are consultants available to help design philanthropic programs. There are experts in liability and casualty insurance coverage for families of wealth. There are educational consultants helping to find acceptable schooling, geriatricians focusing on the needs of aging members of wealthy families, and doctors providing examinations and appropriate treatments with no limits on cost.

All of these consultants and service providers can be viewed as part of the team that manages the client's wealth.

THE WEALTH COUNSELOR

As the foregoing list shows, a myriad of advisors are available to a wealthy individual or family. These may include a lawyer, an investment expert, an accountant, a banker, and a number of other specialists. Each may offer a "full range" of services, yet each has its own "niche." And there are other less traditional players in the "financial advisor" field. Indeed, we have a client who reviews every significant decision with his massage therapist.

When I am in a room with a client and several advisors, we advisors are more sensitive to the differences in our roles than is the client. Our industry is really a shared one of "wealth management and counseling," and we have similar core skills. Our professional designations—lawyer, accountant, investment advisor, or banker—result from statutory and regulatory limitations not inherently logical to our client. Many jurisdictions do not set limitations. In Hong Kong, a bank can write wills, and in other jurisdictions, an accounting firm can be a money manager. Note the number of brokers and investment counselors who are now offering full trust services.

A client recently challenged me by asking whether he could design his wealth management without employing any expert's help. He noted that he could buy index funds for investment, an automated tax return preparation program, and the full services of an Internet bank. In a final stab, he told me that he understood that his state had written laws of intestacy whereby his estate would pass to his wife and children as he desired. Why should he incur fees? he asked. What was he missing?

He was missing "wealth counseling." I proved this by asking him a series of questions starting with: "What is your wealth for? . . . How do you want to utilize your wealth responsibly to create functionality, increase satisfaction, and encourage the happiness of yourself and your family?" Once questions such as those are answered, tax planning, asset allocation, design of entities, and similar details can be addressed and resolved easily and quickly. No technology or fund has yet been established to help an individual answer these questions.

A friend of mine is a specialist in bonds and is compensated on a commission basis—he is a "bond trader." His customer base is made up of some very sophisticated experts in financial services who manage investments for large institutions. They use no other investment advisor—only the bond specialist. He has asked them why they "need" him when they could easily manage their own bond portfolios masterfully. They tell him they pay him commissions because they want the "counselor," the listener who helps them develop their objectives for the management of wealth.

We have watched the good wealth counselor become a close friend and personal confidant of the wealth possessor, in a deep relationship of trust and reliance. The relationship can become multigenerational. Many of our clients are the third generation of families my grandfather counseled. A 92-year-old investment counselor I know has now worked with three generations of one family—attending weddings and funerals, rushing to a client's house to work through a personal emergency, advising a newly married couple on whether they should buy a home. When those clients talk about that investment counselor, they speak about him as a family member.

TEAM COUNSELING

One individual—an investment professional, a lawyer, an accountant, a family office manager, or any other—can be the good counselor. But it is also possible to build a *team* to counsel the client, as shown by the experience of the Overton family. Team counseling can be supportive, constructive, and successful. The operative concept is collaboration, and the principle to be enforced is that advisors working together for a wealth possessor's benefit (or a family's benefit) are more effective in rendering services than advisors working separately or, worse, in competition with each other.

The Proposer

At the outset, some influential person must forcefully propose a collaborative approach. That "proposer" can be the wealth possessor or the head of a family office. It can also be a lawyer or accountant (noting the possibilities of wash-sale exposure among managers, or otherwise expressing the wisdom of collaboration). The proposer must have the power to enforce the collaboration and the vision to understand how it should be structured among the advisors themselves, which principles must be addressed early, and how the chemistry of the team should develop. The proposer is suggesting a mind-set or culture, and the proposer must have enough understanding to comprehend how the team will work together.

The Coordinator

A coordinator must also be selected. This person (or institution) sets meeting dates (usually after endless rounds of surveying the participants to find a date that works for all), ensures that communication and exchange of information are complete, and facilitates expense reimbursements. The coordinator is primarily an administrator and is frequently the family office, a bank, a lawyer, an accountant, or any other member of the team who has some office staff and facilities available.

The Mediator

This is the most important and complicated role of all. Particularly at the beginning, the mediator is the enforcer of collaboration. He or she prevents advisors from using sessions to promote themselves over others, and urges them to resolve their differences by having discussions among themselves. The mediator has the authority to keep a meeting within its time frame and agenda, and to ensure that issues are properly developed and discussed. Frequently, the mediator must ask difficult questions that are being sidestepped by others in order to impel an advisor to defend a position or to consider alternatives. The mediator requires that issues be addressed at appropriate times and does not allow an advisor to use the issue for his or her own purposes. The mediator ensures that the game is fair.

In addition, the mediator helps to design the rules, sets the frequency of meetings and the closing dates for portfolio evaluation, lists the eligible attendees, and circulates the methods of sharing information so that all advisors are equally prepared. The mediator sets the agenda, gives the participants enough time to consider issues in advance, and establishes other ground rules for sessions, including such issues as reporting and confidentiality. The mediator sets the tone at every meeting and keeps the advisors focused on the well-being of the wealth possessor or family.

The advisors can number from three to 20. The mediator must be fully aware of each advisor's technical expertise and must encourage the team to utilize this expertise. Like a conductor of an orchestra, the mediator leads the group in harmony, for the benefit of the client.

The Objective

Your objective should be to build a team of "wealth counselors" for yourself and your family. The relationship between you and your team—and between you and each player—will become as important to you as their professional skills. Some relationships become multigenerational; they grow through family and institutional generations to span many years. Effective wealth counseling is provided by a group of professionals who become your friends and your family's friends as they look after your interests. Stock picks and tax recommendations will be less valuable than their friendship and their common-sense support as you work through the difficult questions of what your wealth is for and how to use it.

Words to the Wise

- Build a team of wealth counselors for yourself and your family.
- Survey your advisors and evaluate their strengths and weaknesses. You need a person or company you can trust—one with skills in which you have confidence. Do not tolerate any advisor whom you consider deficient in any respect.

Words to the Wise (Continued)

- The particular specialties on your team are not as important as your sense that the team is comprised of people you trust—people who can work together to bring in others as needed.

- Tell your advisors that you insist on *collaboration,* not competition. Draw your vision of a group of advisors who are all working together for you and your family. Each advisor must abide by this principle. Express your hope that any differences among them can be resolved before you have to become involved.

- Select the mediator and prepare that person to play the role. Anoint him or her during one of the early meetings of the team.

- Choose an efficient, effective, and neutral coordinator.

- Challenge your team to work through the technical matters and, as the team works together, explore the softer issues of your wealth and how to use it.

- Be open with the advisors—as a group and individually.

- Encourage the advisors to develop *esprit de corps,* by means of: dinners or lunches with all of them; remembering occasions; and noting professional achievements.

- You are likely to find that the most effective wealth counseling comes from a group of professionals who not only look after your interests but become your friends.

Charles A. Lowenhaupt

Charles A. Lowenhaupt is the managing member of Lowenhaupt & Chasnoff, LLC. Founded by Mr. Lowenhaupt's grandfather in 1908 in St. Louis, it is the oldest tax law firm in the United States and now serves families and businesses throughout the United States and overseas. Mr. Lowenhaupt's areas of emphasis include family wealth planning, taxation, estate planning, and wills and trusts. He is the chairman of a subcommittee of the Estate and Gift Tax Committee of the American Bar Association Tax Section, Advisor Faculty Emeritus of the Institute for Private Investors, a frequent writer and lecturer, and a member of numerous professional organizations.

11

BALANCING ACT

The Art of Asset Allocation

JONATHAN SPENCER

A new client recently sold his business. He now had $20 million from the sale and wanted to invest his hard-earned money. Because he had concentrated all his efforts, over many years, toward making his business a success, he had no working knowledge of how to invest. He hoped he could make his wealth grow by investing well. However, he also wanted to protect it, because he knew that the successful sale of his business was a one-time event for him—something he could not easily repeat.

We all want our investments to do well, but "doing well" means different things to different investors. Yet, no matter what an individual's definition of investing success may be, the approach to success is the same. Careful, long-term planning is the hallmark of prudent investing, and the foundation of that planning is asset allocation. Asset allocation helps to create an investment portfolio that achieves a dynamic balance between the objective realities of investing and the subjective realities of *you*—who you are and what you want to accomplish with your investments.

The new client described above is quite similar to hundreds of other entrepreneurs who achieve success through hard work and dedication to their businesses. When all their efforts pay off, they're confronted with questions about how best to preserve their wealth, and these questions are probably not within their expertise. I talked with the client and gave him an introduction to investing wisely. I explained aspects of asset allocation that would give him the confidence needed to make investment decisions in conjunction with a trusted expert. This chapter describes the essential factors of asset allocation that can help wealthy individuals gain that confidence.

OF EGGS AND BASKETS

"Don't put all your eggs in one basket." That phrase is well known for a very good reason: it is time-honored, experiential advice.

For investors, diversification provides the best defense against excessive risk. Spreading one's risk is essential. The early Venetians made this tactic a cornerstone of their success—which lasted for hundreds of years. When ships were outfitted for trading voyages, merchants didn't foot the full bill for any one ship. Each merchant put a bit of money into dozens of ships sailing to Alexandria, Constantinople, and the many Levantine ports. Some ships never returned, but the ones that did brought huge profits for everyone involved.

Asset allocation is the process of deciding how to diversify your investments—how much you should put into stocks, how much into bonds, and how much into other asset classes. The amount you place in each asset class will depend on how much, and how fast, you want your investments to grow—in other words, what level of investment performance fits your goals. To help you gauge the performance of each of your selected investments within its particular asset class, you need a frame of reference: a benchmark. For example, the Standard & Poor's (S&P) 500 Index is frequently used as the benchmark for performance of U.S. domestic stocks. By studying how the Index has performed, you will gain a relative indicator of what to expect over the long term. In any given year, you can compare how the stocks in your portfolio matched up against the Index, and thereby determine whether your stocks produced an acceptable return.

The S&P 500 Index includes the stocks of only 500 large domestic companies. If you are considering buying a selection of stocks of small companies, or adding some international stocks to your portfolio, you should judge that performance against a more comparable index—for example, the Russell 2000 Index for small company stocks, or the MSCI EAFE* Index for international stocks.

When you are determining your asset allocation mix, you will encounter a number of objective variables that will shape your decisions. The three basic variables are: (1) the expected return, (2) the volatility (or risk) of each investment, and (3) the correlation—how sensitive the performance of that investment is to other investments in your overall portfolio.

---

* Morgan Stanley Capital International Europe, Australasia, Far East.

Each investment's level of *liquidity*—how easily an investment can be turned into cash—may become a factor. The most publicly traded stocks and bonds are of course highly liquid. Lack of liquidity becomes a consideration when your goal is to include more specialized investments such as private equity, hedge funds, and real estate.

After they construct a hypothetical portfolio, wealthy individuals should review the returns of the portfolio from two perspectives: a before-tax perspective and an after-tax perspective. For wealthy individuals and families, the results of pretax and after-tax asset allocation can be critically different.

Before we discuss after-tax asset allocation, let's look at the fundamentals of asset allocation in general.

ASSET ALLOCATION—WITHOUT THE JARGON

Asset allocation is the process of determining what, *for you*, is the best mix of investments. For any desired investment objective, you could construct a multitude of different asset allocation mixes, but only a limited number of those possibilities would match your subjective goals and personal life situation. Meshing your subjective and emotional restrictions with the many investment choices available is the art of asset allocation.

Understanding your investment profile and defining your investment goals is a careful and complex process. It involves building a close and trusting relationship with a financial institution. Asset allocation professionals will help you to define your goals and to understand each investment's potential risks and reward. They will then structure and implement an asset allocation strategy with which you will be comfortable. The allocation decisions you make will have a significant impact on your lifestyle and the lifestyles of future generations of your family.

STEP BY STEP

The first step is to identify your primary investing goal—the one *you* regard as more important than all others. "I want to retire at age [40, 50, 60]." "I want my kids to go to Oxford without *needing* a scholarship." "I want to double my money in 10 years." The need to be specific when defining your goals shows up in the example of wanting to double your money. Do you want to double the actual dollar figure, or double what your money is now worth? The intrinsic worth of your money over time depends on inflation. If you are investing during a period of high inflation, doubling the dollar figure will yield significantly less than doubling the purchasing power of your money. If your only goal is to meet inflation, you could place all your investments in U.S. Treasury Bills. These securities generally keep pace with the rate of inflation, (there are U.S. Government Securities called TIPS, or Treasury Inflation Protection Securities, whose value is directly indexed to the rate of inflation; these instruments guarantee that your real return at least equals that of inflation), and, because they are backed by the full faith and credit of the U.S. Government, Treasury Bills are considered essentially "risk-free." Historically, they haven't rewarded investors with much of any returns above inflation (and sometimes they have underperformed inflation), but if T-Bills are your choice, you will not be exposing your capital to any credit or market risk.

If you want to advance your wealth beyond simply keeping pace with inflation, you will inevitably have to assume a greater degree of risk. Consequently, your initial "wish" goal may have to be revised if the prospect of risk makes you uneasy. For example, you may discover that you can't possibly double your money in a 10-year time frame without extensive risk, and you will probably balk at taking huge risks with the wealth you've already accumulated. In that case, maybe a 20-year time frame is more reasonable. Or you may frame your goal within a different and more reasonable set of parameters, such as: "I want to realize a steady 5 percent over inflation on my portfolio annually." The risks will be more in line with what you can tolerate, and the investment mix will be significantly different.

The next question to ask and answer is: Where does asset allocation fit within your overall wealth management plan? Is it just one part of your total wealth, or should all your wealth be viewed as components—allocations—of your portfolio? For example, when determining what percentage of real estate should be in your portfolio, your optimal asset allocation model may say 8 percent to 10 percent. But if your homes—say, in New Jersey, Santa Fe, and Palm Beach—account for a portion closer to 20 percent, you are probably not going to sell one of them. Instead, you might consider limiting your asset allocation portfolio to the investable portion of your total wealth or construct an asset allocation portfolio knowing that you may be over-invested in real estate. Keep in mind that variable life insurance, 401(k)s, and pension funds contain underlying investments and should be included in your asset allocation planning.

WORLD WEALTH CATEGORIES

To diversify your investable wealth properly, you need to be familiar with the various world wealth categories. These include domestic stocks and bonds, international stocks and bonds, cash, real estate, commodities, and gold. Each category has its benefits and its drawbacks. (We'll look at the specialized investment areas of private equity and hedge funds later in this chapter.) Along with the inherent questions of volatility, liquidity, and return, the correlation (or lack of correlation) between asset classes becomes an important factor when you are determining the best combination of assets for your portfolio. Correlation—how closely the rise and fall of one asset class matches another—affects the volatility of your portfolio because different asset classes do well at different times and for different reasons.

Let's take a quick look at the pros and cons of the different asset classes. Stocks may have the best ability to generate substantial returns quickly, but they also experience high volatility. Bonds have lower volatility, but their returns are usually lower. However, there are historical periods, such as the years following World War II and the early 80s, when bonds generated returns of the magnitude usually associated with stocks. Cash investments, such as money market funds or Treasury Bills offer safety and immediate liquidity, but they barely keep you ahead of inflation—and less so after taxes. Physical real estate—historically, the basis of both power and fortune—retains an intrinsic value in all circumstances, but is illiquid as it takes time and costs money to sell. Tangible commodities (agricultural products, livestock, precious and industrial metals, energies, and so on) frequently act as good hedges against inflation. In addition, they don't react to world events the same way as stocks and bonds do. In other words, because commodities have a low correlation to stocks and bonds, they provide a level of balance to a portfolio. On the down side, commodities are highly dependent on supply and demand. In an economic contraction, the demand for commodities can go down while the supply goes up, and the result is lower prices to consumers and investors.

Each investment class raises questions of return, volatility, liquidity, and whether (or how) that asset class matches or doesn't match the price movements of the others. The answer to which asset classes should you include in your portfolio, and how much of each class depends on your assessment of your personal life situation and your investment preferences. The following questions may help to initiate that assessment:

- Which assets are you comfortable owning—for instance, is an investment strategy such as private equity too uncertain for your peace of mind?
- What level of risk do you favor? Can you maintain a strategic holding in the face of short-term downturns? What portion of your portfolio (if any) would you liquidate?
- Have you identified your major investment time horizons, such as how many work years are ahead before you can retire, or how many years from now will all your children have completed a four-year college degree?
- How much money are you withdrawing from your investments as income?
- How much money are you planning to contribute to your portfolio on a regular basis, and for how long?
- What level of liquidity do you require for your portfolio?
- How much are you willing to pay for portfolio "insurance"—such as collars and hedging techniques—to limit your exposure to the downturn of an asset class?

DIVERSIFICATION AND REDUCING RISK

Investment returns at any level above the "risk-free rate" (which is the rate you receive when you own U.S. Treasury Bills) involve a *cost* factor and a *risk* factor. For example, hunting down bargain stocks that have growth potential incurs a cost in time, intellectual output, and money. A risk factor can take its toll on any investment: corporate bonds always carry the potential for default, and any company could go bankrupt and render its stock worthless. Diversification, however, limits an investor's exposure to one asset class and lowers his or her portfolio's overall level of risk unless, without meaning to, your investments are all subject to the same risks.

Two fundamental ingredients will guide your investigation to determine the optimal mix: (1) the risk/return performance potential of an asset class, and (2) the correlation of that asset class with others. Some asset allocation planners focus on economic models to forecast these ingredients. Others prefer to look at historical information. Planners will adopt either a strategic or a tactical approach when they apply their analysis. The strategic approach tends to be more fixed; it adheres to an established plan over the long term. The tactical approach is more fluid; changes to the original plan can be introduced as markets change. We prefer both the strategic and historical perspectives.

The strategic method was formulated by some noteworthy economists, including Nobel Prize winners Harry Markowitz and William Sharpe. In the 1950s, Markowitz made the important observation that certain investment classes may be highly risky if held alone, but when they are combined with other assets in an investor's portfolio, they can actually produce lower overall risk for the portfolio and more attractive potential returns.

The reason for this effect lies in the varying degrees of correlation among different asset classes. One common example is that the market movement of bonds doesn't usually match the movement of stocks. If stocks are down, investors will still have some upside potential from the bonds they hold. We can also measure this non-correlation between narrower asset types, such as high-yield bonds and municipal bonds, or domestic stocks and international stocks. The historical information tells us the general extent to which the movements of any one asset class relate to those of any other. The less their relation, the more attractive they may be as counterbalances for each other, as long as they have some level of positive return.

THE EFFICIENT FRONTIER: THE BORDERS OF PRACTICAL INVESTING

In the 1960s, William Sharpe further refined Markowitz's Modern Portfolio Theory by establishing ways to measure the level of risk for different investment vehicles, and to compare those measurements to expected levels of return. One of the measures developed from this work is the Sharpe Ratio—a measure of the risk-adjusted excess return of a portfolio, and a representation of the excess return gained per unit of risk taken. It is frequently used to compare the performance of two managers, whether they use similar or different investment styles. The two managers may have achieved the same return for a particular time period but incurred different levels of risk. Their Sharpe Ratios will reflect that difference in risk. The performance of the manager with the higher Sharpe Ratio would be interpreted as exhibiting less risk (compared to the other manager's) for the desired return. In general, Sharpe Ratio comparisons help investors to select advantageous return-vs.-risk investment styles and managers for their portfolios, rather than looking at only the highest possible return. This weighing of reward by risk approach becomes increasingly important as investors' wealth increases and wealth preservation dominates their investing philosophy.

Using historical data, asset allocation planners can calculate how particular portfolio mixes might be expected to perform, and at what level of volatility or risk. The results of these calculations can be plotted on a graph that shows the highest rate of return for the accompanying level of risk of each portfolio mix. Such a graph presents what are known as efficient frontiers. Figure 11.1 plots the optimal risk/return for portfolios composed of varying amounts of domestic stocks and bonds.

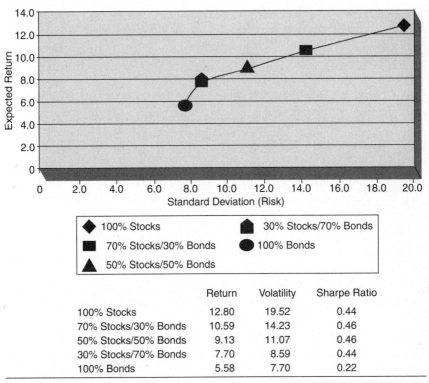

	Return	Volatility	Sharpe Ratio
100% Stocks	12.80	19.52	0.44
70% Stocks/30% Bonds	10.59	14.23	0.46
50% Stocks/50% Bonds	9.13	11.07	0.46
30% Stocks/70% Bonds	7.70	8.59	0.44
100% Bonds	5.58	7.70	0.22

Source: Ibbotson Associates. Stocks represented by S&P 500 Total Return Index. Bonds represented by Long-Term U.S. Government Bond Total Return.

FIGURE 11.1   Historical Performance of Stock, Bond, and Balanced Portfolios from 1926–2001

More diversified examples can show portfolios with varying proportions of domestic stocks and bonds, international stocks and bonds, and commodities. (For an example, see Figure 11.2, shown later in this chapter.)

The efficient frontier will help to guide you toward an asset mix that will meet your requirements for the highest level of return in relation to an acceptable level of risk. This visual history of how different investments have fared over time also helps you to formulate realistic goals. If your initial, idealized goal was to double your money in five years, efficient frontier diagrams can guide you toward a more reasonable objective.

DIFFERENT ASSETS, DIFFERENT HISTORY

To form reasonable expectations for the performance of an asset class, how much history do you need? Researchers and analysts have good data on domestic stocks and bonds stretching back to at least 1929. (Calculations generated by Wall Street often start post-Great Depression.) However, other asset classes either have less historical data or their data are more vague.

For example, the Nasdaq market (mostly technology companies) was not widely followed by investors prior to the early 1990s. Consequently, the focus was contained within the decade of the 1990s. Suppose you had looked at the returns for Nasdaq stocks at the beginning of 2000. They boasted an average annual gain of 24.47 percent over the prior 10 years. Most people concentrated on an even shorter time period—the five years from 1995 through 1999, when the Nasdaq's average annual gain was 40.12 percent. The returns were astounding, and the risks involved were all but ignored. But just two years later, at the end of 2001, the five- and 10-year averages for Nasdaq showed quite a different story: 8.60 percent and 12.76 percent, respectively. Suddenly, risk was back in the picture.

There's a cautionary tale here: History has its limitations. The shorter the history, the greater the risk in relying on its predictive estimations.

Good asset allocation planners should include lack of reliable history as a risk factor. It would certainly have contained some of the irrational exuberance of the late 1990s. Today, that same short-period-of-historical-data risk factor can be applied to hedge funds and private equity.

ALTERNATIVE INVESTMENTS

Hedge funds and private equity have only recently caught investors' attention. Their performance histories are short and appear excellent. Is that enough to go on? In the case of hedge funds, there are added problems. Tracking the entire hedge fund world is not possible, and getting fund performance information on private equity is even more difficult. This is partially due to the newness and lack of SEC oversight, and the desire of managers to preserve privacy. In addition, widely divergent strategies use the umbrella name "hedge funds."

Hedge funds and private equity return histories contain two additional complications: *self-selection bias* and *survivor bias*. Self-selection bias occurs because data-tracking organizations include only hedge funds and private equity ventures that are presented to them by their respective managements. Consequently, ventures that go out of business or have returns that would not attract investors never get included in the "indexing" calculations. Fund managers perceive data-tracking organizations as providing a form of marketing. Survivor bias occurs when one probes the historical performance of the current hedge fund or private equity universe. Any ventures that were once part of the index but have since failed would not be available in any current search for historic performance. These biases consequently skew the results of index calculations toward the performance of winners.

Group performance poses another problem. Not only are alternative investment benchmark performances skewed toward winners, but it is impossible to invest in them. No investable index for alternative investments exists—for example, like the S&P 500 Index for large-capitalization domestic stocks. In addition, few hedge fund managers have been able to match the return of the index they are part of year after year. It's important to understand this, or you're likely to be disappointed with any individual hedge fund managers you use.

All of this, however, does not mean that you should totally avoid hedge funds and private equity. Instead, you should approach them with the knowledge that the historical data—the quantitative assessment of their capabilities—are limited and add an element of risk. From there, proceed with caution as to how much of your asset allocation strategy you devote to them. Fortunately, as years go by, the information and data for hedge funds become better and more plentiful for two primary reasons: (1) each year extends the historical data, and (2) the increasing interest of institutional investors is making hedge funds provide more comprehensive disclosure and create greater transparency.

CORRELATION AND LIQUIDITY

One of the advantages of hedge funds and private equity—beyond the potential for strong returns (albeit with strong risk)—is that both of these categories show low correlation to stocks and bonds. Hedge funds possess this characteristic almost by definition; they frequently employ short-selling techniques (holding positions that will profit if a particular stock goes down) and/or other strategies that counterbalance traditional long-only investments. On the other hand, although private equity is removed from the volatility of the open markets, a correlation with stocks does exist. The exit strategy most often used for private equity is to make an Initial Public Offering (IPO). The number of IPOs increases when the markets are doing well, and vice versa.

Liquidity poses another problem for alternative investments. In general, hedge funds will allow you to cash out only quarterly. Although they are starting to offer monthly cash-out windows, you are still at the mercy of the moment: you can't choose the exact time or price you want. With private equity, liquidity concerns increase. You may be required to hold your investment for five years at the minimum. In addition, you may be confronted by capital calls—requests for additional investment in order to keep the venture going. If the attempt to gather the additional capital fails, your investment may well disappear entirely. If the venture finally succeeds, then your additional investment was worth it. However, the venture may continue to flounder, in which case you will simply have thrown good money after bad. If, for example, you're 55 and looking to retire soon, you probably don't want too much of your portfolio tied up in relatively illiquid investments that have long time horizons.

COMMODITIES

Long-only tangible commodities represent a valuable addition to your asset allocation strategy because of their noncorrelation to stocks and bonds. When you look at the correlation of commodities to either stocks or bonds, it is readily apparent that commodities have a life of their own. Commodities can help bolster your portfolio's return in relation to the risks involved. Commodities have a high correlation to inflation. Thus, investing in commodities can protect against surges in inflation.

Figure 11.2 shows an efficient frontier that compares some traditional portfolio mixes with an optimized mix that includes allocations to commodities (returns presented below are that of The Falconwood Corporation's Tangible Asset Program, a diversified tangible commodity strategy) and hedge funds (returns used are that of the Hedge Fund Research Index which represents all hedge funds in their universe; this index is not investable and you should consult your asset allocation planner to help you choose hedge funds). Notice two important things about this chart. First, the optimal portfolio (B) produces a significantly better expected return in relation to the highly risk-averse portfolio of fixed income only (A), yet the risk of portfolio B is only slightly higher. Second, the mixed stock/bond portfolios (C and D) indicate only slightly higher returns than portfolio B, but carry a much greater level of risk. The all-stock portfolio (E) may generate significantly higher

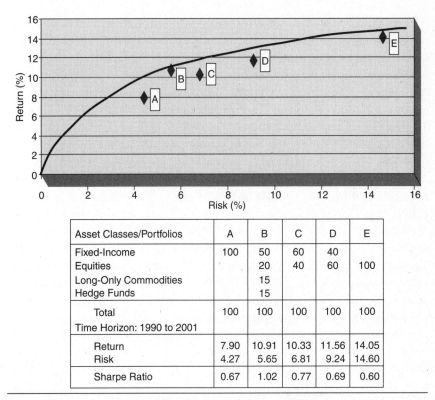

Asset Classes/Portfolios	A	B	C	D	E
Fixed-Income	100	50	60	40	
Equities		20	40	60	100
Long-Only Commodities		15			
Hedge Funds		15			
Total	100	100	100	100	100
Time Horizon: 1990 to 2001					
Return	7.90	10.91	10.33	11.56	14.05
Risk	4.27	5.65	6.81	9.24	14.60
Sharpe Ratio	0.67	1.02	0.77	0.69	0.60

Source: Ibbotson Associates and The Falconwood Corporation.
Notes: Benchmarks: Total Return on 5-Year U.S. Treasury Notes; S&P 500 Total Return; The Falconwood Corporation Tangible Asset Program; Hedge Funds Research All Funds Index.

FIGURE 11.2   Risk Comparison

returns, but its accompanying risks are even greater. The table at the bottom of Figure 11.2 also shows the various Sharpe Ratios for these portfolios. The higher the Sharpe Ratio, the better the portfolio in terms of the relation between risk and return. As you can see, portfolio B has the best ratio by far.

When investing in commodities, we use the highly liquid and transparent exchange-traded futures contracts that are available on a wide range of tangible commodities (energies, grains, metals, and so on). As with any allocation to a particular asset class, proper diversification within commodities should be pursued with the help of an expert professional who is well-versed in commodities markets.

ALLOCATION DECISIONS

When you work with asset allocation professionals to construct your portfolio, they will gauge your reactions to all the pros and cons of each investment class. For example, they might ask how you feel about private real estate investment partnerships. (They offer very little liquidity, and once you're in one, you're in it for about seven years.) What percentage of your portfolio could you comfortably designate? Nothing? Five, 10, or 15 percent? If you balk at the partnership's lack of liquidity, and perhaps designate 5 percent as the maximum, your planner knows that you probably won't be comfortable with alternative investments in general.

The risk-return relationship can be calibrated as finely as an optometrist calibrates eyeglass lenses to your vision. Suppose that your initial goal is to double your money in 10 years. Would you be willing to follow a strategy that could potentially achieve that goal, if the strategy also included a 10 percent chance of losing half your money? Would you accept that strategy if it included a 20 percent chance of losing one third of your money? If safety is a major concern, you will probably want to modify your aggressive portfolio and create a more risk-averse portfolio. This process keeps going back and forth between the objective investment data and the subjective criteria of what you need, want, or hope to achieve from your portfolio.

TAX CONSIDERATIONS

You've put together a portfolio that seems to work for you on a pretax risk-return basis. But the asset allocation process can't stop there, because that first level of portfolio construction doesn't take taxes into consideration. Comparing returns before and after taxes can alter some of your initial asset allocation decisions.

For example, a pretax optimized portfolio would probably avoid municipal bonds. The returns for municipal bonds are generally lower than they are for most other bonds, but that picture changes after taxes are taken into account. Municipal bonds are exempt from federal taxes; they will also save you state and local taxes if they are for your state of residence. But even if you consider only the federal tax savings, you will see how desirable municipal bonds can be. Suppose you're considering a municipal bond that, on the surface, would bring you 5 percent. At the top federal tax bracket (38.6 percent for 2002 and 2003), a taxable bond of equivalent value would have to yield about 8.15 percent. That's a big difference.

Figure 11.3 shows four different portfolios. Portfolios A and B were designed for a "very risk-averse" investor, and portfolios C and D are for a "moderately risk-averse" investor. Portfolios A and C show a logical diversification prior to any tax considerations; in both, municipal bonds don't stand a chance. However, portfolios B and D are reconfigurations that maintain the risk-aversion levels of the investors while making the most of returns *after taxes*. At the bottom of the table, you can see how a change from pretax to aftertax asset allocation affects the returns of the investment portfolio. Portfolios A and C look like winners before taxes, but portfolios B and D—with their municipal bond allocations— emerge as the favorites after taxes are taken into consideration.

Here's another interesting tax consideration. You might design a portfolio heavily weighted in a variety of taxable bonds. Yes, they *are* safer than equities, but the tax consequences are quite different. Historically, bonds primarily produce regular income, and therefore regular income tax (38.6 percent for the highest bracket in 2002 and 2003). Although stocks do produce dividends (taxed as regular income), their primary return to investors is considered as a capital gain, which is currently taxed at 20 percent (if held for more than 12 months). At almost half the tax cost, you might find that your portfolio should have a slightly larger stock allocation that could raise your *after-tax* return with the same level of risk.

Even when particular stocks in your portfolio decline, they can still provide a tax advantage. Stock losses can be used to offset gains elsewhere in your portfolio. Losses can be carried forward to another year, thereby allowing you to leverage those losses to your best tax advantage.

Another tax factor for your overall portfolio involves what assets you choose to place within tax-deferred and tax-exempt vehicles such as IRAs, 401(k)s, and life insurance. For example, private-placement life insurance policies will frequently provide you with access to hedge funds—well known for their tax inefficiency. Within the tax-exempt format of life insurance, the problematic tax considerations disappear. However, you shouldn't concentrate only high-risk, tax-inefficient items in a life insurance policy. If you had only one hedge fund in your insurance policy and that hedge fund fails, you have nothing left in that policy and it would then be worthless. This is why you should diversify your tax-favored vehicles by establishing an optimal mix with an emphasis on tax-inefficient investments.

Time Horizon: 1980 to 2001

Portfolio Names		Very Risk Averse		Moderately Risk Averse	
Investment Options:	Asset Limits	Ptf A Pretax	Ptf B Aftertax	Ptf C Pretax	Ptf D Aftertax
Intermediate-Term U.S. Bonds	0–35	35.00	35.00	—	—
Long-Term U.S. Bonds	0–35	9.97	—	35.00	—
Municipal Bonds: Tax Free	0–35	—	10.00	—	31.15
Foreign Bonds	0–15	15.00	15.00	5.00	8.85
Total Fixed Income	0–60	59.97	60.00	40.00	40.00
Growth Stocks	0–35	—	—	—	—
Value Stocks	0–35	14.10	13.83	30.65	32.32
Mid-Cap Stocks	0–15	15.00	15.00	15.00	15.00
Small Stocks	0–15	2.78	3.84	14.35	12.68
Foreign Stocks	0–15	1.09	—	—	—
Total Equity	0–60	32.97	32.67	60.00	60.00
Commodities	0–15	7.06	7.33	—	—
Real-Estate	0–15	—	—		
Total		100.00	100.00	100.00	100.00

	Ptf A	Ptf B	Difference	Ptf C	Ptf D	Difference
Annual Return Pretax	12.18	11.86	0.32	14.50	13.34	1.16
Annual Return Aftertax	9.39	9.66	−0.27	12.11	12.46	−0.35

Source: Ibbotson Associates and The Falconwood Corporation.
Notes: Benchmark: 30-day U.S. Treasury Bill.
Optimization Option: Risk-adjusted return. Fixed income and equity maximums are 60 percent.

FIGURE 11.3   Sample Portfolios for Risk Averse Investors

ASSESSING THE PROBABILITIES OF
YOUR PORTFOLIO

After you determine your hypothetical portfolio and the investment goals you expect it to achieve, you can subject it to "stress tests" that will probe the probability of your portfolio's achieving those goals. One technique to assess how it will perform, and its likely outcomes under various economic and market scenarios, is ironically called Monte Carlo Simulation. This is a statistical technique based on the theories of randomness and probability. The technique is used in many different disciplines—from physics to finance. For your investment portfolio, it's a way to test whether your goals are reasonably attainable.

For example, Monte Carlo Simulation allows an investor to analyze whether his or her retirement assets are adequate for their expected retirement needs. Unlike more conventional retirement simulations, Monte Carlo Simulation takes into account the fact that the return of the portfolio will fluctuate during the retirement period. Certain parameters for this retirement example are defined up front: the starting investment and the expected return characteristics of investments, contributions, and payouts. Consequently, the Monte Carlo Simulation will generate multiple randomly selected scenarios—typically, thousands of scenarios. The probability of success (defined as having adequate resources to meet your retirement needs) is then estimated by analyzing the number of successful realizations versus the total number of simulations run.

BALANCING THE PERSONAL AND THE PROBABLE

This chapter is by no means an exhaustive look at asset allocation. You would probably want to do this when you and your asset allocation planner meet to discuss and structure *your* optimal portfolio. The process is dynamic and different for each individual. Your portfolio should be reviewed at least once a year, to check on your allocations and determine whether you need to rebalance them. Two distinct methods of rebalancing should be applied to your portfolio. The more frequent method is interim rebalancing, where your intent is to maintain the current strategic asset allocations. For example, if one area has done extremely well, the percentage may have risen beyond the limits you and your financial advisor have set. You would then cash in the excess and invest the proceeds in other asset classes wherein the percentage drifted lower than your desired allocation level. A second, probably less frequent, method of rebalancing should be scheduled when you and your asset allocation planner decide it is time to alter the established strategic allocations. Frequently, this form of rebalancing occurs when there is a significant change in your life. For example, you may have established a strategic plan at age 45. Ten years later, you will need to take into consideration your approaching retirement.

To invest wisely, the most important instruction you need is: "Know thyself." Your subjective parameters—risk tolerance, return requirements, time horizons, liquidity, and tax considerations—will guide your selection of asset classes and your judgment regarding the appropriate amounts you should have in each one.

Words to the Wise

- Enlist the expertise of an investment professional.
- Construct an objective financial profile of yourself.
- Determine your investment goals and establish time horizons for fulfilling them.
- Set your risk-tolerance level.
- Choose benchmarks for your asset classes.
- Select optimal asset allocation.
- Diversify, as much as possible, your holdings within each asset class.
- Stick to your *personal* investment plan.
- Review, revise, rebalance—annually.

The views and opinions expressed herein are personal to Jonathan Spencer and do not necessarily represent those of any employer organization with which he is affiliated.

──────── **Jonathan Spencer** ────────

Jonathan Spencer is an executive vice president and portfolio manager for The Falconwood Corporation, a family office and developer of computerized services, primarily for investment companies. He is president and treasurer of Gresham Investment Management, a commodity-pool operator and commodity trading advisor registered with the National Futures Association, and an affiliate of The Falconwood Corporation. Mr. Spencer is a principal of Enhanced Index Management, a money management company that specializes in enhanced index products. He is also a registered investment advisor with the SEC. His extensive expertise in the futures markets was gained when he held senior positions at Futures Commission Merchants during his 17 years of investment management experience.

12

ADDING REAL ESTATE TO YOUR INVESTMENT MIX

A Complement to Your Stock and Bond Portfolio

RICHARD J. ADLER

The Stanwicks* divide their time among several residences. They own a town house in Manhattan, a condo in Scottsdale, Arizona, and a vacation home in San Miguel de Allende, Mexico. They are considering purchasing a ski chalet in Vail, Colorado.

Like many wealthy investors, Ralph Smithson had a long-standing portfolio made up of stocks, bonds, and his family's business interests. After considering various alternative investments to expand and diversify his portfolio, he bought shares in a real estate investment trust.

Peter Owens is an internist in an affluent midwest community. Joining together in a partnership with other local medical specialists, Dr. Owens purchased and renovated a medical building. The venture gave the team expanded office space for themselves, rental income from other tenants, and some tax benefits.

These hypothetical profiles represent some of the roles real estate can play in our personal lives and our financial well-being. Real estate is often overlooked, but it can be an important part of a diversified investment portfolio. And because real estate has low correlation with either stocks or bonds, strategic investments in real estate may bolster portfolio returns and reduce volatility.

There is more than one way to invest in real estate. Beyond owning homes or professional buildings for personal use, you can invest in debt or in equity, directly or indirectly. You can gain liquidity

---

* Names in this chapter are not those of real people.

via the indirect route of publicly traded shares in individual companies, mutual funds, or real estate investment trusts (REITs). Or, you can look to potential long-term profits in illiquid ownership of property.

HOME SWEET HOME

For most people, their first real estate investment is a family home. Owning two or more homes for personal use—as the Stanwicks do—is one way of participating in real estate. Home ownership has investment aspects; indeed, for many people, home equity is the largest component of their personal wealth. Furthermore, home ownership offers both financial and tax benefits.

From a financial standpoint, residential real estate allows the greatest financial leverage of any personal asset: up to 80 percent mortgage-borrowing capacity. On the tax front, there are two advantages: Mortgage interest of up to $1 million is deductible on first and second homes; a mortgage on a third and additional homes is considered nondeductible personal interest. And, up to $500,000 of capital gain on the sale of a primary residence is now exempt from taxation for a married couple filing a joint federal tax return. The combined benefits increase the long-term after-tax return for housing as compared to many other investments.

Still, homes tend to be consumption items; owners have negative cash flow during the period of their ownership. Investment considerations are secondary: profits, if any, are realized only when a home is sold. This was true even during the heady days of residential price appreciation; it is more true today because prices in many parts of the United States have slowed their rise. According to the Federal Home Loan Mortgage Corporation, house prices across the United States increased from 1976 to 2001, on average, by a compound annual rate of just 5.8 percent (ignoring both the benefits and the cost of mortgage financing). Homeowners in some high-cost regions have had much better results, but sellers can't count on their home's producing significant long-term profits.

Until they are sold, homes are often a cash drain. Mortgage payments, upkeep, insurance, and taxes eat away at potential future gains. This may not pose a problem when enjoyment is the primary purpose of your ownership and you can afford the cost.

THE QUALIFIED PERSONAL RESIDENCE TRUST (QPRT)

Because the carrying costs of a home are high, you may want to look ahead and structure your ownership so that the homes you enjoy today won't become a burden to the next generation. You may love summer holidays and winter skiing at your rustic retreat in the Adirondacks, but having a second house may impoverish your grandchildren if you don't leave the wherewithal needed to maintain two homes.

Worse yet, an appreciating asset can create a major tax burden for your family. The federal estate tax is currently scheduled to go out of existence for one brief year, in 2009. Assuming that it does (most observers do not expect repeal to take place) it will return in 2010. Removing appreciating assets from your estate today is the safest way to keep them from being subject to estate tax tomorrow. One popular way to remove your residence from your taxable estate involves the use of a qualified personal residence trust (QPRT).

With a QPRT, you create an irrevocable trust for a specified number of years; you place your house in the trust while retaining the right to live there. Because the transfer is a gift of "future interest," the gift qualifies for a discount based on your age and the length of the trust. The longer the term of the trust, the greater the discount. But it doesn't pay to be greedy. If you don't outlive the term of the trust, the full value of the property will be right back in your taxable estate.

At the end of the trust term, the property belongs to your designated beneficiary. This need not mean that you will be bounced from your residence, however; you can include, in the trust document, a provision requiring the trustee to lease the house back to you for reasonable periods of time.

A QPRT is restricted to only one personal residence, but each individual is currently allowed to have two QPRTs. Your vacation home and your primary residence can be in separate QPRTs. A married couple can protect as many as three residences if a jointly owned primary residence is owned by one trust, and two vacation homes, owned separately by the husband and wife, are in two other trusts.

Another possibility is to place ownership of your home in a family limited partnership (FLP) or limited liability company (LLC) in which family members own the partnership interests. The transfer qualifies for a discount on the value of the property because the partners receive an indirectly owned illiquid asset. Placing other income-producing assets in the FLP or LLC can provide money for upkeep of the residence so that it will not become a burden to the next generation.

REAL ESTATE IN YOUR PORTFOLIO

Homes, no matter how they are owned, are still primarily for personal use and enjoyment. To diversify your investment portfolio, you should consider *investment real estate*. As an alternative investment, real estate has low correlation with more traditional investment classes.

The investment side of real estate has changed dramatically in the past 10 years. As securitization took hold, the real estate industry took giant steps away from the old form of limited partnerships—where the tax tail wagged the investment dog—and toward real estate as a stable investment alternative.

There are myriad ways to invest in real estate, and a spectrum of potential returns and volatility can be found along the way. One major real estate investment category involves financing. Another involves ownership.

The revolution in real estate as an investment began on the debt side, through mechanisms for financing. Federal agency obligations representing securitized mortgage debt obligations include those issued by the Government National Mortgage Association (Ginnie Mae), the Federal National Mortgage Association (Fannie Mae), and the Federal Home Loan Mortgage Corporation (Freddie Mac). Also on the debt side are real estate investment trusts (REITs) specializing in mortgages, collateralized mortgage obligations (CMOs), and, more recently, commercial mortgage-backed securities (CMBS).

Ginnie Maes, Fannie Maes, and Freddie Macs are pass-through mortgage-backed securities. Principal and interest payments on the underlying mortgages are paid to investors on a monthly basis. The interest portion of each monthly payment, which is higher in the early years of the mortgage pool, is taxed as ordinary income. The rest is a return of principal.

Ginnie Maes were the original mortgage pass-through securities. They can be purchased individually or via shares of a GNMA mutual fund. Because they are backed by the full faith and credit of the federal government, their yield is usually higher than that of Treasuries but a bit lower than the yield on Fannie Maes and Freddie Macs, which do not carry the government guarantee.

Although individual mortgages are typically 30-year obligations, the average life of a new Ginnie Mae pool is now projected at eight years. This shorter life span occurs because of the partial monthly pay-down of principal and because individual mortgages within the pool are paid off early when homeowners refinance their mortgages or sell their homes.

There is a down side to investing in mortgage-backed securities. Monthly cash distributions are variable. The repayment of principal fluctuates with interest rates. Lower rates encourage refinancing, which accelerates principal repayments and thus shortens the average life of the obligations. Rising rates have the reverse effect. The prices of mortgage-backed securities are therefore more volatile than those of conventional bonds. And, because some principal is repaid each month, there is no lump sum to reinvest when the pool matures.

A variation on the theme of mortgage-backed securities—collater-alized mortgage obligations (CMOs)—evolved as a way to manage the risk of fluctuating principal payments on mortgage pass-through securities. When you buy a CMO, you buy a specific group or "tranche" of mortgage obligations that will mature in a narrowly focused time period or "window." Maturities can range from a few months to 20 years. Because of the more controlled maturity date, yields are often slightly lower than those for comparable mortgage pass-through securities. But CMOs are still interest-sensitive and, because repayment is allocated to different tranches, some are more volatile than others. If mortgage rates drop and homeowners refinance their mortgages, the CMO may mature earlier than the designated maturity date.

Commercial mortgage-backed securities (CMBS) are similar to CMOs except that the mortgages in the pool, because they are on commercial properties, are considerably larger. With only a dozen or so mortgages in the pool, there is much more *event risk;* if one of the properties fails, it is a meaningful event within the structure. Nonetheless, because of their efficient management structure during the last five years or so, the relatively new sector of CMBS has come into its own and has largely replaced mortgage REITs as the securitized debt instrument of choice in commercial real estate.

MORTGAGE REITs

Real estate investment trusts are publicly traded entities; their shares are traded on the stock exchanges. They are similar in some ways to closed-end mutual funds. Mortgage REITs pool their investors' money to finance real properties. The more popular equity REITs—discussed later in this chapter—pool investors' money and own and operate properties. Like Ginnie Maes, shares of public REITs may be purchased directly or through mutual funds.

REITs got their start in 1962, when Congress enacted legislation to spur individual investment in real estate. After investors lost money in poorly managed mortgage REITs in the early 1970s, the group was tainted for a decade. Then the tax reform legislation of 1986 undercut tax-favored limited partnerships by lengthening the depreciation periods, limiting the deductibility of interest, and restricting so-called "passive" losses that could be used to offset other income. The same legislation enabled REITs, for the first time, to operate and manage commercial property, as well as own it.

REITs grew dramatically in popularity in the 1990s, in response to the severe downturn in real estate at the beginning of the decade. In the 1980s, commercial real estate had initially boomed in response to tax stimuli, pension fund investments, and the deregulation of savings and loans. The resulting overbuilding ended in a bust after the 1986 tax reform act, the savings and loan debacle, and the Persian Gulf War.

Historically, banks and insurance companies had supplied much of the capital for real estate, but, in response to the downturn, regulators ordered them to secure their real estate holdings with three times as much capital, under new risk-based capital requirements. The only sources of capital large enough to fill the vacuum created by the new requirements were the public markets. The wave of IPOs and secondary offerings of REITs that followed was gradually able to refinance the industry on a sounder basis. The public market capitalization of REITs rose from $10 billion in 1990 to $150 billion in 2001. REITs have become a respected asset class; they are now recognized in three different S&P indexes.

The REITs that have truly come into their own are equity-based; unlike the mortgage-based REITs engaged in financing, these REITS actually own and operate properties. REITs are actively managed, but mortgages don't need active management. Commercial mortgage-backed securities (CMBS) offer a less expensive and more efficient way to pool and manage mortgages. Equity REITs today account for 95.7 percent of the total market capitalization of all REITs. Mortgage and hybrid REITs total just 4.3 percent.

EQUITY OWNERSHIP

Some investors choose to invest in real estate through one or more of the debt obligations described above—federal agency obligations, collateralized mortgage obligations, commercial mortgage-backed securities, and mortgage REITs. Because these obligations entail significant interest-rate risk, however, many others prefer to invest in real estate as a tangible entity. There are several ways to do so: Buy and manage an investment property, participate in venture funds or private partnerships, or own shares of either publicly traded companies involved in real estate development or equity REITs.

Direct ownership—such as buying and renovating individual homes or small apartment buildings, and then putting them up for sale—often requires a lot of hands-on participation. Such ownership is also illiquid (it may not be easy to sell when you want to cash it out) but the rewards may be worthwhile. Rental property can provide a steady stream of income coupled with tax write-offs. Investing in raw land with an eye to development won't yield current income but does contain the potential for long-term appreciation.

The story can be different when you can use the property yourself. For example, professional practices sometimes form partnerships to either build or purchase and renovate an existing building, thereby giving themselves more office space plus rental income and tax benefits. Owning a building that you use eliminates the risk that office space will stand vacant.

Many investors prefer to be less actively involved. They can choose venture funds or private partnerships as investment vehicles.

Some venture funds—for example, those that finance start-up companies in the business world—are development-oriented or focused on creating new properties. That approach is risky but, if successful, it can add considerable value to your portfolio. Other venture funds focus on redevelopment, repositioning, renovation, and remarketing of existing properties.

Both types of venture funds are generally private placements that require participants to have at least $1 million in net worth and $200,000 to $250,000 in annual income. Both are limited to a maximum of either 100 or 500 investors, and both are illiquid investments. Until they run their course and accomplish their objectives, it can be difficult to get money from them.

Private partnerships typically are much smaller. Family members, as an example, may pool their resources and establish a private partnership to buy an office building. In the partnership framework, one or more general partners assume most of the liability. Limited partners are not involved in day-to-day management; their liability is limited to the amount of their invested capital. Today, some pooled ownership arrangements that were formerly structured as private partnerships take the form of limited liability companies.

One problem with much direct investment in real estate is the lack of diversification. It can take $25 million or more to create a real estate portfolio that is diversified both in type and location. Where portfolios are less diversified and less liquid, a higher rate of return is needed to compensate for the added risk. The underlying principle applies to any investment: If you take more risk, you want more potential reward.

One way to minimize risk, retain liquidity, and achieve greater diversification is to invest in publicly traded companies concentrating in real estate. These enterprises, sometimes called real estate operating companies (REOCs), can retain more cash in exchange for giving up the tax benefits inherent in the REIT structure. A ready source of cash can be vital in real estate development, but REITs are required by law to pay out 90 percent of their income each year. This can be a boon to investors who desire income, but it can put a crimp in development.

If you are willing to trade current income for the possibility of future appreciation, shares in a REOC might be a good choice. A number of domestic companies offer investment opportunities, and, if you are willing to assume the currency risk, there are overseas opportunities as well.

EQUITY REITs

Each form of equity investment described above is attractive to some investors, but equity REITs are head and shoulders above the rest in well-deserved popularity. Equity REITs invest in every kind of property, but, according to the National Association of Real Estate Investment Trusts (NAREIT), the largest segments at the end of 2001 were apartments (22 percent) and office buildings (20 percent). Shopping centers accounted for 10 percent and regional malls represented 9 percent of REIT ownership. Industrial properties were at 7 percent, and resorts and lodgings were at 5 percent.

With REITs, you have a liquid investment; shares can be sold at any time. Liquidity has improved dramatically in recent years because of the rapid growth and institutionalization of the market. There are now almost 200 publicly traded REITs in the NAREIT. Shares of most are traded on the New York Stock Exchange. More important, the introduction of REITs has made real estate a fungible investment, one that could be compared to other securities. In making ownership fungible, REITs could be said to do for real estate capital what Eli Whitney's cotton gin did for machine parts.

Buying shares of REITs is much like buying shares of other companies, but there are some differences. Because REITs are involved solely in real estate, depreciation becomes a factor, and the traditional measure of net income is inadequate. Because sizable depreciation charges may significantly understate earnings while overstating expenses, NAREIT uses a measure called "funds from operations" (FFO). FFO is net income after subtracting gains or losses from debt restructuring and property sales and adding back real estate depreciation and amortization charges.

But FFO itself has been criticized in some quarters. In late 2001, Wall Street analysts determined to adopt a new formula for measuring REIT performance. The new formula excludes gains and losses from the sale of property (more properly akin to capital gains) and focuses instead on "operating income per share." The new measure should provide additional transparency and make it easier to compare REIT shares with other securities.

Remember, though, that REITs are an investment for total return. When you invest in equity REITs, you can generally expect both high current income and moderate long-term growth. Dividends, at an average of 7.0 percent at this writing, provide reliable cash flow, and the price appreciation approximates that of the Consumer Price Index.

If they meet certain conditions, REITs qualify for special tax treatment. Unlike conventional corporations, they pay no federal taxation at the corporate level. At least 75 percent of the company's assets must be in real estate held for the long term; at least 75 percent of the company's income must come from real estate; and the company must pay out at least 90 percent of its income to shareholders each year.

Shareholders, in turn, pay ordinary income tax on most dividends. In some REITs, part of the dividend distribution—currently, an average of about 10 percent of dividends—may be treated as return of capital. When investors receive return of capital, it is not currently taxable but it reduces the cost basis of the shares when they are sold. In addition, when property within the portfolio is sold, the investor's share of the resulting distribution may be taxed as a long-term capital gain. You can avoid the annual taxes associated with owning REITs if you hold your shares in a tax-advantaged retirement account such as an IRA, Keogh, or 401(k) plan.

REITs returned 12.5 percent for the period from 1972 through 2001, against 12.2 percent for large stocks and 8.9 percent for 20-year U.S. Government bonds. From 1992 through 2001, REITs returned 11.6 percent against 12.9 percent for large stocks and 8.7 percent for bonds. For the year 2000, when the stock market began to tank, REITs returned 26.4 percent while large stocks lost 9.1 percent and bonds gained 21.5 percent.

A most important fact for long-term investors: including REITs in your portfolio can act to reduce risk and increase return. A review of risk-adjusted returns indicates that the return on REITs has been almost as high as the return on large stocks, but the volatility is considerably lower. REITs therefore represent a middle ground between stocks and bonds: they offer the competitive returns of stocks and the lower risk of bonds. Yet REITs also have little correlation with stocks or bonds, thereby helping to balance and diversify a portfolio.

According to Ibbotson data for 1972 through 2001, a portfolio made up of 50 percent stocks, 40 percent bonds, and 10 percent T-Bills returned 11.3 percent with a risk quotient of 10.9 percent. For the same period, a portfolio of 45 percent stocks, 35 percent bonds, 10 percent T-Bills, and 10 percent REITs returned 11.5 percent with a risk level of 10.5 percent. Change the portfolio mix to 40 percent stocks, 30 percent bonds, 10 percent T-Bills, and 20 percent REITs, and the return becomes 11.7 percent with a risk factor of 10.2 percent. The same principle of improved returns and lowered risk applies when REITs are added to an all-income portfolio made up of bonds and T-Bills.

REITs are multifaceted investments. We like to say that REITs act like bonds in the short run, stocks in the intermediate term, and real estate in the long run. Unlike those from bonds, returns from REITs can rise during inflationary cycles, reflecting increasing rental income. At all times, because rental income is similar to the interest on bonds, REIT dividends can lend balance to stock portfolios.

Although they share some characteristics with convertible securities, REITs are better because they have an indefinite life span, without the fixed ending date of convertibles. In addition, in the REIT world, quality rises to the top; the better ones typically thrive and the poorer ones disappear. Quality convertibles, by contrast, often disappear through calls; poor ones languish.

Put another way, REITs act as a proxy for commercial real estate, with significant fixed-income characteristics. From a financial standpoint, we look at commercial real estate as an aggregation of leases wrapped in land, bricks, and mortar; the leases themselves are fixed-income obligations but the real estate holds potential for appreciation.

Words to the Wise

- Real estate investments can bolster portfolio returns and reduce volatility because they have a low correlation with either stocks or bonds.

- *Ginnie Maes, Fannie Maes, and Freddie Macs* are pass-through mortgage-backed securities. Principal and interest are paid to investors each month.

- *Collateralized Mortgage Obligations (CMOs)* enable investors to buy a specific group of mortgage obligations that will mature in a narrowly focused time period.

- *Commercial Mortgage-Backed Securities (CMBS)* are similar to CMOs, but because the mortgages in the pool are on commercial properties, the individual underlying mortgages are larger and there may be greater risk of default.

- *Real Estate Investment Trusts (REITs)* are publicly traded entities. Because shares can be sold at any time, they provide a liquid investment.

- *Equity REITs,* which pool investors' money to own and operate property, are the most popular of all equity real estate investments. They can be purchased individually or through mutual funds. Investors typically invest in REITs for high current income and moderate long-term growth.

- Other forms of equity real estate investments include buying and managing investment property, participating in venture funds or private partnerships, and owning shares of publicly traded companies involved in real estate development.

Richard J. Adler

Richard J. Adler is managing director and cofounder of European Investors. With over $4 billion in assets under management for major foreign and domestic clients, the firm is one of the leading investors in securitized real estate. Mr. Adler serves as investment strategist for the firm's real estate securities as well as its equity and fixed-income activities, and he is a member of the firm's REIT and U.S. Equities Investment Committees. He is chairman of the Board of Trustees of the EII Realty Securities Fund.

13

WEALTH MANAGEMENT AND TRUSTS

Building a Legacy for the Ages

ALBERT C. BELLAS AND DIANE E. LEDERMAN

Abe and Ida Richman's lives were the classic American success story. Arriving as immigrants, they worked night and day to establish a fine haberdashery. When they retired, their son Leo took over the business and enlarged the store into a full-service clothier. He worked hard but expanded his cultural horizons too; he climbed the social ladder and sent his children to the best schools. Eventually, Abe and Ida's grandchildren inherited the business, but they had no interest in working long hours. They hired a management team to run the business while they enjoyed multiple homes and world travels. They returned home for annual board meetings at which they argued among themselves. They signed off on the management team's plans for expansion into new markets and new businesses, and, finally, they watched the business spiral into bankruptcy and saw their net worth go down the drain.

T here is some wisdom in one of the oldest expressions for squandered wealth: "From shirtsleeves to shirtsleeves in three generations." The experience is universal. The first generations that create wealth leave it to their children, who reap the benefits, entrench themselves in the upper class, and preserve enough to pass on to their

Material contained in this chapter is strictly for informational purposes and should not be considered legal, tax, investment, financial, or other professional advice. If you are considering a trust, you should consult your professional advisor with respect to your individual circumstances.

heirs. By the third generation, the connection between work and wealth has become remote. Having been born to a life of luxury, this group squanders what is left of the money. Their children must then start the cycle over again.

But is this proverbial cycle natural and therefore inevitable? Not at all. Consider the Rockefellers and the Rothschilds. Their names have remained synonymous with wealth for more than one and two centuries, respectively. These families, and other less famous ones, have succeeded in preserving their wealth through multiple generations and across family branches, thanks to sound values, financial acumen, and a well-executed strategy. Put together, these qualities comprise the essence of wealth management.

Wealth management is a discipline that cannot be automated or squeezed into a "one size fits all" package. Every family has unique characteristics, dynamics, and needs. The wealth management issues for a family with hundreds of millions of dollars will be different from those for a family with moderate wealth. Nonetheless, the basic steps for preserving wealth are the same. The first generation must establish a solid foundation for wealth management, both in terms of *attitude* and in its use of the right *wealth management tools.*

Attitude is important for creating and maintaining the values that help drive the generation of wealth. Attitude also includes willingness to listen to and learn from trusted legal, tax, and financial professionals. The practical tools of wealth management include asset liquefication, estate planning and investment management; a variety of tax, legal, and family wealth-transfer issues are encountered at each step. Given the right attitude, good advisors, and the proper application of wealth management tools, a legacy can be built to last through generations—maybe even across centuries.

The first section of this book addressed many of the interpersonal challenges that wealth brings. In this chapter, we will address some of the more practical and functional issues of preserving wealth across generations. Specifically, we will discuss one of the basic building blocks of wealth management: trusts. It is important to remember that because trusts can be tailored in virtually infinite ways, they can accommodate the most sophisticated wealth management strategies or accomplish very simple tasks. This chapter is designed to discuss the basic considerations in the creation of trusts. If you are considering the creation of a trust, we urge you to consult with professional financial advisors.

THE TRUTH ABOUT TRUSTS

One of the fundamental tools of wealth management is the trust. Trusts can help ease your tax burdens, manage your financial affairs, and help you transfer wealth to family members, individuals, or charities that are important to you. Yet trusts remain a mystery to many people.

Individuals who have never been exposed to them think trusts are only for the ultrawealthy, or are designed to keep assets out of incompetent hands. Many people who have had experience with trusts that were created years ago believe they are rigid and restrictive constructs that lock up money and make it hard to retrieve.

In reality, trusts can be quite useful, even for younger people or people with moderate wealth. Today's trusts can be remarkably flexible and useful tools—and with their flexibility comes opportunity.

It is true that for most of the twentieth century, many trusts were inflexible legal structures. But changing laws and a growing understanding and acceptance of trusts have led to a near-revolution in their use. Whatever your situation, if you have more than one million dollars in assets, a trust could probably benefit you.

In case you are new to trusts, let's start with a brief definition. Very simply, a trust is an agreement in which you transfer the legal ownership of assets to someone else (the trustee) who then holds them for the benefit of one or more third parties (the beneficiaries). The trustee may be an individual or a professional corporate trustee (that is, a bank or trust company).

Why would you create a trust? For a myriad of reasons. For many years, one of the most popular uses of trusts was to reduce your taxable estate in order to escape onerous estate and gift taxes—as high as 55 percent! However, the tax law changes of 2001 (officially, The Economic Growth and Tax Relief Reconciliation Act of 2001) have thrown the entire estate tax system into flux. As we write this, the estate tax is scheduled to diminish every year until it disappears altogether in the year 2010. Unless Congress acts to repeal it again, it will be reinstated in 2011. The Act retains provisions for gift taxes (declining to 35 percent in 2010, but returning to 55 percent in 2011).

Most trust and estate professionals agree that the estate tax question is an ongoing political drama that will undoubtedly undergo many twists and turns in coming years. For this reason, we will avoid talking about trusts for tax planning. Instead, we will focus on the other considerations for using trusts. Here are a few examples of how you might use a trust:

- To provide support for your spouse after your death, while protecting your spouse from requests by a future spouse for the assets, and protecting your assets for your children and grandchildren.
- To transfer assets for the benefit of a beneficiary, such as a child or grandchild, while at the same time protecting those assets from a current or future spouse of the beneficiary.
- To provide support for, but protect the underlying assets from, a spendthrift or incompetent beneficiary.
- To fund a charitable organization and provide support for you and/or your beneficiary.
- To manage your business affairs for you.

Those are just some basic uses of trusts. You can tailor a trust to suit your specific needs and objectives, or even combine various trusts to work together.

A FLEXIBLE AND VERSATILE TOOL

Trusts can be supremely flexible structures, if you allow them to be. In general, the more control you attempt to exert over a trust, the more restrictive and less flexible it will be. Often, well-intentioned plans can backfire in the long term. For example, some trusts created in the middle decades of the twentieth century required trust monies to be invested only in U.S. government securities, which, at that time, were considered the only "safe" investment. Over the years, those trusts suffered from miniscule returns after taxes and management fees were paid. If those trusts had utilized more flexible language—allowing the trustee to choose prudent investments, for instance—they could have achieved better results.

A common misperception about trusts is that they won't allow you to change your mind. What if you want to change beneficiaries, for instance? It is true that an irrevocable trust cannot be changed, but the terms can be written to *accommodate* change. For example, you can permit a future change in trust beneficiaries by granting a beneficiary a "power of appointment." This power gives the holder the ability to select who receives the property, from among a group you designate, and in what form (outright, in trust, or a combination of the two). A trustee can also be given the power to pay trust assets to another trust that might have some different provisions.

Not all trusts are irrevocable. A revocable trust, as the name implies, can be altered or revoked by you at any time and as often as you want. Also called a "living trust" by some, this trust structure can accomplish several objectives. First, the trust can specify a variety of actions you want implemented if you are incapacitated or unavailable to make decisions for yourself or your business. For example, a revocable trust can give someone else the authority to manage your financial affairs, including overseeing investments, making deposits, and paying bills. A revocable trust also allows assets to pass outside the probate process. Probate is the court-supervised process of validating a will or establishing a distribution of the assets of a deceased person, including the payment of outstanding obligations. The probate process generally is not inherently onerous, but it can become so when real property is owned in several states. (The probate process is a state-by-state procedure.) Steering clear of probate may also be desirable if you anticipate that someone will contest the probate of your will, or if you have no heirs. Other situations also apply.

Let's look at a few hypothetical examples of common situations and review how trusts can help.

Second Marriage with Children

Mark's first marriage was full of strife, but he had found happiness with his second wife, Elaine. He had two teenage sons, with whom Elaine showed tremendous patience and tact. Now Mark and Elaine were looking forward to the birth of their own child. Mark was almost 10 years older than Elaine, and he wanted to make sure that Elaine, the two boys, and the new baby were all protected in case he died.

Although he had the highest regard for Elaine's judgment, Mark worried about what could happen in the future. What if his two boys continued to sow their wild oats and Elaine lost patience with them? He wanted his assets to provide Elaine with support as long as she lived, but, upon her death, he wanted the assets to be split evenly among the three children. Also, if Elaine were to remarry, he didn't want her new spouse to have access to the assets.

Second marriages often involve children from prior marriages, and even though all parties currently may be living in harmony, the future disposition of your estate shouldn't be left to chance. Using a trust, Mark could ensure that, should he die before her, Elaine would be financially secure, and, upon her death, all three children would receive an equal inheritance. If Elaine remarried, she could tell her new spouse, with perfect honesty, that the terms of the trust did not allow her to share the assets with him.

What about the flexibility we spoke about earlier? If Mark wanted Elaine to retain some power over the disposition of the assets (for example, to satisfy unforeseen needs), the terms of the trust could give Elaine the power to determine how the assets were to be awarded to the children: either in trust or outright, and if in trust, the terms of the trust. Mark could also give Elaine the power to change the trustee during her life and a limited power to demand a small percentage of the trust assets each year, with a lifetime cap on the amount withdrawn from the trust.

Protecting Your Children's Inheritance

Jack and Laura were blessed with wealth and three beautiful daughters. As the years flew by and their little girls turned into young women, Jack and Laura began to see the need for estate planning. They intended to leave substantial inheritances to each of their daughters, but they were concerned about what might happen when their daughters married. What if one of the girls made a bad choice in a marriage partner? It pained Jack and Laura to think of what could happen to the daughter's inheritance. A trust could help.

Remember, a trust is an entity that is legally separate from its beneficiary. A trust can be created so that your child's spouse has no right to the assets in the trust, regardless of what may happen during the marriage, or in divorce court, or at your child's death. In fact, a trust can be created so that even if Jack and Laura's daughters wanted to make a spouse a beneficiary of the trust, they could not do so. Naturally, nothing would prevent the daughters from using distributions from the trust to benefit their spouses or families—and, distributions can also be lost in divorce court. But a trust can ensure that a portion of the inheritance would be protected.

Trusts can also be useful with many of the "parenting" issues that surround children and money. If you're like most people, you want your heirs to benefit from your hard work and good fortune, but you worry that too much money will sap their incentive to make the most of their own life. One solution is to create a trust that does not mandate distributions but gives a trustee the ability to determine your beneficiaries' needs. The trustee can provide your beneficiaries with increasing distributions as they become more mature. This avoids the "windfall" affect.

One caveat: Some parents are tempted to include *incentives* in a trust—specific guidelines intended to encourage certain behaviors or goals in their beneficiaries. For example, some parents encourage the pursuit of lucrative career paths by matching the trust recipient's earned level of income. If he or she earns $100,000 a year, the trust will match it by the same amount, up to a certain level. Others earmark money for educational expenses. Still others, when dealing with children with drug or alcohol dependencies, will tie trust distributions to participation in a treatment program and proof of sobriety.

These well-meaning motives, however, may have unintended consequences. For instance, what if your son went to business school, graduated with honors, but then had a life-altering experience that encouraged him to join the Peace Corps, where he is earning a modest salary but is doing much good in the world? Should he or she be penalized for that decision?

The fact is, the more limited you attempt to make your trust's terms, the more likely the trust will run into unexpected problems. No one can predict what's going to happen in the future. Times change and people change; it's nearly impossible to catch everything with a checklist of dos and don'ts.

One of the most important ways to meet the challenge of children and inheritances is by choosing a knowledgeable trustee who can help you to teach your heirs to be responsible for their wealth and themselves. If your heirs are inexperienced with money, the trustee may involve them in the management of the trust by teaching them about the financial markets. A trustee can also introduce beneficiaries to other children of wealth, giving them an opportunity to share problems and solutions with their peers. Needless to say, choosing a trustee whom you trust and respect is a critical step when creating a long-term trust. (See Chapter 16, "Finding an Outstanding Trustee.") Giving your beneficiary—or another trusted family member or advisor—the power to change the trustee can help alleviate any concern that the trustee may have too much power over your loved ones' inheritance.

SOLVING A PORTFOLIO PROBLEM

Let's look at another way that trusts can solve a common financial challenge: an overly concentrated holding of one stock.

Sarah had been with a small technology company since it was created by five friends working out of a basement. The company quickly turned into a sprawling powerhouse. Sarah's ample salary, combined with highly appreciated stock, encouraged her to contemplate life beyond "making a living." She went to work—gratis—for a charity that helped educate underprivileged children. But her entire life's savings were concentrated in one company's stock, which paid no dividends. She was also concerned that the stock's price far exceeded its real value. She wanted to diversify and she needed an income stream, but the rock-bottom cost basis of her stock would result in a huge income tax bill.

One solution for Sarah could be a Charitable Remainder Trust (CRT). The CRT could provide her with immediate tax advantages, regular distributions for the rest of her life (and the life of a beneficiary, if she wants), and the remainder of the trust's assets would go to a designated charity upon her death or her beneficiary's death, if at a later date.

Here's how it worked. Sarah's advisors established a CRT and funded it with her appreciated company stock. The trust then sold the stock and reinvested the funds in a diversified portfolio. Sarah will receive regular payments from the trust during her lifetime. Because of the charitable status of the trust, Sarah could avoid the immediate payment of capital gains taxes on the sale of the stock. Furthermore, she received a current income tax deduction based on the projected gift to charity at the end of her life expectancy (provided the charity is not a private foundation).

Flexibility? Sarah could name any beneficiary, including a spouse or children, to receive distributions after her death and during their lifetime. She could also retain the right to remove them as beneficiaries during her life. At the end point designated for making these payments, the principal remaining in the trust would go to a charity named by Sarah when she created the trust or at any other time. She could also choose to give the power of naming the charity to someone else, such as a beneficiary or trustee.

The statutes concerning charitable remainder trusts have numerous important technicalities. You need to consider them; otherwise, the trust may not accomplish your objectives. For instance, there are legal limitations on the amount of distributions you can receive each year, and you must give a certain amount of the remainder to charity. Importantly, the sale of assets to or by the trust must follow strict guidelines. When considering a trust, it is always important to consult a tax advisor!

FAMILY FOUNDATIONS

Sooner or later, many families with substantial wealth consider a private family foundation. Foundations may be established as not-for-profit corporations, or they can be set up as trusts. Both structures have certain pros and cons, based on families' individual goals and circumstances, but a family foundation can be an excellent way to ensure that your legacy benefits both your family and a larger community. If you wish to set aside a substantial amount of assets for charity, a family foundation can be one of the best—and most tax-effective—vehicles for charitable giving and for strategic wealth management. It provides major donor control, family involvement, and a framework for multigenerational continuity.

If you establish a private family foundation, you can create a forum for spouses, children, and other family members to listen to each other, be heard, and come to collective conclusions about the values and the strategic mission of family giving. Younger generations develop fiscal responsibility and find satisfaction and self-worth through their participation. They learn, firsthand, the responsibilities of wealth.

Private foundations are complex organizations. They involve significant costs and restrictions, and they require substantial funding, maintenance, and governance. Generally, they have one major source of funding, are in the form of a trust or corporation, and they must pay out at least 5 percent of the value of the foundation's assets in annual gifts, in order to avoid the imposition of an excise tax on amounts not properly distributed.

Many foundations are created with little more than an initial endowment and good intentions. The ones that survive are those that are well planned and professionally administered. (The next chapter, "Prudent Investing for Private Family Foundations," addresses some of these issues.)

SUMMING UP

Trusts are most useful when they are tailored to your individual purposes. Here are a few basic guidelines to keep in mind when you prepare to discuss trusts with your professional financial advisors.

■ Define your long-term values and goals.

The long-term survival of your wealth depends on the patterns established by the first wealthy generation. The basic values and practices you establish can have a ripple effect through generations. The Rothschild family, for example, financed the business development of its second generation through loans rather than grants, to inculcate the lesson that capital has a cost and requires a return.

■ Seek professional advice.

As the old advertising saying goes: "Don't try this at home!" The laws governing trusts and estate planning are complex and ever changing. You need the expertise of professionals who are thoroughly steeped in the nuances of this field. Make them members of your financial advisory team. The creation and administration of trusts require specialized expertise in trust law, the tax codes, trust administration, and/or investment management. Ideally, you will find a team of professionals who have all of these skills, and they will work together for your benefit.

■ Consider a corporate trustee.

For many people, their first choice for a trustee is a close friend or a relative. That's a natural reaction, but having a sole trustee may not be the best decision. A trustee's duties include administering the trust, dealing with beneficiaries, filing tax returns, and investing and safeguarding the trust's assets. Not only are those duties time-consuming, but they require someone with financial sophistication and an understanding of legal issues. Depending on the size of the trust, a corporate trustee may be worth considering. A friend or family member may serve as a cotrustee. A personal understanding of a family's needs would then be added to the professional expertise of a corporate trustee.

■ **Pay attention to the trust's situs.**

A trust need not have its situs (location) in the state in which you or your beneficiaries live. Not all states operate with the same laws. Trusts are legal entities separate and distinct from their creators and beneficiaries, so the location of a trust is an important and specific decision. Your advisors should be able to recommend the most advantageous states.

■ **Foster teamwork.**

A fortune, once made, becomes a business to be managed. Keeping wealth alive for centuries requires assistance from others who have specialized talents or skills, and from the heirs, who are expected to keep the fortune productive in the future. Family members, as well as trusted attorneys, tax accountants, investment managers, and trustees all have a role to play within a governance structure geared toward the implementation of shared values. As in any business, communication is essential to success. To keep your wealth intact and growing, foster teamwork among your wealth management team.

Words to the Wise

- ■ Define your long-term values and goals. This will help to ensure the survival of your wealth through future generations.
- ■ Seek professional advice. Consult experts who have specialized skills in tax codes, trust law, trust administration, and investment management.
- ■ The duties of a trustee are time-consuming. They require someone who has financial sophistication and an understanding of legal issues. That's why it makes sense to consider a corporate trustee.
- ■ Pay attention to the location of your trust. Select a jurisdiction with laws and regulations that are most in keeping with your goals.
- ■ Foster teamwork. Family members, attorneys, tax accountants, investment managers and trustees, working together, can help you preserve your legacy for your beneficiaries.

Albert C. Bellas

Albert C. Bellas is chairman and CEO of the Neuberger Berman Trust Company, N.A., and a managing director of Neuberger Berman, LLC. Mr. Bellas is responsible for oversight of the Trust Company's fiduciary and wealth management services. Since 1981, Mr. Bellas has been involved in wealth management services for high-net-worth individuals and families. He is a frequent guest speaker on investment topics at conferences and seminars for organizations such as the Investment Management Institute, the Callan Investment Management Council, the Institute for Private Investors, and the Family Office Exchange. He is a member of the Investment and Financial Planning Committee of Trusts & Estates.

Diane E. Lederman

Diane E. Lederman is senior vice president, chief fiduciary counsel, and general counsel of Neuberger Berman Trust Company, N.A. Ms. Lederman has over 19 years' legal experience in estate and financial planning. She counsels individuals on estate, gift, and generation-skipping tax planning; retirement benefits planning; charitable giving; and similar topics. She has coauthored articles for Estate Planning *and* Trusts & Estates. *Ms. Lederman is a current and past member of the Committee on Trusts, Estates and Surrogate's Courts of the Association of the Bar of the City of New York, and a member of the Estate Planning Committee of the New York State Bankers Association.*

14

PRUDENT INVESTING FOR PRIVATE FAMILY FOUNDATIONS

Keeping an Even Keel in Stormy Markets

Ralph D. Sinsheimer

David and Ruth created their private family foundation in 1999 with $20 million, which represented partial proceeds from the sale of their business. At the time, investment policy ranked far down on their list of priorities. First and foremost, they were focused on developing a grant-making framework that would have a meaningful positive impact in their local community, where they felt it was most needed. With their attention focused on the business of "doing good" and tending to the administrative details faced by any new foundation, they initially planned to invest the foundation's assets in a stock market index fund, which they viewed as an "automatic pilot" for the long term. Fortunately for David and Ruth, they had an experienced team of financial advisors, who instead recommended that they create an investment policy designed to meet "prudent investor" standards. After consultation with their advisors, an investment committee was formed and the foundation's assets were invested in a broadly diversified, actively managed portfolio that included allocations to various asset classes. Two years later, when the Standard & Poor's 500 Index was down more than 35 percent from its peak in March 2000, David and Ruth were glad they had listened to their advisors. Their foundation's assets weathered the stock market storm. David and Ruth are still focused on the grant-making side of their foundation, but they have developed a healthy respect for the investment policy side.

The 1990s were boom years for foundations and endowments. As the stock market soared, the assets of nonprofit entities swelled with investment gains. The market's "wealth effect" prompted individuals to contribute to charities and, in many cases, to create their own private foundations, which now number approximately

40,000 in the United States. During this time, private foundations were invested in a market that seemed always to be rising. Even mediocre relative investment returns far outstripped historic norms. In this benign environment, some family foundations became complacent and neglected to rigorously review their investment policy. However, with the bursting of the technology stock "bubble," the subsequent broad market decline, and a cloudy economic picture, charitable momentum slowed.

To continue as a powerful and positive societal force, private foundations must reexamine their investment policies in light of an extremely challenging stock market—one that is marked by high volatility caused by exogenous shocks and cyclical economic factors. Many portfolios have been hit hard by losses. Some foundations that had increased their charitable grants significantly during the flush years are now forced to decrease their annual distributions and cut back on discretionary spending.

This crisis has forced foundation boards to revisit the concept of "prudent investing" as codified in various states' Management of Institutional Funds Acts, their Prudent Investor Acts, and other related laws. These laws require fiduciaries, including the trustees of private foundations, to incorporate principles of modern finance and total return into their investment policies. An investment policy must now be drafted in light of the foundation's spending policy and the dynamics of the market.

The recent provisions for prudent investing create a great deal more flexibility than fiduciaries had in decades past. But increased flexibility brings with it increased responsibility and liability. Foundations have long been responsible for investing their assets wisely. However, with the focus on modern concepts of "prudence," which are varied and sometimes controversial, foundations now may be challenged by states' attorneys general (and, potentially, by the foundations' creators) if they fail to exercise common sense and to incorporate the modern meaning of prudence in the management of the foundation.

The challenge is to determine the exact meaning of prudent investing. Fiduciaries no longer have "bright line" tests in making decisions. The various states' Acts require them to take a prudent and thorough approach to decision making. The *approach* to decisions about asset allocation, risk/return targets, and manager selections is more important than the decisions themselves.

THE NEW LOOK OF PRUDENCE

In the days before the first Management of Institutional Funds Act (1972) and the Uniform Prudent Investor Act (1997), many trustees and directors of family foundations believed that they were required to invest the foundations' assets entirely or primarily in bonds. The approach was viewed as ideal, given the conservative nature of high-grade fixed income and the yield advantage of bonds over stocks. Yield was paramount because the practice was to limit spending so as not to exceed investment income. This bond-centric approach, which lacked a growth component, ignored the corrosive effect of inflation on real spending power. In addition, interest rate fluctuations and credit risk issues have rendered bonds more volatile.

Today, fiduciaries are held to broader and more comprehensive standards of investment performance—which include balancing risk and return. The Uniform Prudent Investor Act provides guidance for those with oversight responsibility for family foundations. The Act is concerned principally with investments by private trusts that have one or more individual beneficiaries, but trustees of charitable trusts have similar duties and concerns. The following tenets underlie most states' Prudent Investor Acts:

1. The standard of prudence is applied to the portfolio as a whole, rather than to individual investments. An investment that might appear highly risky by itself can be "prudent" if assessed in relation to the rest of the portfolio.
2. The trade-off between risk and return is identified as the fiduciary's central consideration. A foundation that is created to exist in perpetuity will, by definition, be able to invest in "riskier" (i.e., more volatile) investments than will be acceptable for a foundation with a shorter life span.
3. All categorical restrictions on types of investments have been eliminated. The trustee can invest in virtually any asset class that plays an appropriate role in achieving the risk/return objectives of the trust and meets the other requirements of prudent investing.
4. Diversification is a key component of prudent investing, unless special circumstances indicate that the purpose of the trust is better served without diversifying.
5. Delegation of investment management to investment professionals is permitted and encouraged. Trustees of foundations

may engage investment managers and direct those managers to invest funds for total return, in accordance with modern portfolio theory.

SETTING INVESTMENT POLICY

The process of creating and monitoring investment policy is one of the most important functions of a foundation board and/or its trustees. The investment policy statement articulates the foundation's investment goals and identifies the interrelationship between investing and spending. It provides the broad asset-allocation guidelines within which investment managers may position the foundation's assets. The investment policy statement is a blueprint for current and, importantly, future foundation overseers. The statement also lays down the framework for assessing investment performance.

A sample *Statement of Investment Policy* for the fictitious Smith Family Foundation is provided on pages 168–174. As should any useful investment policy statement, it defines: the foundation's investment objectives; a time horizon; the required return; the need for sensitivity to volatility in the value of the portfolios in any calendar year or other period; and the expected real growth in fund assets. An investment policy statement may also include preferences for or restrictions on investments, such as the expressed exclusion of leveraged investments or the inclusion of a socially responsive investing style.

In the case of our make-believe Smith Family Foundation, the target for a minimum annual return is set at 5 percent adjusted for inflation—a figure that corresponds to the Foundation's spending policy. Foundations have always faced a unique balancing act between maximizing annual grant-making initiatives and maintaining and growing their long-term donative power. To retain its tax-exempt status without penalty, a foundation must give away at least 5 percent of its assets each year. Further, foundations have both regular and periodic spending needs that must be met. These sometimes onerous annual outflow requirements, coupled with the fact that many private foundations have no sources of income beyond investment returns, fly in the face of foundations' perpetual charter. To sustain or increase the real value of their capital, foundations must seek investment returns at least in excess of the required 5 percent, plus enough to stay ahead of inflation and pay investment management and administrative fees. Some foundations may need to earn investment returns of roughly 9 percent on average. That is only 2 percent less than

U.S. equities returned annually from 1926 through 2001, according to research by Ibbotson Associates.

To earn the returns they need to exist in perpetuity, most foundations must invest a meaningful portion of their assets in equities, as opposed to investing the lion's share of their assets in bonds. In the Smith Family Foundation investment policy statement, shown below, equities are targeted at 65 percent of assets, with a tolerance for as much as 75 percent when equity-oriented alternative investments are included. But given the inherent risks of equities, is this an appropriate level of stock market exposure in light of Prudent Investor Acts? There are no hard and fast rules, but the policy clearly strives for diversification, which is a central tenet of those acts.

As exemplified below, investment policy incorporates asset allocation guidelines, which, in addition to setting the target allocations, should include provisions for updating, rebalancing the asset mix, and benchmarking investment performance. Asset allocation guidelines must be both firm and flexible. For example, the operating ranges that are established should consider the long-term historical advantage of equity ownership as well as the higher volatility associated with stocks. These ranges provide for an asset allocation discipline and ensure that the foundation does not fall prey to outright market timing. At the same time, tactical decisions can be made within these ranges to reflect the current outlook for different asset classes.

A Sample Investment Policy*

Smith Family Foundation
Statement of Investment Policy

INTRODUCTION

This is the Statement of Investment Policy (the "Policy") governing the investment management of the Smith Family Foundation funds (the "Foundation") as approved by the Board of Trustees (the "Board") of the Foundation on (date of approval) _____ .

The Board, through the Investment Committee (the "Committee") formed and empowered by the Board, is charged with establishing and carrying out

---

*This sample investment policy is not intended to address the specific needs of every private foundation nor is it to be construed as a recommended asset allocation. It is simply provided for illustrative purposes.

the Policy, reviewing it regularly, recommending improvements as circumstances dictate, monitoring and evaluating the performance of the investment managers, and employing or terminating investment managers.

The Policy has been adopted as a framework for achieving the objectives outlined in the "Statement of Financial and Investment Objectives" below. Implementation of the Policy may be made only with prior approval of the Board.

STATEMENT OF FINANCIAL AND INVESTMENT OBJECTIVES

The purpose of the Foundation is to support grant-making activities through a total return investment strategy and a spending policy set to maintain, or ideally increase, the purchasing power of the Foundation, without putting the principal value of the Foundation's investments at excessive risk.

The primary investment objective of the Endowment is to attain a minimum average annual real total return (net of all investment management fees) of 5.0 percent, as measured over rolling four-year periods. Real total return is defined as the sum of capital appreciation (or loss) and current income (dividends and interest) adjusted for inflation as measured by the CPI [consumer price index]. This investment objective corresponds to the Foundation's spending policy.

Implicit in that purpose and objective are the goals of preserving and enhancing the Foundation's inflation-adjusted purchasing power and providing the necessary liquidity to meet the Foundation's distribution goals.

INVESTMENT PHILOSOPHY

The following principles, which recognize the long-term nature of the Foundation's purpose, are significant factors in the allocation of the Foundation's assets:

- In order to achieve a rate of return that will support the spending policy set forth above while protecting the Foundation from inflation, some investment risk must be taken in the management of the Foundation's assets.
- The most effective way to establish an appropriate risk level of the Foundation is through asset allocation (i.e., stocks, bonds, alternatives, and cash).
- There is significant evidence that long-term investors do not benefit from attempting to earn returns through short-term asset class forecasts or market timing. Therefore, a strategic long-term asset allocation strategy has been adopted for the Foundation. Over time, the Foundation will remain invested in asset class percentages that are close to those called for in the strategic asset allocation adopted for the Foundation.

- Style and strategy diversification will be pursued and will increase the probability, over three- to five-year periods, that the Foundation will achieve its investment objectives with reduced volatility.

INVESTMENT MANAGEMENT STRUCTURE

The Foundation will be managed by external investment management firms, which shall be selected by the Board or the Committee. The Committee will monitor the performance of the investment managers, regularly schedule meetings concerning the performance of the Foundation and its investment managers, and report quarterly to the Board.

Each investment manager shall have discretion to manage the assets in the Foundation's portfolio so as to achieve the investment objectives within the guidelines set forth in the Policy.

Transactions by investment managers should be made on the basis of best execution, which is intended to mean best realized price.

ASSET ALLOCATION STRATEGY

The overall asset allocation strategy shall be to diversify investments to provide a balance that will enhance long-term total return while avoiding undue risk or concentration in any single asset class or investment category. The following table lists the permitted asset classes, their target weights in the Foundation, and the operating range for each asset class.

Asset Allocation Policy

Asset Class	Target Asset Allocation	Operating Range
Fixed Income		
Investment Grade	25%	20–50%
High Yield	5%	0–20%
Alternatives: Fixed Income		
Absolute Return	5%	0–15%
Fixed Income Subtotal	35%	25–50%
Equities		
Large Cap	40%	30–50%
Small Cap	10%	0–20%
International	10%	0–20%
Alternatives: Long/Short Hedged, Private Equity & Other	5%	0–15%
Equity Subtotal	65%	45–75%
Total Portfolio	100%	

The Board, by way of the Committee, will have the responsibility to allocate investment resources within the ranges listed above. In doing so, the Board will seek reasonable assurance that the Foundation, as a whole, is well diversified, so that no single security, class of securities, or specific investment style will have a disproportionate impact on the aggregate investment results.

EQUITY INVESTMENTS

Equity investments may consist of domestic and foreign common stocks and convertibles.

Investment managers of the equity component of the Foundation may use derivative securities in hedged strategies to replicate market exposure and/or to execute a strategy at lesser cost than purchasing or selling the underlying securities. Derivative securities are not to be used to create a leveraged position in the investment manager's portfolio.

The equity component of the Foundation will be broadly diversified according to economic sector, industry, number of holdings, and other investment characteristics. Diversification will be achieved at the Foundation level; therefore, a certain level of concentration at the individual investment manager level will be tolerated. To enhance overall diversification, equity investment managers will be selected to employ different equity management philosophies, which will contribute to the desired degree of diversification.

No purchase will be made that will cause more than 5.0 percent, at cost, of the equity component of the Foundation to be invested in the equity securities of any one issuer. Compliance with this provision will be monitored quarterly by the Investment Committee.

ALTERNATIVE INVESTMENTS

The Foundation may employ investment managers to pursue alternative investment strategies (other than traditional long-only purchases of stocks or bonds) for the purposes of diversifying the market exposure of the Foundation and/or enhancing the overall return. No more than 5.0 percent of the Foundation may be managed by any single alternative manager. Where alternative investments are made through a "fund of funds" structure, in which an investment manager selects other commingled vehicles where the actual investments are made, the 5.0 percent restriction shall apply to the individual investment managers of the underlying investment vehicles, and not the fund of funds. Alternative investments may include: investment managers; partnerships or other similar vehicles investing (long and/or short) in domestic and international securities; venture capital investments; private equity; high-yield and distressed securities and loans; commodities; oil and gas interests; real estate; and derivative instruments. In each case, the investment manager (as with traditional investment managers) will be expected to operate within the guidelines proposed when the Board approved the strategy. Alternative investments shall not, in the aggregate, exceed 20 percent of the Foundation's market value.

FIXED-INCOME INVESTMENTS

Fixed-income investments may consist of bonds (which term is meant to include notes, debentures, mortgage-backed securities, and other publicly traded debt instruments which are not publicly traded but for which a limited trading market is likely to be available) and money market instruments, but equity and convertible securities are excluded. Investment managers may use derivative securities to replicate market exposure and/or to execute a strategy at lesser cost than purchasing or selling the underlying securities. Derivative securities are not to be used to create a leveraged position in an investment manager's portfolio.

In general, the fixed-income portion of the Foundation will be diversified among different sectors of the fixed-income market. Fixed-income investment managers who specialize in debt instruments rated BB or below will not exceed 20 percent of the Foundation. However, the average quality of the overall fixed-income component of the Foundation is expected to be A or better.

With the exception of obligations of the United States Government and its agencies, no purchase will cause more than 5.0 percent of the fixed-income component of the Foundation to be invested in the fixed-income securities of a single issuer. Fixed-income investment managers may have up to 15 percent of their portfolios in bonds denominated in currencies other than United States dollars. Currency hedging may be utilized by investment managers only to offset the currency risk of holding assets denominated in non-U.S. currencies. Currency speculation is strictly prohibited.

GENERAL GUIDELINES

Decisions as to individual security selection, position size, diversification among industries and issuers, current income levels, turnover, and other tools employed by active investment managers are left to broad investment manager discretion, subject to the usual standards of fiduciary prudence and applicable guidelines.

PERFORMANCE EVALUATION AND EXPECTATIONS

Total Portfolio Benchmarks

To achieve the Foundation's stated objective of earning an average annual real total return of 5.0 percent (net of all fees over rolling four-year periods), the Foundation will be invested in accordance with the Asset Allocation Policy previously described. To measure the effectiveness of its investment managers' selections, the Committee will measure total portfolio performance against a target allocation benchmark. This benchmark is based on the Foundation's Asset Allocation Policy and is determined as follows:

Asset Class	Market Index	Benchmark Weight
Fixed Income	Lehman Aggregate	35.0%
Alternative—FI	CPI Plus 3 percent	5.0%
Large-Cap Equities	S&P 500	35.0%
Small-Cap Equities	Russell 2000	10.0%
International Equities	MSCI World ex-U.S.	7.5%
Alternative—Equity	CPI Plus 5.0 percent	7.5%

The investment results for each asset class individually will be evaluated using the broad market benchmarks set forth above. The benchmarks for alternative investments are based on a premium to the CPI because the goal of these investments is to achieve long-term growth with little or no correlation to major asset class benchmarks.

Manager Benchmarks

The Foundation's investment performance, and each asset class, will be evaluated using the broad market benchmarks set forth above. Each investment manager will be judged against a narrower market benchmark that reflects its specific style of management. In many cases, this benchmark will differ from the broader asset class benchmarks set forth above. The combination of investment manager benchmarks within an asset class should closely approximate the benchmark for the asset class as a whole.

Individual investment manager performance will also be measured against a universe of other investment managers who follow a similar investment style. Foundation investment managers are expected to perform in the top half of this universe.

Comparisons with market benchmark and investment universes will occur on a regular basis. Results will be evaluated based on rolling four-year periods.

FOUNDATION CASH FLOW AND REBALANCING

A projection of the resources available for allocation to the investment managers and for withdrawals from the Foundation will be made periodically by the Foundation's administrative staff. The Board will review these projections in order to determine whether it is necessary to rebalance the Foundation's investments to accommodate additions or withdrawals.

Rebalancing the Foundation's investments to target allocations should be reviewed at least annually, when the target ratios are reviewed. The Committee, in accordance with the Board's determination, shall make additions to and withdrawals from investment managers. The Committee will notify investment managers sufficiently in advance of withdrawal orders to allow for time to build up necessary liquid reserves.

MONITORING OF INVESTMENTS

All investment managers are required to report to the Committee any significant changes in their firm's ownership, organizational structure, professional personnel, account structure (e.g., number of accounts or size of assets under management, or account minimums), or fundamental investment philosophy. The Board will monitor both the Foundation as a whole and the Foundation's individually managed portfolios for: consistency in each investment manager's investment philosophy, return relative to objectives and investment risk measured by asset concentration, exposure to extreme economic conditions, and volatility. The Board, at its regularly scheduled meetings, will review the performance of the Foundation as a whole and of the investment managers individually.

Each investment manager will report, on a quarterly basis, its total return net of all commissions and fees, time-weighted and dollar-weighted, and segmented at the level of each asset class. Each investment manager also should present purchases and sales for the quarter, portfolio holdings at cost and at market value, and an analysis of the portfolio by sector. Investment managers should communicate regularly with the Committee concerning their investment strategy and outlook.

The Board may request that investment managers be present at periodic meetings to present their portfolios and results. The Committee will report to the Board, at its regularly scheduled meetings, the performance of the Foundation as a whole and of each investment manager.

A well-thought-out investment policy, such as that of the Smith Family Foundation, helps trustees to maintain an even keel during both calm and volatile markets. To succeed, all investment decisions—from broad-based asset allocation to issue-specific security selection—should adhere to a predetermined investment discipline, regardless of the winds of investment fashion. In this regard, private foundations would do well to emulate the nation's most successful major endowments. They utilize a formal, deliberative process to set long-term investment policy, and they monitor current investment activities in the context of this policy, even when policy decisions invite criticism in the short term. Buying low and selling high—the fundamental principle of sound investing—requires the fortitude to buy when most of the market is despairing, and to sell when most of the market is euphoric.

ALTERNATIVE ASSET CLASSES

Today's foundations face a larger universe of investment possibilities than ever before. Stocks, bonds, and cash are no longer the only asset classes available. Advances in investment research, structured finance, and technology have changed the investment world and created new asset types.

In the past decade, alternative asset classes—for example, hedge and private equity funds—have grown very popular with foundations and endowments. Alternatives to traditional asset classes now account for some 23 percent of endowment investments, including 18 percent that are invested in hedge funds, according to a study by Commonfund Institute. About 60 percent of college endowments make some allocations to so-called alternatives. According to the study, foundations with assets of more than $100 million allocate between 15 percent and 29 percent of their assets to alternatives, and institutions with less allocate 5 percent to 7 percent to such funds. College and university endowments assign an average of about 45 percent of their assets to various classes of U.S. equities, about 21 percent to U.S. bonds, and more than 17 percent to non-U.S. equities.

Large family foundations can qualify to invest in hedge funds that are unregulated and, therefore, closed to small investors. These foundations are attracted to techniques that strive to provide positive absolute returns, regardless of the direction of the traditional markets—including "market-neutral" and arbitrage-based funds that strive for equity-like returns with bond-like volatility. Alternative asset-class managers generally aim for low correlation to traditional stock and bond investments; therefore, their use can have the salutary effect of zigging when the rest of the foundation portfolio is zagging. A study in *The Journal of Investing* suggests that, on average, a 6 percent to 16 percent allocation of such strategies to a diversified portfolio can significantly cut volatility—and, therefore, risk—within the portfolio. It's not surprising that hedge funds mushroomed from $67 billion in 1990 to more than $500 billion in 2001.

Hedge funds are complicated vehicles that require detailed analysis before investment. One must be careful not to assume that absolute-return investing will always produce positive returns with little or no market correlation. In fact, it seems that, once every market cycle, a liquidity-driven crisis has the effect of creating significant market directionality in these strategies. In addition, the use of leverage, which is itself a source of risk, can create unrelated business income that can jeopardize the tax-exempt status of a foundation unless the hedge fund is located offshore. No foundation should consider this asset class without close investigation and a complete understanding of the potential returns, the correlation of those returns with other asset classes in the portfolio, and the risks.

CONCLUSION

Prudent Investor Acts require trustees and boards to take into account today's current and prospective market realities. They permit fiduciaries to use common sense to avoid being hamstrung by outmoded laws. In addition, the language of the trust instrument or of other foundation organizational documents is typically very broad in allowing fiduciaries to make investment decisions and diversify assets. Under Prudent Investor Acts, delegation is encouraged if a fiduciary does not have sufficient investment expertise. However, the fiduciary must use appropriate care in choosing an asset allocator and an investment manager, monitoring their actions, and setting the terms of the delegation. Whether acting alone or by delegation, fiduciaries must ensure that the foundation's assets are adequately diversified, and that the risk/reward trade-offs have been optimized.

Foundations today face volatile markets and virtually unlimited investment choices. Like all investors, foundations must therefore carefully construct investment policies that include guidelines for future spending and investment. They should also choose at least some board members and/or advisors who thoroughly understand the dynamics of prudent decision making—including the principles of modern finance and the best methods to achieve the desired total net return with the least risk.

One solution will not fit every foundation's needs. Investment policies must be crafted to reflect the unique characteristics of the individual foundation. In doing so, the policy should take into account the foundation's purpose, the size and frequency of its grant-making activities, the proposed life of the entity, and any preferences of the founder. Central to the investment policy statement is a set of asset allocation guidelines that defines both the acceptable asset classes (and their subcomponents) and the percentage ranges within which the foundation can invest.

Creating a private family foundation can be immensely rewarding for you, your family, and the causes you choose to support. It is also a serious undertaking that requires careful planning and a disciplined approach to investment management if it is to be a vibrant, positive, multigenerational force.

For more information on private family foundations, two organizations may be helpful: The Foundation Center (www.fdncenter.org) and The Council on Foundations (www.cof.org). Both offer extensive services and resources regarding the formation and operation of foundations.

Words to the Wise

- A sound investment policy, implemented and managed with professional discipline, is essential to the long life of a foundation.

- An investment policy should define: the foundation's investment objectives; its time horizon; its required return; its sensitivity to volatility in the value of the portfolios in any one year or other period; its current and desired future charitable donations; and its expected real growth in fund assets.

- To retain their tax-exempt status without penalty, foundations must give away at least 5 percent of their assets each year. Administration and other fees will require additional costs that may create a substantial "bogey" for expected investment returns.

- Prudent Investor rules create a need for professional standards of investment management for private family foundations.

- Today's foundations face a larger universe of investment possibilities than ever before. New asset types may create opportunities to reduce volatility and risk in portfolios, but they require thorough analysis and expert management.

Ralph D. Sinsheimer

Ralph D. Sinsheimer is senior vice president of Neuberger Berman Trust Company, N.A., where he heads the Wealth Management Group. A certified trust and financial advisor, he works with wealthy individuals, families, and their related charitable entities, toward successfully managing their complex financial needs. Mr. Sinsheimer's experience, gained over 20 years in the financial services industry, encompasses philanthropy management and investment strategy. He has worked extensively with alternative investment vehicles such as hedge funds and private equity, and, where appropriate, has incorporated them into optimized asset allocation models. He has served on a number of corporate and nonprofit boards, including LifeSpan Bio-Sciences, St. Mary's Foundation for Children, the Boston Children's Museum, and the WGBH Corporate Executive Council.

15

FAMILY OFFICES

Why, When, and How

Ellen M. Perry

Back in the 1920s, the Morris brothers, Victor and Charles, the founders of a large regional department store chain, established a family office. Today, this office serves 100 individuals—three generations of the Morris family—with combined assets of more than $2 billion. The office provides complete investment services, philanthropic counseling, financial administration, and legal advice. The CEO is the current patriarch, Arthur Morris, Victor's grandson.

A large professional staff and a private trust company are in place. Governance is provided by a formal Board of Directors. The board is dominated by family members who represent the different generations and family lines that have structured the tenure and the operating procedures. The wealth manager was chosen both for his investment expertise and his facilitation skills. He attends all of the board meetings and plays a valuable role in decision making. A succession plan for the board is in place.

Despite all the enormous changes that have taken place in the outside world during the past 80 years, the office looks and feels almost exactly as it did in the 1920s. Recently, the family has been struggling with the generation gap, epitomized in a demand, by Arthur's children, for significant technological advances, including state-of-the-art video conferencing and a transition to a paperless office. Arthur has resisted these changes to such an unproductive extent that an external wealth management firm has become involved in facilitating the discussions and resolving the differences.

To reduce costs and increase efficiency, the office has accepted outside families as clients. This decision has not been entirely successful and was not wholly supported by the family. Some family members resent the attention paid to outside clients when it interferes with the attention given to their own affairs. And clients from outside the family sometimes feel that they are not fully accepted by the core family.

The Morris family has chosen one of several available approaches to the establishment and operation of a family office. This chapter provides a comprehensive description, including the advantages and disadvantages of each approach.

THE FAMILY OFFICE: A DEFINITION

Family offices are organized to handle a wide variety of tasks for very wealthy families. Many of today's large trust companies, such as J.P. Morgan/Chase, Northern Trust, Harris Bank, and Bessemer Trust Company, began as family offices for their founders. Over time, these single-family offices began to accept outside clients and expand their offerings.

As greater wealth has accumulated in the United States during the past few decades, there has been a dramatic increase in the creation of family offices. Today, industry experts estimate that there are more than 4,000 family offices in the United States. These offices range from the smallest—an assistant or bookkeeper handling the administrative and data-recording functions—to the most complex—a staff of professionals who manage investment assets, prepare tax returns, manage real estate and other "hard" assets, coordinate charitable giving, and enhance the competency of family members to deal with their wealth.

There are two major types of family offices: single-family and multifamily. The former type, as exemplified by the Morris family, is best suited to families with assets of $100 million or more. For those with assets in the $10 million–$100 million range, the most economically viable approach is the multifamily office.

The best-managed family offices of today are redefining ways to manage wealth. Unfettered by tradition and the inflexible trust documents of previous generations, they are seeking solutions to a vastly more complex set of financial, familial, and individual emotional needs and interests.

THE SERVICES A FAMILY OFFICE CAN PROVIDE

A partial list of the possible services that can be offered by a fully operating family office is given below. These services can be provided by internal staff, by external resources, or through a combination of the two:

- Wide-ranging asset management.
- Sophisticated financial planning for multiple generations.
- Trustee and beneficiary coordination.
- Manager selection and monitoring.
- Philanthropic advice and administration.
- Bookkeeping, record keeping, bill paying, and concierge services.
- Education and family facilitation.
- Consolidated reporting on all assets.
- Insurance.
- Master custody and reporting.
- Estate planning.
- Risk management.
- Family meeting coordination and facilitation.
- Succession planning and governance.
- Personal staff management.
- Concierge services.

In addition to all the internal work involved, perhaps the single greatest value that a dedicated office can provide is *coordination*. The office serves as the conductor of the family's financial "orchestra," which includes lawyers, accountants, consultants, managers, and employees. Many families report that their efficiency and work production are vastly improved when the family office is involved.

COMMON FORMS OF FAMILY OFFICES

The two most common forms of family offices are the single-family office and the multiclient family approach. Some multifamily offices are administered by institutional trust companies and investment firms.

The Multiclient Family Office

This type of family office serves the financial and investment needs of families with more than $10 million and presents an attractive and economically viable solution. Large trust companies and brokerage firms offer a wide variety of services to this market. Many firms have invested heavily in this business line. It requires developing sophisticated technology systems to track assets, finding the very best independent money managers, and hiring seasoned professionals as staff members.

Virtually every major bank and financial institution has a special division for the very wealthy. Some multifamily offices make use of the services of such organizations, and many multifamily offices are actually housed on their premises. New technologies, global investment opportunities, sophisticated financial planning and performance reporting, and complex statistical models for considering risk are all serving to attract wealthy families.

Institutions are reaching out to this lucrative market in many ways that families find attractive. In a *Worth* magazine survey of private banking to the wealthy, access to private deals and top-tier external money management were cited as important elements. Wealthy families also seek comprehensive financial planning. Large national accounting firms are offering these families a variety of financial planning, tax, and philanthropic services.

Single-Family Office

Industry experts believe that to create and staff an economically efficient single-family office, a family must possess assets in excess of $100 million–$150 million. This figure takes into consideration the start-up costs, ongoing management and maintenance, and capital expenses.

Long-established single-family offices share many common characteristics. Over time, they have tended to deal similarly with the predictable issues that arise for family offices only after many years in business:

- *Well-developed systems, procedures, management style, and culture.* Like any other mature organization, these family offices have a strong sense of culture, internal identity, and well-established procedures. Often, these traits reflect those of the founding family, which required them of the staff as well. These offices have had many years to consider, design, and test services that meet the needs of the founders or the succeeding generation; historically, they have been developed without much exposure to other offices. In recent years, as this industry has grown, these older offices have both set examples for, and benefited from, improved *modern* thinking.
- For many older offices, the most significant issues arise when the office begins a transition to younger generations. At that point, issues such as succession, governance, and redesign to

meet the different needs of younger members often occur and can create a crisis. As the family grows and more members of new generations become involved in the family office, meeting the wide variety of members' needs becomes ever more chal-lenging.

■ *Mature and time-tested governance systems.* Offices that have sur-vived the test of time have developed ways of making strategic decisions and setting priorities. These offices today are often directed by the generation that did *not* establish the office in the beginning. They inherited the office, along with a plan for gov-ernance that was, at the least, designed by their ancestors. These offices often evolved within the practices and services delivered by an earlier generation; now, they are striving to meet the mul-tiple needs of a larger and more diverse family.

SELECTING THE RIGHT KIND OF OFFICE FOR YOUR FAMILY

When they are creating a family office, families must consider the fol-lowing questions:

■ What are we willing to spend annually for the management of the office? (This will ultimately determine the staff size and management process.) Will the senior executive be responsible for managing the budget?

■ How will the office and the family interface? Who, within the family, is willing and qualified to manage the office staff? Will the family serve as a board or committee, or will one member of the family oversee the staff?

■ How will the family as a whole govern the entity? Whom will it serve? What role—if any—will spouses be assigned within the office?

■ How will the family members pay for services? Will they be charged a percentage of their assets managed by the office, or will there be an expense-sharing calculation based on market rates? Will older family members bear the majority of the costs?

■ How does the family define success? Do the desired goals in-clude financial performance, family unity and collaboration, education of younger generations, and skilled legal and estate work? Families often do not articulate the true goals of an office in a way that allows the professional staff to create annual objectives and performance evaluations for the office staff.

- How much sophistication and expertise does the family want the internal talent to have? What activities are the family members willing to outsource?
- How will the family arrange for succession, both in governance and in senior management?
- Which of the current advisors will remain in place? Who will interact with them, and who will lead them?
- What security and risk-management measures need to be instituted and managed?
- Will a professional search firm be hired to identify and recruit the senior staff?
- How much authority and control should be given to the senior staff?
- How often will the family meet as a governing group?

A variety of skilled specialists can help families to decide what path will best guide them toward their goal. From consultants, attorneys, accountants, and family office industry experts, plentiful advice is available. Relevant contacts can be found among the list of contributors to this book, each of whom can provide a family with timely and helpful resources.

ESTABLISHING A WELL-RUN OFFICE

A well-run office has three major hallmarks: superior management, proactive solutions, and collaborative spirit. This section describes how these traits develop a well-run financial office.

1. *Superior asset management.* At the core of virtually every successful family office is collective dedication to excellent investment performance. Wealthy families seek a diversified approach and the very best management talent available—worldwide. Each family member wants customized asset allocation and attention to his or her goals and objectives. This level of asset management requires sophisticated, consolidated reporting on all the assets.

2. *Proactive financial solutions.* The offices with the highest levels of client satisfaction are those that not only meet the needs of the family, but also anticipate those needs and design creative

solutions. These offices find the best and brightest professionals and assign them to devise innovative ways of managing the very complex finances of their clients. Less successful offices often fail to recognize that, to meet the family's needs, they must operate in a continuing state of flux. It is an art and a challenge to deal with the changing environment that often accompanies great wealth. New business ventures, the acquisition of substantial new assets, constant travel, and geographic changes are only some of the ongoing challenges. Single-family offices tend to have a static client base, and they operate in a noncompetitive environment. The client is not likely to leave the family office but may reject any alternative office solutions. This is one of the two great challenges for single-family offices. (The other is succession.) It is crucial to establish an environment in which family participation is encouraged and creative solutions are rewarded.

3. *Collaborative spirit and mentoring.* During the past few years, many prosperous families have realized that it is necessary to cultivate the skills of a mentor/facilitator/collaborator. Younger generations are not schooled in financial complexities, and great wealth typically complicates familial relationships. As a result, family offices are integrating *collaboration* and *mentoring* into their design. They are also including facilitators in family meetings to help create productive exchanges and to deal with the conflicts that will inevitably arise.

COSTS OF OPERATING A FAMILY OFFICE

Here are the current expense estimates for the two major options: a stand-alone family office and a multiclient family office.

1. *Stand-alone family office.* Industry experts agree that staffing and managing this type of office will cost a family roughly 1 percent of the assets managed each year. The estimate includes staff, software, overhead, systems, consultants, and custody. It does not include managers' fees and brokerage commissions. Thus, a family with $100 million can expect to spend $1 million each year for its office expenses. The largest component of this total is the senior executive's salary, which will run into hundreds of thousands of dollars, based on the amount of asset management oversight and technical experience he or she provides.

The overall cost will vary depending on which services and duties a family chooses to outsource, and the character of the underlying assets. For example, if a family's main asset is commercial property in multiple states, it would probably have higher staff costs than would a family whose assets are primarily marketable securities. A family with 20 adult members whose needs include day-to-day servicing, tax planning and preparation, bill paying, bookkeeping, and the administration of a private foundation, would require a larger staff than a family with five adult members who manage their own households and look to the office only for money management and tax preparation.

2. *Multiclient family office.* As a general rule, fees are divided into two segments. The first segment, the investment management fee, is calculated as a percentage of the assets under management—often 30 to 100 basis points. This may or may not cover the cost of any underlying submanagement fees, but it will include all asset allocation work, statistical modeling, and performance reporting. The second segment of the fee covers services: bookkeeping, bill paying, concierge services, family meeting coordination, private equity due diligence, trustee coordination, and estate planning. This fee is often a flat annual charge, based on estimates of the time and complexity involved. If the multifamily office utilizes a trust company as well, a fiduciary fee may also apply. This can require 10 to 30 basis points, calculated on the trust assets under administration.

In general, large financial institutions that offer sophisticated and comprehensive family office services charge 90 to 110 basis points for a complete menu of services. This figure declines as the size of the asset base increases. We will probably see a decrease in fees as the competition continues to increase and families have more alternatives from which to choose.

SHOULD YOU FORM A FAMILY OFFICE OR JOIN AN EXISTING ONE?

The choice of whether to form a stand-alone office or join an existing one is very important. All involved family members should give the matter sufficient time and attention to arrive at an informed decision that can be embraced by the entire family. Each of the major approaches has varied implications.

Stand-Alone Office

- Families' choice when they are unable to find, through institutional avenues, the kind or quality of services they desire.
- Satisfies investors' desire for complete independence and objectivity in money management.
- Offers a management relationship rather than a client relationship; more control is possible, and staff turnover problems can be avoided.
- Creates a family-focused organization that can hold future generations together.
- Satisfies families' desire for privacy, convenience, and complete customization.
- Offers insulation from merger-and-acquisition risk.
- Makes available a greater range of investment choices than might be possible from one service provider.

Joining an Existing Organization

- Advantages in cost are substantial.
- Operational responsibilities are transferred to staff members.
- Family members can have more privacy from one another's finances.
- An institutional trustee is required.
- Family members have easier access to specialized advice.

NEW TRENDS

Homme D'Affaire   Today, many very affluent families are seeking a trusted advisor—an *advocate,* in the broadest sense of the word. As James E. Hughes, Jr., states in his paper, *A Reflection on the Role of the* Homme D'Affaire *in a System of Family Governance,* "True counselors bring to their clients worldly wisdom and an understanding of the need for orderly change, a deep awareness of human behavior, gentle mentoring, and the ability to subordinate their own ambition to the needs of the client."

As our business world has evolved, and as more and more transaction-oriented professionals are being trained, we have lost the older model of a family retainer or protector. However, an emerging generation of professionals seems to be interested in taking on this role. For this trend to take root, better ways to train and encourage these professionals must be developed, and families will need to demonstrate respect for their services.

Human Capital Management   A truly comprehensive "balance sheet" for a family should account for human talents and characteristics as well as financial assets. Most families fail to devote much time and attention to preparing their members for the responsibilities and advantages that wealth affords. Inheritances are passed along, assets and control are transferred, but little or no competency training occurs.

This training could take several forms: technical training on topics such as financial risk, asset allocation, responsible investing, budgeting, and estate planning; life training in charitable giving and in the role of the wealthy in our society; active beneficiary training; and the impact of wealth on work. This learning process could also create bonding opportunities for siblings and cousins.

A commitment to creating and maintaining educational curricula that will enhance the competence and awareness of family members is emerging in some organizations and industry groups—for example, the FOX (Family Office Exchange) Learning Academy and The Institute for Private Investors (IPI)—and on the calendars of many large trust companies and financial institutions. To date, IPI and FOX are among the few sources that ask participants to pay competitive fees for these services—a signal of their perceived value.

Private Trust Companies   The decision of whom to name as the trustee for your family's enduring legal entities is important. This fiduciary/trustee makes critical decisions regarding investments, grantor intent, trust distributions, and beneficiary preparedness. Historically, wealthy families have named a trusted family member, a lawyer, or a reputable trust company. More recently, families have begun to form trust companies devoted to their affairs alone. For the very wealthy, these firms provide complete privacy; control and flexibility in their fiduciary affairs; corporate insulation from liability; and a governance structure that allows for multigenerational involvement. (See Chapter 16, "Finding an Outstanding Trustee.")

There are now fewer legal, economic, and regulatory barriers to overcome in establishing a limited-purpose trust company, and more and more families are choosing to do so, in states such as South Dakota, Delaware, and Wyoming.

Cooperative Family Offices   These occupy a position midway between a single-family office and a multiclient-family office. Often organized by a core family that is connected to one or two other families, these entities share overhead, staff, and investment opportunities. Some also share space and are identified as joint venture partners of a sort. In other arrangements, the affiliation is loose and the focus is on one or two key areas, such as manager selection and monitoring. The advantages of this arrangement are: cost reduction; collaboration with other financially sophisticated families; more privacy and control than in a multiclient office; and a greater ability to attract and retain professional staff.

Words to the Wise

- Family offices, which can range in size from one employee to a large staff of professionals, handle a wide variety of financial tasks for very wealthy families: asset management, estate planning, philanthropic advice, record keeping, and succession planning.

- Multifamily offices best serve families with assets in excess of $10 million; single-family offices are viable for families with assets of $100 million and up.

- The management of great wealth has become so unbelievably complex, and so driven by sophisticated assets and complicated trust documents, that a team of skilled and experienced professionals is necessary.

- In increasing numbers, large trust companies, major banks, and financial institutions are offering services to the family office marketplace and will create new options and improve affordability.

- Single-family offices can fall prey to problems, including a younger generation's dissatisfaction and familial succession disputes. However, today's generation is writing new rules. They are forging powerful alliances with other families, creating exciting opportunities for their children, and developing resources to recruit and train the high level of talent they require.

- Trends for the future include the emergence of an *Homme D'Affaire* and formal training in human capital management.

Ellen M. Perry

Ellen M. Perry is founder of Family Office Solutions LLC, a consulting firm specializing in family office design, governance development, and objectives identification. During her career, she has developed business models for financial institutions and professional associations wishing to establish family office practices, and she has worked with single and multiclient family offices on the specific design of their businesses. Ms. Perry is also cofounder and former CEO of Asset Management Advisors, a multiclient family office, and Teton Trust Company, an affiliated private trust company. She serves on the board of directors of several family offices, philanthropic organizations, and private family foundations, and she is dean of the FOX Learning Academy, a membership organization for family members and family office executives.

16

FINDING AN
OUTSTANDING TRUSTEE

What Wealthy Families Look for in a
Trustee and How They Get It

JOHN P. C. DUNCAN

The Passant family was at a crossroads. Unfortunately, being told—even by well-meaning advisors—that their problem was "a nice one to have" was not as encouraging as intended. The family was the beneficiary of substantial trusts (more than $100 million of assets) and had funded a substantial charitable foundation. But the family had outgrown, or perhaps outworn, its trustees—an old-line, traditional corporate trustee and individual trustees who were senior, trusted family members.

The individual trustees, who were past the retirement age even for most avocations, were not likely to be able or willing to continue as trustees much longer. To some family members, the corporate trustee's product and services offerings seemed frozen in time. Worse yet, some of its actions—and its reluctance to act when requested—could be explained only by a tendency to regard family assets as its own legacy rather than the family's.

Individual trustee succession was problematic. No obvious Passant family member seemed to be available to step into these difficult and responsible roles for the entire family. The family, and therefore the trust beneficiaries, had descended vertically to four living generations and had spread horizontally to include five main branches as well as distant cousins, stepchildren, and estranged spouses raising fourth-generation children. This breadth and diversity made a subjective consensus about new individual trustees difficult. Also, there were objective concerns about exposing family members, or even friends who were trusted professionals, to the potential liability of acting as trustee. And there were seldom-aired but genuine concerns about whether any individual would have the time or skill to meet the entire family's growing expectations of its trustees. These considerations foretold a heavier—and someday, probably, an almost exclusive—reliance on corporate trustees, at least for the major trusts and the foundation.

191

Further complicating matters was the fact that not all family members were dis-
contented with their long-standing corporate trustee. Family members and branches
receiving more than adequate income from conservatively invested but subpar-
performing trusts, or who never required a service other than a quarterly distribu-
tion, did not seek or necessarily understand the need that others felt to change the
corporate trustee. But given the large number of second-generation family members
who were dissatisfied with the corporate trustee, a major decision was at hand.

A s is often the case, riding on the outcome of that decision was more than a choice of trustees of the family trusts. Also at stake was whether the family, or major parts of it, would continue, in crucial respects, to operate as "a family" and, perhaps, come closer together. If a consensual, family-wide solution for the trustee problem could not be found, the family risked fragmentation: separate trustees for each trust serving a major family branch or, worse, a trustee (or trustees) of major, indivisible trusts whom not all family members had chosen or accepted.

What initially seemed to be a narrow problem of finding the right trustee for the family threatened to escalate into a major family management crisis if a family-wide solution could not be found.

Family Resources   Fortunately, the Passant family had some significant and critical resources available. First, and perhaps most important, the members of the oldest two generations and of many of the families that made up the younger generations shared the view that substantial social and financial benefits were to be gained if family groups and branches acted together as much as possible. In other words, acting as "one family," rather than going their separate ways.

Another major resource was the family office, which could take the lead in a trustee succession project by helping the family to articulate its criteria for its trustees; identifying the available alternatives for meeting the family's fiduciary needs; and performing due diligence on the candidates. Also valuable were the family's awareness of and access to experienced professional advisors who could help to identify the strengths and weaknesses of not only corporate trust company candidates but also the major types of trustees available—individual trustees, institutional corporate trustees, and private ("boutique") trust companies.

Critical Early Decisions   A first and, in retrospect, a vital step taken by the Passant family to resolve its trustee problem was to open the lines of communication among family members. In phone calls and meetings, representatives of the family branches that were dissatisfied with the current trustee explained their concerns to those who did not initially share or understand them. This led to a meeting of family representatives in which three decisions were made. First, it was agreed that a corporate trustee was necessary for the major trusts, even though individual trustees could act as cotrustees of those trusts, if desired, or as sole or cotrustees of the smaller trusts that benefited only individual family branches.

The family representatives considered, but then set aside, the option of forming their own "private trust company." They concluded that although the family's wealth was at least marginally sufficient to support an exclusive, family-owned-and-managed trust company, the commitment of family members' time and the effort necessary for such an undertaking was not there.

After accepting the need for a corporate trustee and rejecting a family-owned private trust company, the family representatives made a third important decision. They assigned the executive director of the family office to identify possible succession candidates, including the existing corporate trustee. Toward that goal, she would first articulate and prioritize the criteria the family members should consider when they selected trustees.

These criteria were to be proposed based on her familiarity with the family's needs, the issues and concerns family members had expressed, and any objective standards that she would develop with the assistance of legal and financial advisors. Using the criteria she put forth and any other criteria that resonated with family representatives, she would propose a list of candidates for corporate trustee. The family would choose, at another meeting, three or four leading corporate trustee candidates to investigate in depth. Personal interviews of senior trust company personnel would be conducted by family members.

Identifying Types of Corporate Trustees   Responding to these decisions, the Passant family office executive, in consultation with outside advisors familiar with a broad range of potential corporate trustees, developed a list of 12 companies that potentially could offer the desired products, services, philosophy, and pricing. These companies were consciously drawn from three groups:

1. Traditional institutional trust companies.
2. New-style "boutique" or independent wealth management trust companies.
3. Multifamily private trust companies.

Given the family's unsatisfactory experience with its traditional institutional trustee, the advisors suggested including other prominent examples of that genre mainly to ensure that the family was exposed to the current offerings and price structures that the best of them had to offer. If the family chose to stay with a traditional institution as its main trustee, it would probably stay with the one it already had rather than bear the burden of replacing one trustee with another in the same mold.

The more interesting candidates, the family office executive felt, were the "boutique" and multifamily private trust companies. These two types of corporate trustees are very similar in services, size, and methods of operations. Their definitive difference lies in the fact that multifamily private trust companies are family-owned but also serve unrelated families of similar wealth and disposition. Boutique wealth management trust companies tend to manage larger amounts of assets than private trust companies and are not primarily owned by the families they serve or by traditional banking institutions. Both types of candidates focus exclusively on wealth management, but private trust companies' clients usually average more than $50 million of assets under management. A boutique trust company is more likely to serve families with lower levels of wealth as well. Distinguishing between these two types of corporate fiduciaries can sometimes be difficult, especially because many boutique trust companies started as private trust companies.

Discovering and Applying the Family's Criteria   The Passant family office executive grouped a long list of the criteria she felt were relevant for selecting a corporate trustee into seven categories. Based on her understanding of the family's needs and expectations, they appear here as she prioritized them:

1. Responsive and flexible.
2. Loyal and independent.
3. Multicompetent.
4. Efficient; controls costs.
5. Convenient and accessible.

6. Secure and private: protects assets and family.
7. Promotes family's nonfinancial objectives.

Applying these criteria, the office executive recommended to the family four companies that seemed to excel under the first two categories and perform at least adequately under the others. All four "finalists" were private or boutique trust companies; neither the current institutional corporate fiduciary nor any other was recommended. Notably, all four finalists performed especially well on the criteria in the final category; they were aware of and they promoted their clients' nonfinancial objectives.

The importance of the first two criteria in separating the finalists from the pack was, of course, not accidental. Many companies have the essential professional qualifications embodied in the third through sixth categories, but few exhibit the client orientation necessary to excel in loyalty, flexibility, and responsiveness to families' financial and nonfinancial needs.

The family office head and her advisors were confident that the family could not go wrong by choosing any of the four finalists. Ultimately, the choice made by the family was as much a result of gut reactions to the interviews of the four finalists as of any quantifiable differences among the four. The success of the Passant family in resolving its trustee succession problem was perhaps best demonstrated by the fact that most family members who did not initially seek or see the need for a new corporate trustee were pleased with and approved the one selected.

Drawing Lessons from the Passant Family's Story

This story about the Passant family's success in overcoming its trust succession crisis offers a lesson that may be imparted to other families confronted with a similar need. As the Passant family showed, the keys to finding a corporate trustee without undermining family unity are:

- Articulate all of the family's needs and expectations, including those of each branch and generation.
- Recognize that there is a wide range of alternative trustee types, and look for the *type* of trustee who can meet your family's requirements.
- Find the right trustee within that right type.

A critical first step is to have the family decide whether it really prefers to be "a family" rather than a group of related families. In this context, the test of whether relatives are "a family" is whether they want to and can work together, to a significant degree, on trustee succession. For some families, uniting to choose a fiduciary will only serve a limited purpose: it allows them to combine their assets in order to access corporate fiduciaries with minimums of millions (or tens of millions) of dollars held in trust accounts. For others, collective action will be both a result of and a tool for family social unification as well as financial unification. Both types of families can benefit from a clearly articulated understanding of their needs and their expectations of their fiduciary's role, and instruction on what is available from corporate fiduciaries and how to find the right one.

No amount of experience with wealthy families or corporate fiduciaries qualifies a family advisor to generalize about the best fiduciary for every family or the most important criteria for a particular family. However, the criteria for a corporate fiduciary that families typically deem important, and what they should expect from corporate fiduciaries, can be learned from experience. Our experience has led us to believe that the seven broad criteria considered by the Passant family represent those that are most important to a majority of families. Each family then must confirm whether all of its important criteria are included among these seven, add any others that seem appropriate, and then determine which criteria reflect its highest priorities.

Our experience has also led us to believe that some types of corporate fiduciaries perform better on some of the criteria than on others. Whether a particular trustee runs true to its type, or even excels within that type, is for a family to investigate and decide with whatever help its advisors—and the trustee candidates themselves— can provide.

DEVELOPING WEALTH MANAGEMENT FIDUCIARY CRITERIA

In the remainder of this chapter, we will flesh out the seven criteria for trustees that were found meaningful not only by the Passant family but also by many others. We will then detail the typical strengths and weaknesses of the three types of wealth management corporate trustees available to families: traditional institutions, private trust companies, and boutique trust companies. (We will also explain why another type, which we dub "product channel trustees," should probably be avoided.) Finally, we will elaborate on the process by which trustee succession decisions can be made confidently, and provide tips for binding your trustee to a performance that fulfills your expectations.

Table 16.1 breaks down, into numerous component parts, the seven broad wealth management fiduciary criteria we have put forth. When reviewing the table, it is important to keep in mind that there is really only one criterion for the family's trustees: they must meet the family's needs. All the other criteria and their components merely represent attempts to identify the ways in which trustees can meet those needs. A family may choose to de-emphasize, or even disregard entirely, any criterion that does not "speak" to that family.

Table 16.1   Key Criteria for Fiduciaries

A. Responsive and Flexible

Networks with third-party providers. Provides choice of trustee's contact personnel. Settlor/beneficiary involvement. Willingness to amend trust instruments.

B. Loyal and Independent

Avoidance of conflicts. Avoidance of sales culture.

C. Multi-Competent

Trust administration. Investment management/alternative investments. Safekeeping/custody. Financial reporting. Tax. Specialized expertise.

D. Efficient; Controls Costs

Controls overhead costs. Provides economies of scale.
Has/Uses leverage with third-party services providers.

E. Convenient and Accessible

Online. Delivers locally useful out-of-state trust/tax laws.

F. Secure and Private: Protects Assets and Family

Quality fiduciary risk management. Capital adequacy.
Adequate regulation/supervision. Privacy culture.

G. Promotes Family's Nonfinancial Objectives

Succession planning. Family member development.
Wealth issues expertise. Facilitates charitable objectives.

Responsive and Flexible   Families are complex; invariably, like the Passants, they develop multiple branches. Also, a family's needs, the economic and social milieus in which it exists, and the offerings of the financial services industry change frequently. Consequently, trustees of trusts intended to fulfill their purposes for generations must be aware of those changing needs and be flexible enough to respond to them, not only over the near term but, hopefully, far into the future as well. This is what the first category of criteria—responsiveness and flexibility—is all about, and it is why families typically place it first.

Today, responsiveness and flexibility are indicated by awareness of families' needs, an ability to customize products and services to meet those needs, and encouragement of family involvement in important trust decisions and the choice of trust officers. Tomorrow, it will still mean being aware of family needs, but it is impossible to predict the financial products and services a trustee will be asked to provide to meet those needs. Therefore, a viable trustee candidate must be able to explain convincingly why it will be able and willing to respond to changing needs and opportunities as they arise in the future.

Loyal and Independent   The second criterion is equally important to most families. Being loyal and independent means putting the family's needs first. This requires acting as the family's advocate, not as its arm's-length purveyor. More specifically, it means "buying" for trusts only what they need and, if possible, the best of what is needed, rather than "selling" to the trusts only the trustee's own products or those of third parties that are most profitable.

The need for and the desirability of a loyal and independent trustee are obvious. But, ironically and unfortunately, wealthy families, like other trust customers, are often seduced by cost considerations to forgo these vital qualities in their corporate trustees. That fate can be avoided by a sophisticated customer of trust services, but, to become a sophisticated customer, some insight into the history of corporate trusteeship will be helpful.

Historically, banks and trust companies have provided all the services of trust administration, other than investment management, for fees that were below their cost of providing those services. The not-wholly-unintended result of this approach to trust marketing has been a subsidy that must be repaid through the other services provided—notably, investment management. This historic pattern continues today at many institutions, even when the trustee does not itself provide the investment management. The low fees quoted and paid for trust administration must be made up through investment services, whether those services are provided directly by the trustee or through affiliates or third parties.

Clients who pay less than cost-plus-a-reasonable-return for trust administration may think they have struck a good bargain, but losses must—and will be—made up through investment management fees or, perhaps, through brokerage services or other financial products provided to the trust. In such an arrangement, the trustee can only break even—let alone become profitable—by selling other products and services to the customer. Its loyalty and independence can be undermined, and it may turn into a sharp seller to the trust instead of an astute buyer for it.

Sophisticated trust customers, recognizing this dynamic, not only want trust administration, investment management, and the other elements of trust services unbundled (separately offered and priced); they also want to pay a fair price for trust administration. This eliminates the need, if not the entire incentive, for the trustee to put its own interests first when providing or buying products and services for that trust. Hallmarks of independent trustees, then, are not only their willingness to unbundle all their products and services but also their insistence on a fair and reasonable fee for accepting the significant burdens and responsibilities of acting as trustees. The hallmark of the sophisticated trust client is that he or she willingly pays a fair and reasonable price for trust administration.

Our emphasis on these criteria for trustees—flexibility and responsiveness; loyalty and independence—is not to slight any others, such as: convenience, efficiency and cost control; security of family assets and privacy; and breadth and depth of product and services offerings (whether provided internally or through third parties). No trustee will qualify as even an "adequate" trustee if the scores for any of these criteria are poor. However, performing well in the first two areas tends to distinguish an excellent trustee from a merely good one.

The Importance of the Trustee's Own Product Offerings—A Reassessment   This criterion, the breadth and depth of product and services offerings, requires further mention. Sometimes, when selecting a trustee, undue emphasis is placed on its internally provided financial products. These should not be disregarded, but a sophisticated buyer of financial services will realize that at least three disadvantages may be associated with a trust company business plan that emphasizes internally provided products over those obtainable from networking with third-party providers:

1. Such emphasis may stem from incentives to prefer the company's profits over the client's interests.
2. No company, however large, can internally provide every product required by wealthy families today, or be a leading provider of even most of the products such families require.
3. Financial institutions are far less reluctant to change third-party providers as clients' needs and financial markets change, than to abandon a faltering, or obsolete, internally provided product.

Business plans that emphasize internally provided products are more often associated with traditional institutional trustees than with private or boutique trust companies. At a minimum, a sophisticated client should look for a range of product offerings that balance high-quality internally and externally provided financial products, and a trustee who is equally willing to provide a third party's products or its own products, particularly when third-party offerings provide a performance or cost advantage for the trust customer.

Should Nonfinancial Objectives Be a Factor?   For most families, wealth management is not just about maintaining and enhancing wealth or using it for the necessities of life and for such luxuries as a family member may consider consistent with his or her means. A family's concern with other uses of wealth is often reflected in a mission statement, which may deconstruct as the goal of "assisting every family member in reaching his or her potential in life." A trustee can either aid or impede the accomplishment of a family's mission.

Many families will also want their trustee to be sensitive to: their charitable leanings and goals, both as a family and as individuals; their desire to keep in the family certain assets, such as commercial enterprises or the family's manor or ranch; or their goal of promoting individual development through formal education or, equally important, life experiences.

For many families, the difference between a "great" trustee and an excellent one will be whether the trustee scores well on this final criterion and not just on the other six.

DOES THE IDEAL TRUST COMPANY EXIST?

Perhaps you are saying, "This is all very well, but isn't the unavailability of trustees who meet all these criteria—and have a fair chance of continuing to do so in the future—driving wealthy families, who can afford to do so, to form their own private trust companies?" Well, yes—and no.

Yes. Many families have become dissatisfied with the offerings that seem to be available to them from corporate trustees, and they prefer to form their own trust companies rather than to hire a private trust company or a boutique wealth management trust company. But having its own private trust company is not right for every wealthy family. It requires not only an extraordinary level of wealth, but also an extraordinary level of commitment and personal involvement, by at least some family members, to the business of wealth management. Not every family has members able and willing to shoulder those burdens, and it can be even more difficult (socially, if not legally) to walk away from a family-owned trust company that is not meeting a family's or a family branch's needs than from an unrelated trustee.

And, no. There are excellent alternatives for families that do not qualify or prefer to have their own private trust company. The key to finding an excellent corporate trustee is to commit to a trustee succession process such as the one that was completed by the Passant family. And the keys to that process, again, are: a full and clear understanding of the family's needs and its expectations regarding its trustees; the ranking of trustee criteria consistently with those needs and expectations; and the rigorous application of those criteria to the available trustees.

Trustee Strengths and Weaknesses, by Type   To help narrow the search to include only the types of trustees most likely to exhibit the characteristics sought by a family, it is useful to consider the strengths and weaknesses typically exhibited by the various types of corporate trustees that provide wealth management fiduciary services. These again are: the traditional institutional trustees, multifamily private trust companies, and the similar boutique wealth management trust companies. Our view of their strengths and weaknesses within the seven criteria we have been considering are set forth in Table 16.2.

When reviewing this table, it is important to keep in mind that our assessments of various types of trustees involve *classes,* not specific trustees. Individual trust companies within each class can and

Table 16.2   Perceptions of Fiduciaries by Type

Fiduciary Needs/Wants	Individual Trustee	Institutional Trustee	Multifamily Private Trust Company	Boutique Trust Company
Responsive and Flexible	🏛🏛	🏛 ~ 🏛🏛	🏛🏛 ~ 🏛🏛🏛	🏛🏛 ~ 🏛🏛🏛
Loyal and Independent	🏛🏛🏛	🏛 ~ 🏛🏛	🏛🏛 ~ 🏛🏛🏛	🏛 ~ 🏛🏛🏛
Multi-Competent	🏛	🏛🏛 ~ 🏛🏛🏛	🏛🏛 ~ 🏛🏛🏛	🏛🏛 ~ 🏛🏛🏛
Efficient and Controls Costs	🏛 ~ 🏛🏛	🏛 ~ 🏛🏛	🏛🏛 ~ 🏛🏛🏛	🏛 ~ 🏛🏛🏛
Convenient and Accessible	🏛 ~ 🏛🏛	🏛 ~ 🏛🏛🏛	🏛 ~ 🏛🏛🏛	🏛 ~ 🏛🏛🏛
Secure and Private	🏛	🏛🏛🏛	🏛🏛 ~ 🏛🏛🏛	🏛🏛 ~ 🏛🏛🏛
Promotes Family Objectives	🏛🏛🏛	🏛	🏛🏛🏛	🏛🏛 ~ 🏛🏛
Average Score	1.9 🏛's	1.9 🏛's	2.5 🏛's	2.3 🏛's

do significantly vary, for good or ill, in their performance. Conse-quently, generalizations may be useful to narrow the list of candidate trust companies, but until the criteria are carefully applied to a spe-cific company, it cannot be told whether that company outperforms or underperforms its peers or will meet a family's needs.

Individuals as Trustees   Table 16.2 also considers how individu-als score on our seven criteria. As the table suggests, in addition to their limited life spans, individuals typically have some weaknesses that are not found in corporate trustees. These weaknesses, combined with the increasing difficulty families experience over time in finding individuals who will serve as trustees and will meet all of their sub-jective and objective criteria, often spur a family to search for a cor-porate successor trustee.

Institutional Trustees   In our experience, a second main spur to commencing a search for a new trustee is dissatisfaction with an ex-isting institutional trustee. Many of the reasons for such dissatisfac-tion are suggested in Table 16.2. But, as the table also shows, there is a great range in performance by institutional trustees under most of the criteria. A particular institution may well perform better on one or more criteria than its peers or even than all the other trust companies considered by a family.

A particular strength of traditional institutional trustees is their strong capital bases, which are suited to the requirements of any trust instrument. Also, traditional institutional trustees are often strong in product and services offerings (such as providing an international network), in providing security for financial assets, and in trust administration expertise. They also have great potential to deliver economies of scale to their large client bases; many have offices convenient to client families whose members are dispersed through many states; and many can offer trusts sited in states with advantageous trust or tax laws. But, in practice, many institutional trustees do not pass along the cost savings from their economies of scale, nor do they promote conservative but sensible tax and fiduciary strategies that take advantage of the trust laws of states such as Delaware or the tax laws of states without trust income taxes.

The benefits from an institutional trustee's broad product offerings, and from its trust and financial services expertise, are sometimes overwhelmed by the impact, on families, of a particular institution's inflexibility, unresponsiveness, or lack of independence. Inflexibility and lack of independence can be manifested by an unwillingness to unbundle investment management from trust administration or, even though unbundled, by a replacement of the trust institution's historical "client relationship" culture with the now more fashionable "sales" culture. As a result, the company's and its preferred providers' products may be oversold to trust clients. In the area of nonfinancial needs of clients, institutional trustees' efforts often are limited to seminars for family members and other educational offerings that have not been customized to meet the needs and interests of particular clients.

Private and Boutique Trust Companies Taking each as a class, multifamily private trust companies and boutique wealth management trust companies have some significant strengths. Again, these strengths are not shared by every member of either class of trustee.

Such companies almost invariably take a "best of breed" approach to the investment managers and other financial products providers they make available to clients, instead of attempting to provide most investment management or financial products themselves. This is one of the reasons they tend to have relatively small back-office staffs and low overhead expenses to pass on to clients. This also results in greater flexibility in product offerings. When performance flags, outside managers can be more readily abandoned than employee managers. When financial products are found less effective than had been touted, it is easier to replace an outside provider's products than those the trustee provides itself.

Multifamily private and boutique trust companies are in a superior position (compared to single-family private trust companies and individuals) to achieve economies of scale because they generally have a larger client/asset base over which to spread their fixed costs. Because of their typically low overhead, economies of scale are more likely to be passed on to clients as cost savings by independent trust companies than by institutional trustees.

Independent trust companies usually seek to offset not offering expensive expertise in-house for every financial product needed by clients by offering strong networks of independent financial products providers and consultants. By not bundling investment management with trust administration (unless desired by the client) and by generally not providing investment management and financial products in-house, they may limit their need or desire to make up for low-margin services through the investment services sold to trust clients.

Because these companies tend to limit themselves to serving wealthy families, they clearly have an exclusive focus on—and perhaps greater familiarity with—the needs of wealthy clientele than would a company that also provides retail trust and investment services and products. Also, as private and boutique trust companies grow in size and sophistication, they are increasingly adding offices in states that provide advantageous fiduciary and tax laws and effectively promoting those advantages to clients who can benefit from them.

A significant disadvantage of most of these relatively small trust companies, however, is their lower capital as compared to institutional trust companies. Consequently, some "legacy" trusts require successor trustees with capital levels that exceed those of many private and boutique trust companies. If such a trust cannot be amended, a company without requisite capital must be eliminated from consideration.

All of the private and boutique trust companies considered here are regulated by state or federal regulators and therefore must have strong risk management and adequate capital. On the other hand, they may be less likely to be excessively conservative than traditional trust institutions, when they respond to clients' requests for assistance in solving their problems. For instance, in our experience, they are far more likely to be willing to assist a family in amending trusts to meet its evolving needs.

Product Channel Trustees   As we suggested earlier, there is one type of trust company that wealthy families may want to view with circumspection and perhaps even avoid. We call these companies "product

channel trustees" because they were formed more as marketing channels for an affiliate's financial services products than as a platform for
providing top-drawer trust services. At first blush, they may look like
boutique trust companies, but they can be recognized by a pronounced
tendency to low-ball trust services in order to sell their financial products; an unwillingness to unbundle trust administration unless they
(or an affiliate) provide a substantial portion of the investment management; and, in general, an emphasis on selling financial products
over personalized trust services. They often have a large retail trust
business. Obviously, such companies tend to perform poorly on the
vital criteria of loyalty and independence.

Boutique trust companies, in contrast to product channel trustees,
have a clear focus on providing quality trust administration and objective investment advice. A boutique company may also be affiliated
with an investment services provider, but it will not favor its affiliates'
products over others' unless they are objectively superior in performance, price, or suitability to client needs.

A SIX-STEP TRUSTEE SELECTION PROCESS

The trustee selection process diligently and successfully pursued by
the Passant family is summarized in this chapter's "Words to the Wise"
section. As we have seen, the first three steps in the process are introspective: (1) identifying the family's circumstances and goals, (2) examining its fiduciary services needs, and (3) determining its key
criteria for its trustees. These are the most difficult and most rewarding steps, for in choosing the right trustee, as in life's other arenas,
knowing who you are and what you want is better than half the battle.
The final three steps in the process are the most easily completed not
only because they consist of objective analysis rather than soul searching, but also because the information required by these steps is readily available from legal and financial advisors and from the trustee
candidates themselves.

Two critical elements of the selection process warrant a final word.
First, to realize maximum value, the family must decide at the outset
if it is at least unified enough to pursue this process jointly and to try
to meet collective and individual needs through a shared trustee. If
not, the process will still prove invaluable, but the result may be the selection of multiple trustees for family branches rather than one for at
least the major trusts.

Second, after deciding to embark on a joint process, the family must commit substantial time and resources to it. Trade-offs can be made between family members' time and the use of the family office or other nonfamily resources, but, ultimately, to get it right, family representatives of all adult generations and all branches must devote time and effort to both the introspective part of the process and the selection of the trustee(s) from among the final candidates. As with the Passant family, substantial levels of communication among family members will be necessary to complete the process successfully.

THE FAMILY FIDUCIARY CONTRACT

Even after it selects a corporate trustee, the family's task is not quite complete. The trustee must still be "bound" to the family's vision and expectations for its fiduciary services provider. This is largely accomplished by picking a trustee who shares that vision and those expectations in the first place, but more can and should be done. After the trustee is chosen, the process usually ends by having the trustee accept the family trusts and adding the family's signature(s) to whatever forms the trustee presents regarding its fees. This means, though, that the trustee's only legal obligation to the family will be to meet the minimum requirements of fiduciary responsibility set by laws and trust instruments. Even the least qualified of the trustee candidates considered by the family was prepared to undertake, and probably was competent to perform, this minimum obligation.

One may well ask: Where, in this scheme of things, is the obligation of the new trustee to provide the attentive level of service that it marketed to the family? Where is the obligation to communicate with the family in extraordinary detail regarding investment performance, and to learn of and respond to evolving family needs? Where is the obligation to make available the most current financial products and technologies? Finally, where does the trustee agree to relinquish amicably the reins of the trusts in the future if that is the desire of the family?

All of these, and any other expectations of the family of the trustee that are consistent with law and trust instruments, can be incorporated into a "Family Fiduciary Contract" between the family and the trustee, confirming the trustee's performance promises and the family's expectations. After all the work of finding the right trustee, it would be a pity if the result was not as expected merely because the mutual understandings of the family and the trustee were not reduced to writing at the outset of the relationship.

Now the job is complete. The family that carefully pursued this trustee selection and binding process has not been guaranteed an ideal trustee relationship or assured that an excellent initial relationship will not someday sour. But that family will have dramatically improved its odds for a long-lasting partnership with an excellent fiduciary.

Words to the Wise

The trustee selection process has six steps. The first three consist of family introspection.

- **Step One.** The family identifies: its decision-making style, mission, objectives, and strategies; the wealth that will be managed and distributed by fiduciaries; and where family members and their assets are located.

- **Step Two.** The fiduciary services needed by the family for existing and planned trusts are identified, as are nontrust assets requiring investment advice and management, and the need for fiduciary services such as global custody, guardianships, and charitable-giving support.

- **Step Three.** The family determines and prioritizes its key criteria for its trustees, using the seven categories the chapter discusses and any others the family cares about.

In the last three steps, the family applies these insights to an objective analysis of trustees.

- **Step Four.** The family confirms the "universe" of trustees available for its needs: individuals, traditional institutions, private trust companies, and boutique wealth management trust companies.

- **Step Five.** A comparison of available trustees, using the family's own criteria, allows the family to focus on the most promising types and candidates.

- **Step Six.** The trustee candidates are analyzed for their match to the family's criteria, and the final selection is made.

————————————— **John P. C. Duncan, Esq.** —————————————

John P. C. Duncan is the founder of Duncan Associates, LLC, a Chicago law firm with a nationwide clientele. The firm concentrates on the representation of private, boutique, and traditional trust companies; family offices; and other wealth management companies. Mr. Duncan has formed or is in the process of forming more than 25 trust companies in eight states, and he lectures and writes regularly on wealth management topics. He is the author of the CSBS State Trust Company and Trust Modernization Act, *the model for trust company acts adopted by about a third of the states.*

PART THREE

Private Lives

Without a doubt, wealth is a responsibility. However, wealth opens up innumerable possibilities for enhancing your life. It allows you to extend the reach and depth of the activities you pursue for both enjoyment and purpose.

A prime example is Roy Neuberger's life story (see Chapter 4). As a young man, Roy went to Paris with dreams of becoming an artist. He soon realized that his talents as a painter didn't match his dream, but he never lost his love of art. When Roy first started working on Wall Street, he would regularly visit galleries and museums after work. When his amazing financial management talents brought him monetary rewards, he started buying the paintings of many new artists that caught his eye and his heart. Today, Roy has amassed an outstanding collection that chronicles the immensely rich and varied history of twentieth-century art. Roy used his wealth to honor his dream, to receive great enjoyment from it, and to establish a significant museum of contemporary art.

His purpose and enjoyment were united—to everyone's benefit.

Collecting offers innumerable ways to unite purpose and enjoyment. The key is to collect what captivates you. Kathleen Doyle's chapter on collecting gives a variety of examples of collectors and their collections, but they all share a critical element: they took delight in what they collected, and that delight shows through in the knowledge and quality of their collections.

An especially adventurous area in which to collect is contemporary art. We tend to think of *our* contemporary art scene as

more confounding and difficult to know than any other historical period. But that has often been the case. Paris, in the 1860s,
was outraged by the new Impressionists. Picasso shocked the art
world in the early twentieth century, as did Jackson Pollock and
others as the century progressed. But, at each step, there were
collectors who were there to support, encourage, and keep art
alive. Michael Danoff's chapter offers worthwhile and practical
advice on how to approach collecting contemporary art. Again,
one of the basic, critical ingredients is your own enthusiasm—
your enjoyment.

Enjoyment of your wealth can also provide a practical purpose. Although a discussion of real estate for investment purposes
appears in Part Two of the book, vacation homes are included in
this section within the context of "practical luxuries." Items such
as vacation homes, jets, and yachts can serve multiple functions.
Milton Ferrell's chapter about these practical luxuries offers pertinent information about the tax deductions involved, the legal
issues to keep in mind, and—in the case of private jets—the benefits of greater privacy, security, and ease of travel.

With our world becoming increasingly unsafe, sophisticated
security—for you, your family, and your possessions—should be
considered a luxury you cannot afford to do without. The Internet's ability to provide immense amounts of information about
anyone also means that criminals can more easily discover people
to target. You no longer need to be famous or prominent in the
Fortune 500 world; your wealth alone can attract unwanted attention, and today's general concerns for the safety of your children didn't significantly exist 10 or 20 years ago. The book's final
chapter discusses many aspects of security—from fundamental
safety precautions for your home to important advice for corporate executives who travel internationally.

How wealth affects your life is up to you. You can let it take
over. You can let it rule you. Or you can harness the freedom,
power, and potential that wealth offers by keeping it as a function of your life, not the reason for your life.

Wealth can help you achieve many satisfying goals if you can
judiciously balance the pull of the opposites. We have addressed
emotions and objectivity; risk and trust; enjoyment and purpose.

Resist turning wealth into emotional currency. Find an investment management approach that makes you comfortable, not anxious. Use wealth to enrich your spirit. A tremendous feeling of peace and satisfaction accompanies the stewardship of wealth. And, of course, there is satisfaction in helping those you love achieve their happiness as well.

Having wealth is great. Living happily and wisely with wealth is far better.

17

THE JOY OF COLLECTING

From Simple Pleasures to Rare Treasures

KATHLEEN M. DOYLE

The year was 1964, and Ralph Esmerian was in his twenties. He had graduated from Princeton University two years earlier and had been living in Greece, teaching on a Ford Foundation fellowship. As he traveled around the country, he picked up ancient shards of pottery—tangible connections to an ancient world in which people took a handful of earth and turned it into a useful, decorative object.

Nearly four decades later, when Ralph spoke at Doyle New York's Connoisseurship lecture series, he explained how that early experience with relics of another culture led him to start what would become one of the finest collections of American folk art in private hands.

Soon after he returned from Greece, Ralph was buying a gift at a New York folk art gallery, and he noticed a small reddish-brown Pennsylvania German plate. He turned it over, saw the rough unglazed underside, and thought, "Here's the earth again!" He bought the little plate, and it stirred him enough so that he began looking for other examples of American folk art that reflected the same sensibility.

Ralph's background prepared him to recognize quality, but the objects he grew up with were almost the opposite of those he began to collect. He is a fourth-generation dealer in fine gemstones, and he was brought up in New York, surrounded by eighteenth-century French furniture, paintings, and objects. Yet, as I have learned from 40 years in the auction business, great collections in any category share certain characteristics: quality, rarity, condition, provenance, and context. Collectors are similar in important ways, too: they are passionate, they assemble items that reflect a distinctive taste, and they are usually interested in the people and culture behind the objects.

The first step for an aspiring collector is to become educated in the field. After the plate aroused Ralph's interest, he began to read books and catalogs, visit museums, and seek out dealers who were known for their ethics and expertise. Nearly all serious collectors develop relationships with dealers they trust and who will keep them in mind and seek out special pieces for them. Joe Kindig, Jr., a specialist in Pennsylvania German folk art, became one of the dealers Ralph Esmerian counted on. When they met, Joe Kindig's crammed shop was deceptively simple, but the best objects are not always found in the most elegant surroundings. Mr. Kindig had helped Henry du Pont form his collection at Winterthur in Delaware, and counseled Abby Aldrich Rockefeller in Williamsburg.

As Ralph Esmerian's connoisseurship and budget increased, his collection came to encompass painted furniture; pottery and sculpture; paintings; *fraktur*, the illuminated documents that are distinctive to the Pennsylvania Germans; and all sorts of other objects that appealed to him—even handwrought hardware. His collection is unmistakably cohesive, but unlike some collectors who aim to acquire an example of each important type of object or artist in a category, his ambitions were never encyclopedic. He simply looked for the best of the pieces that touched him. Increasingly, people who had treasures to sell sought him out. If the piece didn't "speak" to him, he didn't buy it.

In 1984, he made one of his great purchases. He paid a record $1 million for a portrait, "Girl in Red Dress with Cat and Dog" by Ammi Phillips. He had become president of the American Folk Art Museum, and he generously turned the painting over to the museum. Then, in 2001, he made the stunning gesture of donating 400 of his most important pieces to the Folk Art Museum. The museum celebrated the opening of its new building by exhibiting the collection, which is also the subject of a book, *American Radiance: The Ralph Esmerian Gift,* published by Harry Abrams.

Ralph Esmerian's story is one model of the way an important collector evolves. Generosity is often the ultimate step. "Collecting can be selfish," Ralph says. "You've been good to yourself, and there comes a time when you have to give it back into a community."

ASKING QUESTIONS

Whatever the category or reason for collecting, in order to be informed, a collector will ask:

- What is it?
- How do you define the terms that apply to your category?
- How is value determined?
- Is it in good condition?
- What is its history—where did it come from, and where has it been?
- How old is it?
- Is it unique or rare; how many are there like it?
- Is it "good, better, best"? Is this a good example? Is there a better one? Is this the best example available?

THE COLLECTING PERSONALITY

Just as no two collections are alike, people have different motivations for collecting. Some, like Ralph, are profoundly moved by a certain kind of object, period, or style. Others are interested in building value, or furnishing a home. And some people are born accumulators. My husband, William Doyle, who founded our auction house, was one of those.

Bill was eight years old when he started pulling his little red wagon around his neighborhood in Newton, Massachusetts, collecting newspapers and tin cans to sell to the local junk dealer. His family was well off; his father ran a successful business and his mother had graduated from Radcliffe College and had her master's degree in English. She cringed at the thought of her little boy running a second-hand business, but that was the way he began. By the time he was in high school, he was going into Boston to talk to antique dealers about the fine points of American furniture.

After college, he came to New York and worked as a banker. On the weekends, he would rent a truck, drive up to New England, and fill it with antiques. On Sunday nights, he sold his finds from the back of the truck to dealers in New York. Inevitably, he had to choose between banking and the antiques business. In 1962, he opened a store in Manhattan. He held American furniture auctions in East Hampton, Long Island, beginning in the summer of 1968, and then opened William Doyle Galleries in 1972.

We were married in 1969, and I worked with him, learned from him, and studied at the New York School of Interior Design. I had a particular interest in jewelry, and after I took courses at the Gemological Institute of America (GIA) in gem identification and diamond valuation, I became head of our jewelry department. To train my eye, I looked at everything. We lived half a block from the Metropolitan Museum of Art, and, in the early 1970s, the museum was nearly empty. You could wheel a baby carriage through the halls, and our children practically grew up there. We spent hours exploring every room. The more you see, the more you absorb, until, after a while, you can distinguish quality. It was fortunate that I understood and loved the business; after Bill died in 1993, I became chairman of William Doyle Galleries.

When Bill collected for himself, he found a category that interested him, learned everything about it, and collected avidly. For a while, he was interested in American mechanical banks; they appealed to his sense of whimsy and his pleasure in the hunt. When the original molds turned up and new banks were made and "aged" by burying them and distressing the paint, it became increasingly difficult for even sophisticated collectors to tell the difference between the old and the new ones. Scarcity plays an important role in an object's worth and in the enjoyment of collecting. When the reproductions clouded the value, Bill stopped collecting the banks.

He began to assemble a collection of old Russian enamel, but again, reproductions were introduced and he sold his collection before the newer examples flooded the market. The same was true of Giacometti lamps and furniture. Giacometti was widely copied and it became increasingly difficult to identify authentic pieces, so the value of the originals was greatly reduced.

Bill's collecting was varied and often unexpected; other collectors are attracted to categories that grow out of important aspects of their lives. Peter A. B. Widener III, whose family donated the Widener Library at Harvard University, collected fine and often early editions of books, principally on sporting subjects. The Widener family has been prominent in racing circles since the nineteenth century; Peter's grandfather founded the racetrack at Hialeah, Florida, and he inherited a premier thoroughbred horse farm, owned large horse and cattle ranches, and was an avid fisherman and bird hunter. His rare book collection reflected his interests, and it was both consistent and deep. When Doyle New York sold his library in May 2000, the value of individual books was enhanced by the strength of the collection as a whole.

FURNISHING A HOME

When a collector is furnishing a home, the choices take into account lifestyle and the environment in which objects in different categories must complement each other. In 2001, Doyle New York sold the collection of Marguerite Dorment, whose original intention had been to furnish her homes in Manhattan, New Jersey, and Palm Beach, Florida. Mrs. Dorment began buying in the early 1940s when she traveled with her husband. She was drawn to eighteenth-century French furniture, Chinese Export porcelain, and paintings. When she developed an educated interest in Chinese Export porcelain, she became friendly with dealers who sought the rarest and most exquisite examples for her. She insisted that every object be in perfect condition, and although the Dorments had many children and grandchildren, she maintained the pieces in pristine condition.

Porcelain's value is judged by age, rarity, condition, the number of related pieces, and whether an object is part of a large set or stands alone. Among the items that were particularly coveted when she decided to sell her collection were a Famille Rose and Gilt "Enfants Charmants" tureen, cover, and stand, circa 1750, named for its design of two children by a rose hedge. Our Asian art specialist found that the design was unrecorded and possibly unique and the high realized price reflected its uniqueness. A pair of nineteenth-century Famille Rose/Verte owls also brought a high price because the owl model was so scarce. And a late Quianlong period (1736–1795) Famille Rose sauce tureen and cover in the form of a purple-breasted duck was exceptionally valuable because it is unusual to find purple enamel.

Certain periods in the history of porcelain are more important than others, even though only a well-trained eye may be able to tell the difference. Tobacco Leaf has been a popular Chinese Export porcelain pattern since it was introduced in the 1770s, but the early examples are considered of better quality and are more valuable than the later ones. Mrs. Dorment's pieces mostly were made during the first decade of production, and she preferred unusual shapes and designs. The date, the rare shapes, and the quantity of Tobacco Leaf porcelain she owned all added to the value.

When her entire collection—furniture, objects, paintings, and porcelain—was displayed together in the exhibition and the catalog, it reflected a sense of her grace and refined taste. The context complemented each individual piece.

Ralph Esmerian started by accident. Bill Doyle loved the process of finding things, learning about them, and acquiring them. Peter Widener III was drawn to his collection by his professional life in the horse and cattle worlds and his sporting avocations. Marguerite Dorment chose beautiful objects that created graceful homes. But all of them were attracted to certain categories. They learned more about each particular category, and along with their knowledge, they acquired pieces that were increasingly rare and valuable.

WHAT ADDS VALUE?

When considering value, the most frequently asked question for an inexperienced collector—"Is it real?"—can have many answers. "Real" can refer to the date a piece was made, and whether it is in original condition or has been changed or repaired. Even antiques can be copies of earlier pieces. Is a 200-year-old American chair "in the style of Chippendale" real, or are the only "real" Chippendale chairs those made by Thomas Chippendale and his workshop in late eighteenth-century England? To be real, does a piece have to be original, without any repairs? What does "Chippendale" mean to professionals?

There are stars in every category: furniture designers, porcelain makers, artists, and jewelry designers. Sometimes the star is an individual, sometimes it is a company. Either way, signed pieces—especially furniture—are nearly always more valuable than those that are unsigned. The finest examples of American furniture are from Massachusetts, Philadelphia, Rhode Island, and Baltimore. One chair signed by a great maker can cost more than $1 million. There is nothing more "authentic" than an original Thomas Chippendale chair; yet an American Chippendale version can command a higher price because it is rarer. What a collector can afford to buy is a big factor in collecting. If a chest by the eighteenth-century Newport, Rhode Island, furniture maker Townsend Goddard is out of range, the collector who knows what a Goddard chest looks like can try to find something close to it in style. At our Fine Furniture and Decoration auctions, we offer examples that are "made in the style of" to distinguish them from period pieces in our other auctions.

The importance of condition varies from one category to the next. In American objects and furniture, there is a premium on original, rather than perfect, condition. A weathervane might show the effects of having been exposed to the elements for centuries, but there may be very few similar examples. It might have been hanging over a historic church for a couple of hundred years, where many people saw and loved it. Perhaps it was the model for a particular design, and although others have been made since, the first one will have greater value, even if it is more battered than the later examples. Or perhaps it is unique, a product of the imagination of a local craftsman. By contrast, in eighteenth-century French furniture, a commode or console will be more valuable if it is in excellent condition.

The importance of workmanship and attribution can transcend materials, even in jewelry. In the 1930s, stones were often synthetic; an informed buyer knows why a bracelet with synthetic sapphires—but exquisite workmanship or a design by an important jeweler—might be worth as much as another piece with natural stones. In the 1950s, Chanel designed marvelous costume jewelry. It is not currently being reproduced because the skilled workmen are not available. If something is no longer being made, that adds value.

Among the elements that affect what someone will pay for an object, the most difficult element to quantify is *provenance*—the history of who has owned a piece previously—which can add immeasurably to the perception of an object's value. Owning something that has been a part of history or has belonged to a person of historical interest—or something that the collector can imagine in an exceptional setting—has an appeal all its own. When we sold the equipment from the kitchen of the internationally known chef and author James Beard, items like a copper pot that would bring a few hundred dollars if it had come from anyone else's house took on an aura beyond price, and sold for considerably more. For someone who loves to cook, there is magic in following a recipe from a James Beard cookbook, using one of his sauciers.

Another collection that gained value from its provenance belonged to Lady Sarah Consuelo Spencer-Churchill, a sister of the eleventh Duke of Marlborough and a cousin of Sir Winston Churchill. Her grandmother, Consuelo Vanderbilt, married the ninth Duke of Marlborough in one of the most famously unfortunate marriages of the Gilded Age. (They divorced and she was later happily remarried to Jacques Balsan.) Lady Sarah had inherited much of what she owned, and her glamorous background gave her possessions a distinct mystique. Many of the pieces had come from Madame Balsan's house in Paris, which her father, William K. Vanderbilt, an important late-nineteenth-century collector, had helped furnish. There were chairs that royalty had sat in, and that had witnessed the dramatic unraveling of the Marlboroughs' highly publicized match. It was easy to imagine that Sir Winston Churchill had written a letter at a certain table, or that Edward VII had glimpsed his reflection in a particular mirror. The quality of some pieces of furniture also added to their value; Lady Sarah owned signed examples from some of the great furniture makers. The pieces' condition varied; it was evident that they had traveled and been used, but provenance compensated for scratches and nicks.

Even when a collector is buying out of love for a style or period, rather than strictly as an investment, it is critical to understand the current state of the market and its influence on availability and price. The economy affects price, but so do decorating trends. When the English Country House look was wildly popular, Staffordshire china dogs flew out of the auction galleries at enormous prices. Now, that style of decorating is not as "trendy," and Staffordshire dogs are available again, at reasonable prices. Oriental carpets are currently undervalued, partly because they are not generally in style right now, but also because most people can only buy just so many, and if they are not being used, they are extremely difficult to display. But, as always, there are exceptions. We recently sold a custom-made Axminister carpet of unusual dimensions and in perfect condition, which attracted clients from all over the world and brought a huge price at auction.

Changes in lifestyles can enhance or decrease value. Currently, fine silver can be bought very reasonably at auction. Not many people serve formal afternoon tea with elaborate silver tea services, so extraordinary silver services come up at affordable prices. However, Europeans still serve tea, and a bidder may be competing with European dealers, who will drive up the prices. Although silver is a good category to collect because so much is available at such good prices, there are exceptions: Georgian and Early American silver—in particular, anything made by great silversmiths like Paul Revere or Paul Storr— continues to appreciate. Georg Jensen pieces have become trendy and expensive because Hollywood celebrities are collecting them, often to complement Arts and Crafts furniture and objects. That is an indication of how the popularity of one category can affect another. Hollywood and celebrity affect price in unexpected ways. When Renee Zellwegger wore a gown to the Academy Awards that was bought at our couture sale, she was cited in *People* magazine as one of the 10 best-dressed actresses, and that encouraged other people to buy vintage couture clothes.

Value is not always immediately apparent; research can broaden and enhance the market for an object or an entire category. We recently offered an Eastman Johnson painting dating around the time of the Civil War. It is a poignant image of a young boy in a Union uniform far too large for him, with a rifle that is also too large; he seems to be wearing the uniform of a fallen older brother or father, testimony to the dwindling resources in the final years of the war.

Six months earlier, a virtually identical Eastman Johnson had been sold by another auction house; that sale achieved only moderate success. However, our research showed that the painting we were offering defined a moment in history. The uniform was key; the flowers in the background determined the time of year in which it was painted; when we consulted a Civil War expert, we found that the rifle was not American, which pinpointed a period late in the war, when people were importing weapons from Europe to continue the fight to the bitter end. Putting the detail of the image into perspective helped bring the painting to life, not just for art collectors but for those who are interested in the Civil War. When we sold the painting, it brought ten times the price of the recent sale of the similar example, and we tripled the world auction record for any Eastman Johnson painting.

That was more than a marketing strategy. It was a prime example of one of the most basic elements of collecting: knowledge adds meaning to an object and increases the emotional involvement that characterizes all true collectors.

Words to the Wise

- Decide early whether you want objects to live with, to use, or to display but rarely handle; whether you want to collect in an encyclopedic manner—one of everything in a category— or make your own taste the final criterion, even if it means leaving holes in your collection.

- When evaluating a piece for purchase, carefully consider its condition, history, age, rarity or uniqueness, provenance, and value in relation to similar objects.

- Value is not always immediately apparent. It requires research.

- Educate yourself continually. Train your eye. Consult with experts and dealers you can trust.

- Be aware of the elements that create value in your category, and keep current on the market value of similar objects. The Internet simplifies this process.

- Be patient, but be ready to act quickly when something you love comes on the market at a price you are willing to pay.

- If an object doesn't sing out to you, even if it meets all the criteria for excellence, it is probably better to wait for one that catches hold of your eye and your heart.

——————————————— **Kathleen M. Doyle** ———————————————

Kathleen M. Doyle is Chairman and CEO of Doyle New York, a premier Manhattan-based auction gallery. Founded by her late husband, William Doyle, the gallery auctions prominent collections in such categories as European and American fine furniture, paintings, estate jewelry, and decorative arts. Ms. Doyle worked with her husband at the gallery's founding in 1972. After pursuing other interests for several years, she returned to the auction business 9 years ago and broadened relationships with trust and estate bankers and lawyers who advise their clients on building and valuing collections. She is committed to the gallery's focus on education and furthering connoisseurship in the arts.

18

COLLECTING
CONTEMPORARY ART

Traditional Values, New Meaning

I. MICHAEL DANOFF

The Des Moines Art Center occupies buildings designed by three of the most renowned architects working in the second half of the twentieth century: Eliel Saarinen, I. M. Pei, and Richard Meier. The strengths of the Center's art collection are historically consistent with the architecture, and those buildings contain many internationally known works of art.

While Director and Chief Curator from 1991 to 1997, I maintained a list of "desiderata"—highly desired artists not yet represented in the collection. Private collectors may proceed as they wish when they are deciding what works to purchase. But, as a public institution, a museum that regularly enjoys acquisition funds should have a list of priorities that is annually approved by the acquisition committee.

High on my list, from my first days at the museum, was Gerhard Richter. It was not until early in 2002 that Richter, who lives and works in Germany, had a major museum show in New York. But by the end of the 1980s, Richter had come into his own in Europe and was well on his way to doing so in North America. In 1988, I co-organized a museum retrospective that was seen in Chicago, San Francisco, Toronto, and Washington.

No one knows where an artist of today will be ranked during the centuries ahead. But I believe that by taking the time to look at many works by an artist—exercising substantial comparison and contrast—there is a good chance that the works that are the most successful, the fullest realization of the artist's unique vision, can be identified. In searching for a work by Richter to buy, I saw quite a few paintings that I liked and admired and would gladly have accepted as a gift to the museum—but none on which I wanted to spend the museum's money.

Then an auction catalog crossed my desk and featured a reproduction of a landscape painting that could have been the right work for the museum. The auction was a benefit for a museum in Germany, where the auction was being held. But I couldn't get there for the auction.

In 1994, I got a call from a dealer who knew of my search and said there was a Richter painting for me to see in New York. I flew in, walked into the gallery, and my heart leapt up. (I sometimes think of this as the "Oh, wow!" test.) I had the work switched to a wall where the daylight was different, and I even played with the incandescent light levels. I came back the next day, and the work remained captivating.

Ultimately, it was purchased by the museum for $410,000. I'm sure that is more than the amount it sold for in Germany—it was the work that had been in the benefit auction. But my quest was for quality, not a bargain, and the price was not outrageous. Even if a work is priced somewhat ahead of the market, from time to time one has to accept that fact and go with quality. As it turns out, the value of this painting recently was estimated at approximately $2.5 million. But the real value is the enrichment it has given and, hopefully, will continue to give.

I include this anecdote because it illustrates the approach I use in collecting art. My approach includes familiarity with the artist, a sense of current and potential value, passion for both the work itself and for collecting, and, ultimately, confidence in my purchase decision. As a director of a museum then and of an art program in a corporation now, I collect art professionally, but my methods may prove helpful to anyone who wishes to create an art collection.

People collect art because it adds meaning to their lives. The nature of that meaning varies, but most collectors are exhilarated by the objects they collect and the act of collecting them. Collectors often insist that collecting makes them feel more fully alive. At the heart of the thrill is love for the objects that fascinate them. Like a movie, art can take you out of your seat and transport you to another world.

Many people who embark on a quest to build an art collection sense this excitement, but they realize there is a learning curve. How do you know where to look for art to buy? What considerations are important for the particular work you are considering? How do you learn about the artist and the work? How do you make an offer and close the deal? Here is my approach to these and other fundamental collecting practices.

LEARNING THE WORDLESS LANGUAGE

Art is a language. Until you learn the language, you might draw a blank when you look at art. Once you know the language, however, a work of art takes you inside the world of the human being who made it—and that can be a magical, intoxicating journey across oceans and time. When you walk into a gallery and see a painting by Rembrandt, you get a unique "Rembrandt" feeling because Rembrandt—like all successful artists—learned how to be himself in his art and how to develop a unique visual language.

It doesn't take much to learn the languages of art, although it helps to get rid of any preconceptions of what art is supposed to be. There are no set rules; an artist strives to be herself or himself in the work of art. Whatever medium or style is necessary to realize that creation—canvas, clay, wood, abstract, representational—must supersede any notion of preexisting rules. The end result is: When we are in touch with art, we are in touch with the inner life of the person who created it.

When you are learning about art that is new to you, it can expand your horizons only if you are open to what is being communicated and how the communication is transacted. Works that connect strongly are often the ones that do NOT end up permanently in museum storage. There are no objective criteria for good and bad art; in my view, it is more fruitful to think in terms of which works of art connect best and repay repeated visits. One of the criteria I use is: Does the work of art I'm looking at have its own voice or does it remind me too much of other art—thereby diminishing the uniqueness of its creator? The bottom line: The more you compare and contrast works of art, the more informed your judgment is going to be.

THE CHALLENGES OF CONTEMPORARY ART

Contemporary art—today's art—may appear unfamiliar at first. Artists reflect what they experience, and today's experiences are different from yesterday's; therefore, to varying degrees, today's art will look different from what has come before, and it will be as diverse as the people creating it.

Some people resist learning about contemporary art because they mistakenly assume it requires rejecting earlier ("traditional") art. Quite the contrary; it simply means expanding one's horizons and adding new experiences and pleasures.

It may help to remember that all art was once contemporary. Today's art can be uniquely engaging because it is *our* art. Through it, people in the future will know what it felt like to live in our times.

Contemporary art offers many possibilities for purchase, but history has not sorted out the major artists' names. That's a big part of the excitement of contemporary art: you are very much on your own in making decisions.

LOOKING AND LEARNING

Collecting art demands input on your part: first and foremost, you must look at art. The more you participate—as with learning about wine, tennis, or just about anything else—the more you understand. Immerse yourself in the visual experience. Gain a fluency in the multifaceted world of contemporary art by going to art museums and galleries—the primary places to increase your understanding.

When you visit an exhibition, browse through the catalogs and check the list of lenders. You probably will see the names of galleries that show these artists. That's one way to decide which galleries to visit.

Although buying and selling art is a business, generally those in the art gallery business love art and believe in the talent of the artists whose work they show. First and foremost, gallerists are looking for talent. Consequently, they have done some of the most important sifting for you. Different dealers have different visions of what constitutes excellent art, so make sure to visit a wide range of galleries.

When visiting a gallery, don't be intimidated! No one is going to force you to buy. Look at the art displayed on the walls. Ask about the artists. By all means, ask about prices. Learning about relative cost is an important aspect for any collector.

In addition to galleries, some cities present international contemporary art fairs. Dealers rent booths and display the art they hope to sell. Many art fairs have stringent standards for the galleries that are allowed to participate, so browsing at a fair can be a wonderfully concentrated way to get an overview of contemporary art. Cities that have had such fairs annually include Basel, Berlin, Chicago, Cologne, Madrid, Miami, New York, Paris, and San Francisco. You should be aware, however, that the dealers almost always will want to close any sales during the several-day period scheduled for the fair. Therefore, your time to make a thoughtful decision may be less than desirable, and if you are relatively new to collecting, you may want to concentrate your purchases on artists with whom you already are familiar.

KEY STEPS FOR SMART BUYING

You might feel swept off your feet if you see one work by an artist in a gallery, but before you let your enthusiasm overwhelm you into purchasing it, take a step back and do some in-depth investigation.

In books or art magazines, read enough about the artist's work to gain a sense of where this particular work fits into the artist's output as a whole. Galleries often will provide photocopies of reviews written by critics. Remember that critics can disagree, but their thinking will prod you along as you develop your own judgments.

If the work fascinates you, is it a minor example or a major one? Is it from an early period? If so, has the artist's work matured or changed since then? Is it part of a series? If so, what else is in the series? I might have a strong response to one work, but I always try to see more than one example by the same artist. By immersing yourself in the body of work, you can better understand the "language" of the artist who created it. As you look further, you will begin to make increasingly informed comparisons and contrasts, such as where the work stacks up in relation to others made by the artist, and whether the work of one artist reaches further and digs deeper than the work of another.

What if you are looking at works by emerging artists—works usually created by young artists who are relatively new to the art market? These artists may not have a great body of work, and you may want to wait until you can see more. But if you wait, you might have a difficult time finding available works when you are ready—and the price may have gone up. It's a judgment call—another part of the challenge of collecting.

PRACTICAL CONSIDERATIONS

Now let's tackle some practical aspects of collecting. First, when you decide to dip your toes into the art-buying pool, you should consider the collecting style and focus that best suit you. Do you want to limit your collection to say, color photography, or works only by three particular painters, or do you want to be open-ended? There is no "correct" way. Buy works that make you feel more fully alive.

Second, once you find a work that engages you, double-check your response to it. Look at it on more than one day and at different times of the day. Anything can influence a single viewing—your mood, the lighting (electric or natural), or even your blood-sugar level. Ask to see the work mounted on a different wall in the gallery, or to have the lights turned up, down, or off (assuming there are windows). You might also ask to see the work in your home, although most galleries are unlikely to comply with that request unless they know you.

Third, consider where you will put the work and whether that will be a safe place for it. Your pleasure can turn to aggravation if the work develops problems. Consider, for example, the lighting levels. Colored inks are not permanent, and works on paper are subject to fading from light. At the least, keep them out of direct or bright sunlight (this also applies to color photographs). In most instances, you will want to have the works glazed with ultraviolet-filtering Plexiglas™, which helps protect against fading.

Will the work be easily bumped by humans or pets, or subject to significant changes in temperature and humidity? Office-building energy-saving systems that lower the heat or air conditioning during the evenings and on weekends can create problems. Atmospheric changes that cause expansion and contraction might warp works made from wood, but they can also affect paintings. The paint and the canvas expand and contract at different rates. They will rub against each other, and, eventually, the paint may crack. Ask the dealer to be frank about what the work is made from and whether problems are likely to develop. Some contemporary art is made, all or in part, from unusual materials, and you have a right to ask candidly about their stability.

PRICING AND BUYING

Once you know what you want, how do you get indications that the price is appropriate? It is human to want to feel that you are paying a fair price, but the art market is unpredictable and you should buy a work, first and foremost, because it excites you.

Several factors will have an impact on the price of a work of art. They include: number (one-of-a-kind works have higher values than prints or photographs produced in multiples); medium (some works require expensive raw materials or involve specialized and costly fabrication); size; and the track record of the artist. Well-known artists obviously command a top-dollar price.

Begin by finding out how much the artist's work has sold for recently. A publication like the *Art in America* annual offers lists of dealers in other cities. Call or e-mail some of them and ask what they have by this artist and what prices they have set for works of a comparable medium, size, year of creation, and so forth. You can also investigate auction prices for many artists' works on Internet sites and in libraries.

For emerging artists, exhibitions in one-person museum shows, group museum shows, or the artist's inclusion in private or museum collections will usually increase prices. Generally, if an exhibition features new works by an artist, you can expect an incremental increase since that artist's previous show. The amount of increase depends on factors such as the level of demand since the last show, and recent purchases or exhibitions by museums or notable collectors.

A dealer might try to impress you by saying that an artist's work has entered the collection of a celebrity, but unless the celebrity happens to be a knowledgeable collector, that information is irrelevant. (You might ask a museum official in the celebrity's hometown if the collection is known to include museum-quality works.) Ask the dealer: What was the price range for comparable works in the previous show? Where has the artist exhibited since then? If you are looking at the artist's first solo show, chances are he or she has sold something from a group show or directly from the studio. The dealer should know those prices.

Dealers may be willing to negotiate prices unless a contractual arrangement with the artist prohibits it. Similarly, artists may sell directly if their gallery contract does not preclude such sales. There is no harm in asking the artist, or the gallery, whether a discount is possible; everyone understands that people have budgets.

PRIMARY VERSUS SECONDARY MARKETS

The most recent contemporary art, commonly purchased from galleries or directly from the artists, has pricing issues that differ from those of older works (including older contemporary works and works by artists of previous eras). These works are secured on the secondary market through dealers or auctions. Such works have come back on the market after having been in one or more collections.

If you are buying art on the secondary market it is often more difficult to evaluate the fairness of the asking price; the seller obviously wants the dealer to secure the highest price possible. Do some independent research and ask the dealer to justify the price in relation to comparable works that have sold recently.

If such works are available, you will want to examine the "provenance" or history of their ownership. The dealer can supply this history, and, for works by many well-known artists, the information can be corroborated in specialized publications dedicated to providing information on almost every work by the artist (a "catalogue raisonne"). These publications are generally available in the art libraries of museums or universities. This is especially important for historic art because it pertains to issues of authenticity, price (previous ownership by a celebrated collector or museum can have an impact), and legality.

Notable legal issues could include ownership claims, which are much in the news lately regarding some art looted during World War II. Ownership rights also can be an issue for Native American objects. Certain laws govern export and import from abroad, but these laws rarely apply to previously sold contemporary works.

BUYING AT AUCTION

Many secondary market transactions in art are conducted by auction. The works that are to be sold are on view at the auction house for a specified period of time prior to the auction. Study the work in person and discuss with the departmental expert at the auction house the basis of the estimated price spread. If you cannot bid in person, you may do so by phone. Predetermine your limit and keep it firmly in mind lest you get swept away by the excitement. And remember, there is a buyer's fee (you will be told the amount in advance) and, possibly, a tax.

You also should be aware that a work at auction might not reach the minimum price set by the seller and will then remain unsold. In these instances, the person selling the work might be willing to sell it privately, after the auction, in a transaction brokered by the auction house. To find out, simply call the auction house.

Auction houses occasionally will help you to find a work on the secondary market and arrange the sale as a dealer would. Specialists at auction houses are extremely knowledgeable about who owns what, among private collectors, and they can put that knowledge to work for you.

TIMING A PURCHASE

Two terms you might hear are "buying against the market" and "buying ahead of the market." The first term means buying art that has fallen to below-average market interest, as is reflected in a reduced price. There is little point in using this concept—finding an alleged bargain—as a *primary* reason to make an acquisition. The art market is unpredictable; what happens if the work remains out of favor for the remainder of your life? Then it was no bargain. And if you don't love looking at the work, it does you no good.

"Buying ahead of the market" means buying something that seems more expensive than your research indicates it should be. Unlike "buying against the market," "buying ahead of the market" implies pursuing what you love, despite the price. These situations are judgment calls that involve your disposable income as well as the work itself. You cannot be certain that it will appreciate further in value.

With contemporary art, try to stay focused on the individual work and what you can learn about the artist. Don't worry about whether the artist represents a rising trend. A trend is identified *after* the fact. Often, quite varied works are awkwardly lumped together and critics, collectors, and curators are trying to figure out what is going on. Collect wonderful art, work by work, and don't be swayed by someone else's concept of what constitutes a trend.

USING A CONSULTANT

If you want to be a collector, you must develop your own judgment. You should not rely on a consultant or any third party to replace your own response to art. The consultant should bring works to your attention and offer an opinion if asked—but *you* make the final decision. A consultant also may assist with the purchase price and postpurchase activities such as installation and cataloging. Make sure you see, *in writing,* the consultant's credentials and list of clients. This can be tricky. The person may be highly experienced, may have a minimum of academic training, and may wish to keep his or her client list confidential. Two professional organizations for consultants are NACAM (National Association for Corporate Art Management) and APAA (Association of Professional Art Advisors). Not everyone in the profession joins, but these would be places to start.

If you are purchasing an older work on the secondary market, you might consider having a professional art conservator of your choice examine the work and give you a written report about its physical condition. This is especially critical for very old works, which, by virtue of their age, can have an accumulation of physical problems. Buying on the secondary market can be complicated. You may also wish to pay for outside expertise from someone who has some demonstrated experience with the overall body of a particular artist's work and the market for that artist. (Again, your local museum may help you to contact an outside expert or may recommend a consultant.)

SELLING AND DONATING

Some collectors are proud of never having parted with a single work they purchased, even if they feel that their early purchases were not discerning. Many people view their collections as a history of where they have been physically and emotionally—a reflection of their inner travels over time—so parting with any work is hard. Other collectors feel almost an ethical imperative to refine their collection, hone it, and make it ever better through selling and buying. Still others sell art because they intend to purchase other works of art that are more interesting to them at the moment, or because they need money for personal reasons.

If you are going to sell a work of art, the dealer you bought it from would probably appreciate your offering it back for him or her to sell. Dealers want to further the careers of their artists as much as possible by placing their work in respected collections. They also want to protect the artist's market and sell the work for the highest possible price, which also benefits the seller. In most instances, they will not purchase the work from you; instead, they will sell it on consignment.

Donating is another way to part with a work of art. This is an act of patronage toward the institution receiving the work. Any not-for-profit organization is eligible for a charitable donation, but the artist certainly would most appreciate having his or her work of art find its permanent home in an art museum collection.

Normally, a museum reviews potential gifts with a trustee acquisition committee to determine whether the work advances the mission of the institution and is likely to be exhibited. If display is unlikely, the museum may not accept the gift, out of fairness to the artist and consideration for the cost of housing and caring for it.

The museum will want to issue a deed of gift with "no strings attached," which means the museum may do what it wishes with the work in regard to display and deaccessioning (i.e., removing the work from the collection and from the museum through sales or another transaction). If the donor insists on restrictions regarding, for example, how long the work needs to be on display or where in the museum it must be displayed, the museum is likely to decline. Museums need flexibility to carry out their mission.

When you proffer a work to a museum, and the museum expresses interest, you carry the responsibility for obtaining an appraisal for possible income tax deductions. Appraisals may be done, for a fee, by the Art Dealers Association of America (www.artdealers.org /appraisals.html) or by a certified appraiser or auction house. Check with your tax attorney if you have any assumptions about the consequences of a deduction; gift laws can be complex. In addition to selling or donating, another option is bequeathing. This can involve complicated tax issues, so the bequest should be reviewed by trust officers to make sure you do not inadvertently impose a difficult financial burden on your heirs.

EMBARKING ON A LIFETIME JOURNEY

Collecting art never grows dull. The more you search, investigate, and inform your relationship to art, the more exciting and fulfilling it becomes. It's a training process. You train your eye like a bodybuilder trains his or her body. You can't train your body by watching others work out: you have to pump those weights yourself! You can't train your eye by making decisions based on what others collect: you have to "pump" your own eye.

Words to the Wise

- Develop your own judgment. Don't rely on a consultant or other third party to replace your own response to art.

- The more you compare and contrast works of art, the more informed your judgment is going to be.

- Because the art market is unpredictable, you should buy a work, first and foremost, because it excites you.

- Among the factors that will affect the price of a work of art are number (is it one of a kind?), medium, size, and the track record of the artist.

- Each dealer has a different vision of what qualifies as excellent art, so be sure to visit a wide range of galleries.

- Consider the collecting style and focus that best suit you. Then, find a work that engages you. If possible, make repeat visits and double-check your response to the work.

- Read enough about the artist's works, in books or art magazines, to gain a sense of where this particular work fits into the artist's output as a whole.

—————————— **I. Michael Danoff, Ph.D.** ——————————

I. Michael Danoff is director of the art program at Neuberger Berman. He has had extensive experience developing art collections and has served as director of several art museums specializing in contemporary art—the Des Moines Art Center, Museum of Contemporary Art (Chicago), and San Jose Museum of Art. Mr. Danoff has organized and co-organized many exhibitions, including the first one-person museum shows in the United States of artists such as Georg Baselitz, Peter Halley, Jeff Koons, Gerhard Richter, Ronald Jones, and Cindy Sherman. He has published internationally, held faculty positions at Dickinson College and the University of Texas at Austin, and lectured at the University of Chicago, Stanford University, and numerous art museums.

19

ENJOYING THE GOOD LIFE

Money and Time Well Spent

Milton M. Ferrell, Jr.

A client was recently agonizing over his bid for a private jet valued at around $18 million, an amount he could easily afford. "If my offer is accepted, I'll be miserable because I'll be sure I overpaid," he said. "If my offer is rejected, I'll be miserable and angry because I won't have the plane." I asked him, "Why would anyone sell something below the market price, unless there was something wrong with the product or something wrong with the seller?" To move him past this obstacle, I tried to shift his focus from getting a good deal to thinking about how much he was going to enjoy owning the plane. Once he experienced the convenience, comfort, and opportunities it afforded him, I suggested, he might discover that the value of his happiness exceeded the plane's cost. In the end, he bought the plane and quickly came to consider it one of his best acquisitions.

Too often, a misplaced focus on the *cost* of a luxury item, such as a plane, a vacation home, or a boat, impedes the ability to enjoy and share the blessings of wealth. I believe wealth is a gift and a privilege. Thank God for it. Share it generously. Use the influence it creates for good and fully experience the pleasure that comes from being able to help those you love and live out your dreams. When you can afford it, why not travel in style, on a moment's notice, to places you love to visit? Money commonly becomes a source of conflict or guilt when it should provide comfort and ease. At the point in life when the available money exceeds the available time, I believe the money should be used to enhance the quality of the time. Success in this regard sometimes requires people to change attitudes that may have helped them to get rich. Self-denial may be necessary while making a fortune, but once you are rich, its value in anything other than spiritual terms is debatable.

Wealth is far more likely to disappear through bad investments than through extravagant spending. The best way to preserve a fortune is to let a qualified money manager make prudent investment decisions to preserve your principal. Then you can spend the income without worrying about becoming poor. Planes, vacation homes, and boats are more appropriately viewed as a luxury than an investment, but the items at the highest end of the market are likely to hold their value or appreciate over time. Their purchase represents another level of diversification, one of the most basic tenets of any sound financial strategy.

Some questions to keep in mind when you're considering the purchase of a luxury item include:

- What dreams will this item help me fulfill?
- What new professional and personal opportunities might this item create?
- How will this item enhance the quality of life for those I care for most?
- Do I really want this item?
- What is the item's true cost when compared with the opportunities it will create and its potential for appreciation? (A house in a ski resort area was purchased for $5 million in January 2000 and sold for $7 million two years later. It yielded a much better return than most stock portfolios during the same period.)

These are the important issues that only you can resolve. Your lawyer or accountant can readily assist with key details such as the most advantageous ownership structure, tax implications, and the logistics of purchase and maintenance. A little time and money well spent on the front end of a big purchase can leverage the amount of time available later to enjoy it. After helping many of my clients through both the decision and the transaction phases of buying a plane, home, or boat, I offer the following advice on taking advantage of the opportunities involved.

OWNING YOUR OWN JET

Aircraft owners waste virtually no time on the problems common to commercial passengers: canceled flights, long lines, lost luggage, and travel fatigue. At the same time, their plane helps to increase their productivity, create new business opportunities, build good will, and ensure better security.

For business executives, the advantages of private jets have increased, given the recent security concerns and the cutbacks in commercial service. The National Business Aviation Association (NBAA) estimates that private jet usage grew by a factor of 5.5 between the late 1960s and the late 1990s, when 11,000 companies and organizations were operating 17,000 private jets. No longer is private jet use regarded as a perk reserved solely for the CEO: 86 percent of corporate jet users are now senior and middle managers.

A key benefit of plane ownership is increased productivity. On a company jet, flying time commonly becomes meeting time for briefings and strategy sessions en route and debriefings on the way home. Today's aircraft mirror the comfort and proximity of a deluxe conference room, complete with conventional air-to-ground or satellite phones, fax machines, power for laptops, tables for spreading out large documents, and face-to-face club seating in a private, uninterrupted setting. In addition, much less time is wasted waiting in airports. One study shows that weekly business travelers who use a private jet rather than commercial airlines save up to one month in work time per year. Perhaps it's no coincidence, as the NBAA notes, that among the top 50 Fortune 500 companies, as ranked by returns to shareholders in dividends and capital gains for the past 10 years, 90 percent either own or operate business aircraft.

Owning a plane creates opportunities that you cannot even imagine until you have the experience. Many years ago, when I was considering buying my first photocopier, I remember carefully analyzing the labor and per-page costs involved in having copies made outside the office versus the expense of owning and maintaining the machine. After we bought the machine, we made more copies in three months than we had made in the entire previous year, rendering most of the analysis irrelevant. The same principle holds true for a plane: the sheer convenience of having it at hand will inspire you to use it.

From a business perspective, a plane enables you to rapidly achieve the in-person contact often required to close a deal, demonstrate a service commitment, or resolve a crisis. You can also offer people a luxury ride, complete with leather seats, one-to-one service, refreshments, and privacy, and gain their undivided attention for the length of the flight. Once when I really wanted to speak to a particular corporate executive who didn't own a private jet, I found out where he needed to be and offered to take him in my plane. The six-hour trip there and back turned into a private meeting in a comfortable environment with a delicious lunch, and helped to establish a long-term and mutually beneficial relationship.

You can also offer the plane for customers' or employees' personal use in case of emergencies or coincidental travel plans. Extra passengers cost the plane's owner virtually nothing if the plane is going to be in the air anyway. The reward for allowing others to use the jet is often long-term loyalty.

In the context of increased travel security concerns, private planes bring peace of mind. Knowing exactly who is in control of the plane, who is on board, and whose luggage is in the hold allows you to focus 100 percent on your business at hand. The privacy and reduced visibility afforded by business aircraft can also shield passengers from uncontrolled public exposure, and limit the risk of industrial espionage. Passengers are free to bring more hardware and documents aboard, without worrying about space constraints or the possibility of inadvertently violating the confidentiality of a document or file. Nearby seats cannot be booked by competitors, or their agents, for the purpose of overhearing your conversations during the flight. Cabins can be configured to accommodate virtually any special needs of the passengers.

The Excitement of Acquisition

Buying a plane is very exciting. A private, built-to-order jet gives you a chance to indulge your taste; you can specify everything from the cabin configuration and layout to the kind and color of the leather used for your seats. When you are establishing your unique alphanumeric tail identification, the Federal Aviation Administration (FAA) will even let you use letters and numbers that have special significance for you or your company.

The many details of acquisition and ownership are streamlined when you work with an experienced lawyer or accountant who can negotiate on your behalf and protect your interests before an agreement is signed. This kind of assistance not only ensures that you will contract for a good jet at a fair price, but also leaves more time for you to enjoy the process.

One thing you will want your lawyer or accountant to do is have the plane inspected by a qualified independent individual or facility, before you accept delivery. If you're buying a used plane, people familiar with the aircraft's particular make and model should be able to determine the plane's condition and the state of its maintenance records. These inspectors should include an FAA-certified airframe and power plant mechanic, or an approved repair station. If you are considering buying a plane from a foreign operator, remember that U.S. maintenance standards may not have been followed. To further protect your safety, have background checks conducted on the pilot, crew, and mechanics you hire.

Your lawyer or accountant can provide the hourly operating and annual maintenance costs of any kind of airplane you might be considering. Several reliable sources that publish such information annually are available. This same professional can also help you compare salaries for pilots and maintenance workers, obtain adequate insurance, and maintain the travel logs and documents required for the plane's FAA-regulated safety inspections. Alternatively, you can hire a management company—either a large national firm such as TAG Aviation or one of the smaller pilot-owned-and-operated businesses—to perform all necessary management services. Aircraft management companies can serve as a means for an aircraft owner with limited aviation experience to "buy" the necessary experience.

International travel on a private jet also requires research on visa requirements, permissions to use the air space of countries you may be flying over, and special arrangements for landing, fueling, and fulfilling security requirements in foreign airports. Your pilot may be able to make these arrangements, but, rather than risking an error or an incident, consider engaging a firm such as Universal Weather and Aviation, which specializes in these services, to make the arrangements for you. The cost of an annual contract with a "handling" company like this is a minor variable expense relative to the cost of the plane, and it is well worth the money if you plan to do much international traveling.

Government and tax regulations must be understood: for example, if an elected official is a passenger in your jet—perhaps you're taking him or her back to Washington, DC, or to a company event—be aware that government or agency rules may require reporting, disclosure, reimbursement, or restricted availability of sponsored travel for some public officials, depending on their position. As explained in Table 19.1, your lawyer or accountant must calculate the imputed income for passengers traveling for nonbusiness reasons, as well as the potential business tax deductions for depreciation and operating expenses.

Table 19.1   Comparison Shopping: Representative Specs

Type of Jet	Length (ft.)	Wing Span (ft.)	Cabin Volume (cu. ft.)	Maximum No. of Passengers	Price	Operating Costs/Hour
Gulfstream IV	88.4	77.1	1,525	19	$32,100,000	$5,000
Gulfstream 100	55.7	54.7	375	8	$12,100,000	$2,000
Hawker 800XP	51.2	51.4	604	15	$12,300,000	$2,000
Learjet 31A	48.8	43.9	271	7	$ 6,500,000	$1,700

Convenience and Flexibility

For business owners who require use of a private aircraft for both business and personal travel, one option is to have the corporation buy the plane and treat personal use as a fringe benefit. In this case, the business owner benefits from the conveniences of ownership, and the company takes advantage of the tax deductions for the depreciation and operating expenses associated with a business asset.

The fringe benefit of using a company plane for personal travel is considered taxable income to an employee, but this is a small price to pay for the flexibility afforded. One method of calculating this "imputed income" is to apply a formula using the IRS's published Standard Industry Fare Level (SIFL) tables. This method is intended to approximate commercial first-class fares for "control employees" and to approximate commercial coach fares for all other employees. The cost to the employee is just the income tax on the SIFL value of the flights taken. The company's payroll department will normally handle this through withholding, and will include the amounts on the employee's W-2 form, thereby eliminating any administrative burden on the employee.

The IRS's complex definition for "control employee" requires an attorney's or accountant's help for precise interpretation. In oversimplified terms, a control employee is someone who can authorize his or her own use of the plane. This category would include board members, officers, highly paid employees, and 5-percent owners.

Under the current tax laws and recent court rulings, even though an employee is only paying tax on a small percentage of the actual cost of the personal trips, the company is still allowed to deduct the entire cost of owning and operating the aircraft. Such tax savings can substantially reduce the actual cost of the trips to the company, while providing the business owner with the convenience and flexibility of having a private jet available at all times.

Consider these examples for a round-trip flight from Miami to New York City on a Gulfstream G-IV. This trip will require about five hours of flight time and will have a direct cost of approximately $25,000 (five hours at $5,000 per hour). With a 40 percent tax rate, the net direct cost to the company would be about $15,000.

If you and your spouse decide, on a Friday afternoon, that you want to go to New York for the weekend, you need only call the flight department personnel and tell them to prep the plane. You then just show up and go. Applying the SIFL formula and control employee rates to this trip would result in a taxable value of about $1,750 per person or $3,500 imputed to you. Your personal cost for this trip is your marginal tax rate applied to this amount, so, at 40 percent, it would be $1,400—considerably less than last-minute first-class tickets might cost.

Suppose now that you are informed that an employee has a very sick child who needs to see a specialist in New York immediately. You can make that happen with a phone call, and you really can't put a price on the type of loyalty that can inspire. The cost to the employee is next to nothing. Applying the SIFL formula and noncontrol employee rates would result in taxable income to the employee of about $200 per person, or $400 total. If they have a marginal tax rate of 28 percent, this trip, for the parents and the child, would cost them $112.

Airplane ownership does come at real cost and can be complex to administer, but if you can afford it, you will be able to appreciate the convenience, flexibility, and luxury known to very few.

A HOME AWAY FROM HOME

The purchase of a second home raises several of the same issues as the purchase of a plane. A second home—presumably in a place you love—affords the luxury of a refreshing change of scene in a fully equipped setting that saves the time and trouble of having to bring everything you need with you.

According to the National Association of Realtors, sales of second homes rose 27.5 percent between 1995 and 2001. The surge was prompted by the growth of two-income families, the stock market's appreciation in the 1990s, early retirements, and the generational transfer of wealth through inheritance, which adds up to hundreds of billions of dollars in additional spending power.

Before purchasing a second or third home, ask yourself some questions: Is the location right for you and your family? For example, is this a place where your grandchildren can have fun while visiting you? What will be the cost of utilities and maintenance? How much might the property's value increase? Will you be able to rent the property if you choose to or need to?

As with any home you are considering, you will want to have an inspector look for potential problems and ask an appraiser to give you an estimated fair-price range for the size and location. You may wish to consider purchasing the home during the off-season, when a smaller number of prospective buyers may make sellers more willing to negotiate.

Maintaining a second home from a distance can be challenging and expensive. Hiring a professional caretaker to check the property and manage any routine or ad hoc work that needs to be done will save you considerable time and aggravation. This person can also increase your enjoyment of the house by stocking the refrigerator; making sure all systems are working prior to your arrival; arranging housekeeping services while you are there; and closing the house up after your departure. Organizations such as the National Association of Residential Property Managers can refer you to licensed professionals in your area.

Possible Tax Benefits of Vacation Homes

An owner of a second residence (defined as a house, condo, trailer, or boat that is suitable for overnight use and is held solely for personal use) is entitled to deductions for real estate taxes and mortgage interest. The mortgage interest deductions, however, may be subject to limitation. If you take out a mortgage to buy a second home, the interest is deductible *if* the mortgage is secured by the home and you itemize deductions. Your deduction may be limited if the mortgage exceeds the fair market value of the home or if the mortgages on your main home and your second home exceed $1.1 million ($550,000 if you are married and filing a separate return).

If you rent the home for any period of time, you may also be eligible for additional deductions (up to the amount of rental income received), for costs such as association fees, cleaning, maintenance, management fees, repairs, utilities, and depreciation, depending on the relationship between the number of days the house is rented and the number of days you use it yourself. Sometimes a very small change in plans can produce substantial tax benefits.

Using a reputable real estate management company is a great way to coordinate rental time with personal use. The management company can also coordinate the maintenance and upkeep of the home, as well as keeping and providing records that document use and expenses.

Second homes in attractive locales also create business opportunities that should not be missed. If you are likely to let business colleagues or clients use the property, you might consider having your company rent the home from you at a rate comparable to other properties in the area. Not only will the income help defray the cost of any mortgage, upkeep, or depreciation, it may also entitle you to tax deductions for various other expenses.

Keeping a Vacation Home in the Family

You may want to pass along your second home to your children or grandchildren some day. But whether you bought it as an investment or as a vacation getaway, the IRS will treat it as just another asset in your estate. One way to reduce the estate tax on the home is by forming a Qualified Personal Residence Trust (QPRT).

With a QPRT, you transfer ownership to the trust but continue living in the home during the term of the trust. After that, ownership transfers to your descendants. The value of the home is determined at the outset, and while it may be worth more at the end of the term, the gift tax is based on the original value, not the appreciated value. You get use of the house and avoid saddling your descendants with a big tax liability. The gift tax is further reduced because the IRS allows your descendants, the trust beneficiaries, to take a discount for not being able to use and enjoy the home during the term of the trust. So, the longer the term, the smaller the gift will be for tax purposes.

There are a few catches, however. You must outlive the term of the trust, or the IRS will include the property with the rest of your estate as though the QPRT never existed. Moreover, if you want to continue using the home after the term ends, you may do so by paying the new owners "fair market" rent. However, that decision has to be made at the end of the term and cannot be a condition for making the transfer of ownership. A QPRT can be a useful estate-planning device for transferring ownership of a second home to your descendants, but only if it is done carefully and correctly.

LUXURY BOATS

If you enjoy being on the water, you may also be in the market for a boat. Demand for luxury boats was spurred by the repeal, in the early

1990s, of the federal luxury tax on recreational boats over $10,000. Growing demand has fueled rising prices, bigger boats, and longer waits for their delivery.

More than 500 luxury boats over 80 feet long were on order in January 2002. This was an 18 percent increase over the previous year's orders, according to *ShowBoats International* magazine. Demand has been so high that customers of leading manufacturers such as Palmer Johnson, Feadship, and Burger Boat Company are waiting up to three years for a luxury yacht. Smaller vintage GarWood, ChrisCraft, and Hacker runabouts, as well as handmade classic reproductions, can be equally luxurious and are highly sought after by collectors.

The annual operation, maintenance, upkeep, and insurance on a large luxury boat or a vintage classic can cost from tens to hundreds of thousands of dollars, depending on the care required for the materials used to build the boats. Like any water vehicle, luxury boats require bottom cleaning, painting, and finishing; engine, propeller, and shaft work; interior refurbishing; and carpentry—not to mention the occasional repair of the sophisticated gadgetry used to operate the vessel.

As the size of the boat increases, so do the maintenance costs. Simply putting a fresh coat of paint on a 100-foot luxury boat can cost in excess of $100,000. And docking in a popular yachting community can cost several thousand dollars a month. Then, there are the payroll costs. A top-rate captain with global credentials often commands a salary in excess of $80,000, and additional crew members, at lesser salaries, are usually required. Refurbishing when the boat changes hands often costs 10 to 50 percent (or more) of the purchase price. The best bet is to find a facility with a commitment to quality, experience, and skill, and hire it to do the necessary jobs correctly.

Are all these costs justified? If you are wealthy and you love being on the water and taking family and friends with you, the answer is YES. Like second homes, boats offer opportunities for business entertaining and tax advantages. Once again, you need to take counsel on the rules and restrictions, given the frequency with which they change.

LUXURY ITEMS AS INVESTMENTS

When you make a misguided equity investment, you run the risk of losing everything. When you invest in a jet, a second home, or a boat, however—particularly at the high end of the market—you acquire a tangible asset that will always have some value and may increase in value. A large Gulfstream jet originally purchased for $18 million could be worth as much as $22 million in the used-jet market a few years later. One reason large planes appreciate is because of their long delivery lead times. Therefore, a plane that has already been built may be worth more, to some people, than the promise of one to be delivered from the factory in two years or later.

Depending on their location and the overall economy, vacation homes can also appreciate in value. According to the National Association of Realtors, a house in snowy Stowe, Vermont, which sold for $130,000 in 1996, sold for $325,000 in 2001; a $349,000 house purchased in sunny Sanibel, Florida, in 1996, sold for $750,000 in 2001; and a house that sold for $665,000 in 1996, in Incline Village, Nevada, went for more than $1.2 million in 2001.

The best big boats, such as Palmer Johnsons, Feadships, and Burgers, sometimes gain value, too. For example, a 10-year-old large boat in excellent condition from one of these manufacturers can cost more used than it did when new.

Although such gains are offset by the cost of annual maintenance, the impact of the upkeep is often reduced by tax advantages. The reduction is most significant when the items are used for business purposes as well as personal ones. For example, a number of recent cases have held that employees' use of company jets, second homes, and luxury boats for entertainment and recreation purposes does not bar business deductions for the full maintenance and operating cost of the assets, as long as the standardized value of the perquisite is treated as compensation to the employees. The courts have often rejected IRS claims that the deductions should be limited to the amounts treated as income to the employees; instead, they allow the full expense amounts to be deducted. Consult with your attorney or accountant on these and other tax issues. He or she can provide invaluable assistance in maximizing the benefits from the ownership of luxury items.

Some people make big purchases because they believe that they can always rent or charter their asset if they fall on hard times. In general, however, I believe it is better *not* to consider a plane, home, or boat as a potential source of income. In renting or chartering it, you must compete with businesses that have enough volume to create economies of scale, and the transactions involved can easily turn an item you once loved into a source of anxiety and annoyance. One of the greatest benefits of ownership is to have the plane, second home, or boat available whenever you want it.

Even though a plane, vacation home, or boat might never "pay for itself" in quantitative terms, cost is not necessarily the most important measure of its value. The qualitative pleasure you derive from these possessions, as well as the personal relationships they can help you establish and nurture, can be worth far more than the price you pay.

ENJOYMENT: THE ULTIMATE GOAL

To increase the enjoyment value of a plane, vacation home, or boat, be sure you can easily afford both the purchase price and the incremental cost of maintaining and using the item over time. Try not to let your desire to "get my money's worth" become an obsession to keep the asset in constant use; your possessions should not possess you. Business assets may require 100 percent utilization, but these personal assets acquire a certain charm in being underutilized. Support a maintenance program that makes your plane, home, or boat available to you when you want to use it; accept that it may be idle at other times.

Even the most complicated issues raised here should not undermine your desire when you can afford the things you want. Every challenge becomes manageable in the light of the relevant experience and ability that a good lawyer and accountant can provide. Count their fees among the small incremental costs that make the difference between owning something and enjoying it.

If you are fortunate enough to be rich or to become rich, be happy about it. Be generous with yourself and others. When your boat needs upkeep or something in your home needs repair, give the workmen a tip larger than they'd expect. Make them pleased to get your call or see you coming in for service. When you're spending millions on large purchases and their upkeep, the cost of generous tipping is inconsequential, and your generosity, I believe, will ultimately add to the responsiveness of those on whom you rely for repair and maintenance, thereby increasing your enjoyment of your luxury item and the quality of your life.

You should never lose sight of the opportunities that wealth brings for great joy through freedom and self-expression. Let the things you can afford to own add to your delight and the happiness of those you care about. Learning how to properly purchase and manage luxury items will enable you to spend more time enjoying life and to waste less time on anxiety, guilt, or conflict. Remember, life often runs out before the money does. As the saying goes, "Fly first class (in your own plane, of course!). Your heirs will."

Words to the Wise

■ When buying a plane, vacation home, or boat, remember that its value to you—how it enhances your pleasure in life—will often exceed its monetary cost.

■ Focus on why you want the luxury item and how it will help you enjoy life, rather than on trying to get the best deal. Market value is usually a reasonable price to pay. If an item is selling under market value, there is usually a problem—with either the item or the seller.

■ Rely on your lawyer or accountant to assist you in making and maintaining such purchases, as well as maximizing their potential tax advantages.

■ Keep in mind that high-end items are most likely to retain their value or to appreciate.

■ Use your money to enhance the enjoyment of your life.

Milton M. Ferrell, Jr.

Milton M. Ferrell, Jr., is the CEO of Ferrell Schultz Carter Zumpano & Fertel, a Florida-based law firm offering professional services to individuals, their families, and their enterprises throughout the world. The firm offers a full range of legal services and implements advanced concepts of wealth preservation and international tax minimization. Mr. Ferrell has represented clients in major civil and criminal jury trials, and has advised clients regarding complex business transactions. Mr. Ferrell has a Gulfstream jet, a GarWood runabout, a Burger yacht, and several homes.

20

SAFE AND SOUND

Developing a Sensible Strategy for Your Personal Security

MILTON M. FERRELL, JR.

A client calls to report that her babysitter has disappeared with no forwarding number, and several pieces of her jewelry and silver are coincidentally missing from her home. The following dialogue ensues:

MF: *What's the babysitter's name?*
Client: *Clara.*
MF: *Clara what?*
Client *(sheepishly): I'm not sure.*
MF: *How did you hire Clara?*
Client: *She was a friend of Mary, who watches the children next door.*

Did Clara steal the jewelry and silver? Our investigation could not confirm it. But the client never hired anyone again without first arranging for a thorough background check.

Every activity in life, from walking to the corner to eating a meal, entails some risk. Most threats to our well-being are random, but wealth and visibility do increase the risk of being targeted by people who may view you as an opportunity for theft or extortion.

The possible human responses to real or perceived threats cover a wide spectrum. At one end are those who exercise caution to an almost paranoid extreme because they have exaggerated the risk. At the other end are people who actively pursue risk with no precautions. Neither extreme is useful in the quest to live an empowered life. A more centered approach is to evaluate the risks you face and then take sensible precautions to reduce them.

Some risks are easier to measure than others. An information technology specialist can perform quantitative tests to measure the security of your computer system, but what tests can identify people who might be targeting you for burglary or kidnapping? The best security plans are based on awareness and avoidance of danger. This chapter will cover some basic but often overlooked steps you can take to protect your most valuable assets: yourself, your family, and your homes. In many cases, your lawyer or accountant can provide the services you need or refer you to a suitable specialist.

KNOW THE PEOPLE YOU EMPLOY

A few years ago, before we required candidates to show a photo ID, our firm interviewed a woman for a paralegal position. She had excellent skills, and a preliminary background check turned up no criminal record. As the process went further, our investigator noticed some gaps in her employment history. Then he determined that she had provided an incorrect middle initial and date of birth on her application. Along with the correct data, we uncovered a past that included convictions for drug distribution, prostitution, and embezzlement. When confronted, the woman said, "Of course I lied. If I had told you the truth, I wouldn't have gotten the job." I'm confident that she got a job somewhere else, where perhaps the background check was not as thorough.

My firm routinely implements and manages employment procedures for the people our clients hire to work at their businesses and in their homes. Our experience shows that at least half of our clients' job applicants omit at least one negative item from their application or employment history. The risks associated with an uninformed hiring decision are higher among home workers—housekeepers, gardeners, drivers, nannies or babysitters, handymen, or contractors—who are likely to have direct access to your family and property. Many people seek these types of home workers through advertisements or referrals, and the challenges are increased for those who are managing multiple homes in different locations.

Although you may be pressured to make a quick decision—or tempted by someone who will work more cheaply if you pay in cash— why take the chance of exposing your home and family to strangers, or harboring someone who could harm you? We often find that just having a process in place automatically weeds out people who have something to hide. Key components of this process are: a detailed request for information on the application, a signed authorization consenting to a background and credit check, and a thorough background check. If the worker is going to be using one of the client's vehicles, we also review his or her driving record. We look not only for a valid driver's license but also for a good driving safety record. All this research should be conducted before a job offer is made; it's much easier to avoid a problem by not hiring than it is to fire people after they start working for you.

A complete cross-country background check can typically be conducted within 72 hours or less, and it costs around $500. This relatively small investment of time and money is rewarded by knowing that your employees have represented themselves truthfully and that you will be able to find them (or someone who knows them) later, if something does go wrong. Another incentive for conducting a proper background check is the legal theory of negligent hiring. If your employee harms a third party on your premises or on a job-related errand, you may be held liable for not doing all you reasonably could have done to ensure that you were hiring a safe worker.

When you hire people for full-time or long-term work, you and the new employee should both sign an employment contract that gives you the right to conduct background and credit checks periodically, and spells out any severance policy. Because it's also in your security interests to retain good workers, you should provide them with reasonable benefits such as Social Security entitlement, paid vacation, and an additional retirement plan. Health insurance should also be part of the package, not only for their benefit but also to minimize any health risk they might pose to you and your family. The people who work in your home have a big impact on your quality of life, and your investments to reinforce professionalism and mutual respect are money well spent.

SECURITY BEGINS WITH THE BASICS

Reducing the risk of random threats to your personal safety is largely a matter of common sense and periodic reviews to be sure you are taking advantage of basic precautions. Fundamentally, security begins at the refrigerator door: food gone bad can kill you. Does that mean you should not eat? Obviously, no. Simply be careful about how you store perishables and how long you keep them.

Similar common sense applies to your protection against a common personal security risk: home burglary. Whether random or targeted, burglaries occur more often in neighborhoods that have things worth stealing. Most burglars will bypass a home, however, if someone appears to be in it, or if it requires too much effort to gain entry.

Creating the appearance of occupancy when no one is home is easily accomplished with the use of timers that automatically turn on interior and exterior lights as well as TVs or stereos. Canceling your daily paper and having someone pick up your mail regularly while you are away eliminates the pileups that can clue a burglar to your extended absence. Even better, hire a trustworthy housesitter (only after conducting a background check, of course) to occupy the residence when you are not there.

It may seem obvious that you should keep your doors and windows locked when you're not home, but, in fact, 30 percent of home burglars gain access through an unlocked entrance. High-grade locks with tamper-resistant features are worth the cost when you consider what they are protecting.

Dogs, especially more than one, will sometimes deter a thief, but an electronic alarm system generally offers a higher level of security. A quality home alarm system can cost anywhere from a few thousand dollars to more than $100,000, depending on the location and size of the house or office space being protected.

The most effective alarm systems are those connected to a reliable central monitoring station. Alarms equipped only with sirens may startle a thief, but they are generally not activated until an unauthorized person has already entered the house. The more effective goal is to prevent the intruder from getting in. The system should cover both the exterior and the interior of the house. Keep in mind that some alarm monitoring companies rely on the use of a phone line (which can easily be cut) to communicate problems. High-end systems typically use what is known as a cellular line seizure device. With this feature, the system notifies the central monitoring station when the phone lines are disabled, and the station then calls the police.

An alarm system with "multiple zone" capability protects certain areas of your property but allows authorized people to move about freely in other parts of the house. With this type of system, the front door of a house can be alarmed and the door to the pool can be left accessible to your family or guests. This system also allows for motion sensors to be disabled in certain areas, for example, where pets are left to roam. "Panic buttons" distributed throughout the house and grounds—especially near parking areas, pools, and tennis courts—can be quickly pressed to send an emergency signal to the central monitoring system. These cost as little as $15 each and increase a system's usefulness.

Before selecting a system, consider having an independent expert conduct a home security survey. Many alarm companies offer this service, but you can generally obtain a more thorough, objective, and cost-effective assessment from a person who can also solicit competitive bids for you. Moreover, don't forget to communicate with the person who installs the alarm system. There is little point in having it if you do not understand how it works.

Many people think that owning a gun increases their personal safety, but a 1998 report in the *New England Journal of Medicine* reported that a gun kept in a home is 22 times more likely to kill a family member or a friend than it is to be used against an intruder. If you sense or see an intruder, it's much safer to remain in your bedroom with the door locked and call 911 than to turn on the light, silhouette yourself in an open doorway, and risk confronting people who are likely to be frightened, armed, and more willing to kill you than you are to kill them.

As another fundamental precaution, ask your lawyer or accountant to periodically review your insurance policies to make sure they adequately reflect the things you own, the risks you face, and the precautions you have taken.

SAFEGUARD YOUR COMPUTER

Home computers loaded with personal, financial, and corporate data represent a relatively new security risk. Your hard drive or home network probably holds information that would enable others to take advantage of you in some way. The chances of unauthorized access are increased by the more common use of digital subscriber lines and cable modems, which provide a continuous Internet connection when the computer is on and can facilitate a hacker's effort to enter a vulnerable system.

The first line of defense includes good virus and "worm" protection software that can be updated regularly, and the use of alphanumeric passwords that are difficult for others to guess. You might also consider installing the "firewall" devices that companies use as gatekeepers between the Internet and their internal systems.

If the nature of your data gives you cause for greater concern, you can engage a service that will test your system by actively hacking or attempting to enter your system without authorization. In addition to issuing a report for a fee, these services will recommend the best method to close potential holes in your computer/data security. If your business employs information technology professionals, it's a good idea to have one of them examine your home computer setup, especially if your connection to the Internet is through your business systems. If not, your attorney can help you find a consultant who can suggest the type of firewalls you need, install them, and maintain them periodically.

TRAVEL SAFELY

Travel for business or pleasure continues to be an essential part of life, despite increased domestic and international security concerns. Dangers to Americans traveling overseas —particularly wealthy American business executives with high public profiles—have increased dramatically in recent years with the rise of terrorism and the expansion of anti-America sentiment.

The most basic protective measure is to understand any particular dangers that exist at your destination. One way to keep informed is to consult the online U.S. State Department advisories prior to departure. Because these advisories can be up to 30 days old, travelers should also check the most recent news reports. The best source may be your lawyer, who can provide you with a current security report on your destination. Such research will increase your awareness of the area's potential risks, from crime on the street to the geopolitical situation.

With kidnapping a serious threat in many places, Americans need to exercise caution on foreign and domestic streets. Street criminals, who prey on targets of opportunity, and organized gangs try to identify lucrative and easy victims—including wealthy tourists who are traveling alone. If your size or skin tone prevents you from blending in completely, at least do your best *not* to stand out as an affluent American.

Kidnappers and extortionists identify their targets and then watch these potential victims and memorize their daily patterns. Therefore, especially in high-risk countries, be alert for such surveillance and vary your routine. To eliminate, or at least reduce, the possibility of inadvertently doing something that would bring your activities to the attention of criminal elements, the best advice is to avoid high-risk behavior, exercise good judgment, and be observant of your surroundings.

Kidnapping and extortion insurance is a reasonable investment for people who frequently travel internationally. A policy offering $10 million in protection for you, your employees, and your family members typically runs about $4,000 to $8,000 a year (twice that amount if you include coverage in Colombia).

KEEP PERSONAL INFORMATION PRIVATE

The amount of publicity you court can have a direct effect on your level of security. For example, in one major American city, a few years ago, a local magazine listed the top 10 law firms and wrote up a special section on the firm's partners. The day the article was circulated, the managing partners from two of the profiled firms were robbed at gunpoint in their driveways, when they returned home from work.

Limit publication of your home address to the extent possible. For security purposes, luggage tags, driver's licenses, and vehicle titles should include business addresses rather than home addresses. Credit card bills should be mailed to a business address. In the same vein, keep a valet key for your car separate from your house key, to prevent your house key from being duplicated while your car is parked. If you are selling a car or a valuable piece of art, jewelry, or furniture, arrange for its sale by a dealer or agent instead of showing it at your home. All these steps will help prevent unscrupulous people from discovering where you and your family live.

CONSIDER A PROTECTIVE VEHICLE

Getting from place to place on the ground can also pose some dangers. Threats of terrorism and street violence have increased the demand for, and the supply of, protective cars featuring thick glass, Kevlar and other bullet-resistant materials under their skins, and tires that will not go flat when punctured. The kinds of vehicles that protect diplomats in places like the Middle East and Latin America—and business executives from Mexico City to Moscow—are becoming increasingly common in America's largest cities.

Ten years ago, the only armored vehicles available looked like limousines or trucks. They were used primarily by government officials and cost hundreds of thousands of dollars. Today, thanks to the use of composite materials, the cost of armoring can be as low as $50,000 and the methods can be applied to conventional-looking sedans and sports utility vehicles. BMW, for example, sells the 740iL Protection and 750iL Protection, and Mercedes Benz began making armored vehicles available to U.S. buyers in the 2001 model year. O'Gara, a U.S. manufacturer, specializes in light-armored vehicles that protect against handgun violence, submachine guns, kidnapping attempts, and other attacks. Their vehicles include an armored passenger compartment, ballistic glass, run-flat tires, and a bulletproof battery.

For those whose life requires frequent travel to faraway dangerous places, the private jet manufacturer Gulfstream recently began offering a military-style surface-to-air missile detection system. The system, which can initiate countermeasures to deflect a missile fired by a terrorist from the ground, has become especially popular among wealthy businesspeople who need to travel to remote and dangerous areas.

ENGAGE AN EXECUTIVE PROTECTION SPECIALIST

No matter how many precautions you take, some people will stop at nothing to achieve a criminal goal. If your wealth or fame increases your chances of becoming a target, you might consider engaging the services of a bodyguard or an "executive protection specialist" to help you during a particular period of time or with an identifiable security risk. As with any professional service, you need to find a reputable and qualified person who can work smoothly with you and will understand your specific needs.

The most effective bodyguards do not match the muscle-bound stereotype. They blend in completely with their client's environment and appear to be nothing more than colleagues or assistants. If their previous training emphasized confrontation, they have retrained themselves to focus first on avoidance and escape from danger. Discreet and trustworthy, they can be counted on to protect your confidentiality as well as your safety, given what they inevitably will come to know about your personal life. They are usually very intelligent and capable, which often tempts clients to entrust them with more diverse responsibilities. This is a mistake, however; any distractions from their primary purpose—ensuring your safety—should be minimized.

Generally, the best way to find a good bodyguard is by referral; this is not an area where you want to turn to the Yellow Pages or the Internet. Former employers may give the best references, but they may be difficult to contact if they are celebrities or high-ranking executives. Legal concerns may also make them reluctant to speak honestly about former employees. Lawyers or accountants who know you well are usually good sources of guidance. They can also help you to evaluate what the assignment should entail, develop a realistic statement of work, review the fee structure, and set a manageable timetable.

As a first step, an executive protection specialist will conduct a personal security survey. A few days during the week will be spent shadowing the client to learn his or her daily professional and personal routines, which are usually easier to observe and predict than we like to admit. The specialist will observe and ask questions about the client's habits, family interactions, and methods of communication.

Trust is important at this stage; any withholding of facts will only make it more difficult for the security professional to gauge the potential risks. The specialist may caution the family against the use of cordless or analog phones and provide other suggestions, such as learning evasive driving techniques. Even if the survey shows that a bodyguard is not really necessary, the process usually makes people more aware of their different environments and better able to identify places and situations where they might be vulnerable. In my experience with surveillance, I have found that most people would not notice a fire truck following them, let alone a common car.

The best way for anyone, including a bodyguard, to deal with a dangerous situation is to avoid it or get out of it, rather than take an additional risk by trying to overcome it. Overcoming or apprehending criminals is a task best left to law enforcement personnel.

THE OBJECTIVE: GREATER ENJOYMENT OF LIFE

The closer and more prevalent threat of terrorism in recent years has been a wake-up call: Prepare and protect. In response, the security industry has grown in size and in the diversity of its services. A qualified executive protection specialist can warn you of risks before they materialize, identify specific and relevant threats and vulnerabilities, and defend you against them. The use of expert services increases your return on investment by enabling you to leverage security resources to

meet the most critical needs, reduce the likelihood of future cata-
strophic incidents, minimize any damages incurred, eliminate recov-
ery costs, and safeguard your most important assets.

Remember, though, that personal security is an individual responsibility that can never be totally delegated. You cannot rely on
someone else to protect you if you insist on engaging in high-risk behaviors. Your own common sense has to be the cornerstone for any effective security plan.

As with insurance for other assets, an appropriate security strategy affords peace of mind and a greater ability to enjoy your life. You
will know that you have done everything possible to keep yourself, your
family, and your possessions safe.

Words to the Wise

- Have a thorough background check conducted before you hire
  any prospective employees to work in your home or business.
- Take commonsense precautions to protect your home(s) from
  burglary: take steps to make your house seem occupied at all
  times; put good locks on your doors and windows; install a
  high-quality alarm system; and make sure you have adequate
  insurance.
- Make sure your home computer system has the same security
  protections as your business information technology.
- To protect yourself against being victimized when you travel,
  make sure you understand the security risks that may exist at
  your destination, and act accordingly.
- If your situation warrants it, consider purchasing kidnapping
  insurance, using a protective vehicle, or engaging the services
  of a bodyguard.
- Consult your lawyer or accountant to find the security services you need.
- Be aware of your environment, and deploy strategies for avoiding or escaping danger rather than confronting it.
- Don't let excessive fear interfere with your enjoyment of life.

Milton M. Ferrell, Jr.

Milton M. Ferrell, Jr., is the CEO of Ferrell Schultz Carter Zumpano & Fertel, a Florida-based law firm offering professional services to individuals, their families, and their enterprises worldwide. As part of its range of services, the firm has created an affinity group specializing in investigation, compliance, and enforcement. Mr. Ferrell frequently advises current and former heads of state and CEOs on personal security matters. He has also assisted in gaining the release of kidnappees.

ABOUT THE EDITOR

Heidi L. Steiger is executive vice president of Neuberger Berman Inc., a publicly held, New York-based investment firm that manages over $60 billion for individuals, families, and institutions through private asset management, a family of no-load mutual funds, and professional securities services. Ms. Steiger serves on the firm's five-person Executive Committee and is a member of its Board of Directors.

Ms. Steiger has served in the investment management field for more than 25 years. Before joining Neuberger Berman in 1986, she was senior vice president in charge of special products at Herzfeld & Stern, an investment banking and brokerage firm. Earlier, she held several positions, including director of marketing at Fidelity Management Group. She began her career in 1975 at the New England Mutual Life Insurance Company.

Author of numerous articles on financial decision making and investments, Ms. Steiger is a frequent public speaker and television commentator on topics ranging from estate planning to asset allocation and mutual funds.

Ms. Steiger is very active in nonprofit organizations and sits on the boards of the Metropolitan Museum of Art (National Committee, Business Committee, and Visiting Committee of the Department of Photography), the Juilliard Dance Committee, the Miami Museum of Contemporary Art, the Whitney Museum of American Art (Chairman's Council), and the Financial Women's Association (past president).

A summa cum laude graduate of Boston College with a BA in English/Communications, Ms. Steiger was elected to membership in Phi Beta Kappa Honor Society. She holds an MBA in finance from Columbia University. She received her certification as a Chartered Life Underwriter (CLU) from American College.

INDEX

Accountants/accounting:
  consulting on hiring/purchase
    decisions, 238–239, 256
  family office and, 181
  on team of financial advisors, 115
Acquisition:
  excitement of, 238–239
  as obsession, 7–8
Advisors. *See* Financial advisors,
  team of
Airplanes, private, 236–241,
  245–246, 255
Alarm systems, 251–252
Alienation, avoiding, 10–12
American Folk Art Museum, 214
Anderson, Robert (*I Never Sang for
  My Father*), 78
Art, contemporary, 223–234
  auctions, 230
  challenges of, 225
  collecting as lifetime journey, 233
  consultants on, 231
  donating/selling, 231–233
  key steps for smart buying,
    226–227
  learning wordless language,
    224–225
  looking/learning, 226
  practical considerations in
    owning, 227–228
  pricing/buying, 228–229

  primary *vs.* secondary markets,
    229–230
  provenance, 229
  timing purchase of, 230–231
Art Dealers Association of America,
  232
Asset allocation, 122–139
  alternative investments (hedge
    funds and private equity),
    131, 132, 133, 175–176
  assessing probabilities in your
    portfolio, 137
  balancing personal/probable,
    137–138
  commodities, 132–134
  correlation and liquidity, 132
  defining, 122–124
  diversification and risk
    reduction, 127–128
  efficient frontier, 128–130
  historical performance of stock,
    bond, and balanced
    portfolios (1926–2001), 129
  investment classes/categories,
    126–127
  professional consultants, 134
  risk comparisons, 133
  step by step, 124–125
  strategic *vs.* historical methods,
    127–128
  tax considerations, 134–136

Asset management. *See* Investing/
  investment(s); Wealth
  management
Association of Investment
  Management Research (AIMR),
  104
Association of Professional Art
  Advisors (APAA), 231
Association of Small Foundations,
  67
Auctions, buying contemporary art
  at, 230

Banks (on team of financial
  advisors), 114
BBB Wise Giving Alliance, 67
Beard, James, 219
Berman, Robert Bennett, 46
Boats, luxury, 243–244, 245
Bodyguards, 255–256
Bonds (asset allocation), 126
Boutique trust companies, 194,
  203–204
Breadwinner role, 10
Brokers (on team of financial
  advisors), 114
Buffett, Warren, 19
"Buying against"/"buying ahead"
  of the market, 230–231

Career(s):
  changing, 50–55
    childhood interests and, 54–55
    long-term strategy, 53
    motivation for, 51–53
    sufficient wealth, 51
  choices (and wealth), 7, 8
  definition of "occupation," 9
Cash investments, 126
Certified Investment Management
  Analyst (CIMA), 103, 104
Charitable lead trusts (CLTs),
  64

Charitable remainder trusts
  (CRTs), 64, 159–160
Charity. *See* Philanthropy
Chartered Financial Analyst (CFA),
  103
Children:
  in blended families (second
    marriages), 20–21, 156–157
  challenges of parenting in a
    wealthy family, 17–28
  incentives in trusts (unintended
    consequences), 158
  inheritance issues:
    parenting decisions (impact of
      wealth), 19, 25–26
    protecting with trusts, 157–159
  instilling values/beliefs, 3, 4, 8,
    12, 24–27
  involving in philanthropy, 66–67
  marriages of, 25, 33–35
  peer relationships, and wealth, 17
  "safety net" for, 15
  talking about money with, 12
  trusts for, 157–158
Chippendale, Thomas, 218
Churchill, Winston, 219
Collateralized mortgage obligations
  (CMOs), 143, 144, 150
Collecting, 213–222
  contemporary art, 223–234
  furnishing a home, 216–218
  personality and, 215–216
  questions a collector asks,
    214–215
  what adds value, 218–221
Commercial mortgage-backed
  securities (CMBS), 143, 144,
  145, 150
Commodities, 126, 132–134
Complications (of wealth),
  simplifying, 9–10
Computer/data, safeguarding,
  252–253

Concealing wealth:
  in divorce, 38
  for psychological reasons, 8
Concierge services, 116–117, 181
Consultants. *See* Financial advisors,
  team of
Contract, family fiduciary,
  206–207
"Control employee," 240
Corporate trustees. *See* Trustee(s)/
  fiduciaries
Correlation and liquidity, 132
Council on Foundations, 67
Counseling:
  team, 117–120
  wealth, 117–118
CTC Consultants, 104

Des Moines Art Center, 223
Distortions (of wealth), minimizing,
  7–9
Diversification, 105, 127–128
Divorce, 19–20, 30, 36–40
  avoiding common financial traps,
    37–38
    clouded judgment, 38
    excessive spending, 36–37
    failing to hire good financial
      manager, 38
    hiding money, 38
  emotional *vs.* business impact of,
    19–20
  hiring good lawyer, 38–40
  protecting yourself, 36–37
  second marriages, 20–21,
    156–157
Donations:
  of artwork to museums, 231–233
  to charity (*see* Philanthropy)
Donor-advised funds, 65
Dorment, Marguerite, 217
Doyle, William, 215–216, 217
du Pont, Henry, 214

Efficient frontier, 128–130
Ellig, Bruce, 51–52
Emotional impact of wealth, 1–4,
  5–16
  avoiding isolation and alienation,
    10–12
  making money easier to talk
    about, 12–13
  minimizing distortions, 7–9
  simplifying complications, 9–10
  stages of adjustment to wealth, 2
  writing personal mission
    statement, 13–15
Employees, knowing your
  employees, 249–250
Employee Stock Ownership Plan
  (ESOP), 95
Equity ownership, direct (real
  estate), 146–147
Equity REITs (real estate
  investment trusts), 147–150
Esmerian, Ralph, 213–215, 217
Estate planning:
  charitable vehicles, 64
  and children (*see* Inheritance
    issues)
  postnuptial agreements, 35
Event risk, 144
Executive protection specialist,
  255–256

Falconwood Corporation's Tangible
  Asset Program, 133
Family, 17–28
  challenges of wealth for, 18–22
  history (legacy conversations), 84
  inheritance issues, 19, 25–26,
    157–159
  involvement in philanthropy,
    65–67 (*see also* Family
    foundations)
  legacy, 4, 81–82
  rituals, 27

Family *(Continued)*
  second marriages and blended
    families, 20–21
  spouse (*see* Divorce; Marriage)
  trustee selection and unity of,
    194–196
  values:
    case illustration, 21–22
    communicating, 24–27
    defining, 22–24
Family business/enterprise, 69–70
  dealing effectively with conflicts
    in, 75–77
  examples of conflict and
    resolutions in, 72–75, 77
  isolation and ("not one of the
    gang"), 11
  issues *vs.* conflicts (definitions),
    70
  money in family dynamics, 71–72
  relationships and, 77–78
  signs of potential conflict, 75
  structure/governance, 76
  vision/mission of, 76
Family foundations:
  prudent investing for, 164–178
    alternative assets classes (hedge
      funds/equity funds), 175
    defining, 164–165
    new look of "prudence,"
      166–167
    sample *Statement of Investment
      Policy,* 168–174
    setting investment policy,
      167–175
  strategic approach to
    philanthropy, 64–65, 67
  trusts and, 160–161
Family limited partnership (FLP),
  95, 142
Family meetings, 80–93, 181
  example, 80–81, 88–89
  formats, 82–88

ground rules, 83–87
hurdles, common, 87–88
  keeping people to their
    agreements via a follow-up,
    88
  people who are highly
    impaired, 87–88
  people who can't get beyond
    their own opinions, 87
  people who don't want to
    participate, 87
  people who don't want to upset
    others, 88
professional facilitator for, 83
reasons for, 81–82
steps for facilitating, 89–91
talking about money in, 81
Family offices, 113, 179–190
  collaborative spirit and
    mentoring, 185
  cooperative, 189
  costs of operating, 185–186
  definition, 180
  forms, 181–183
  governance systems, 183
  homme d'affaire, 187–188
  human capital management, 188
  multiclient, 181–182, 186, 187
  new trends, 187–189
  private trust companies, 188
  proactive financial solutions,
    184–185
  selecting right kind for your
    family, 183–184, 186–187
  services provided by, 180–181
  stand-alone (single family),
    182–183, 185–186, 187
  superior asset management, 184
  and team of financial advisors,
    113
Fannie Mae (Federal National
  Mortgage Association), 143,
  150

Fels, Florent (*Vincent van Gogh*), 44
Fiduciaries. *See* Trustee(s)/
   fiduciaries
Financial advisors, team of,
   111–121. *See also* Professional
   money managers
  accountants, 115
  banks, 114
  brokers, 114
  concierge services, 116–117, 181
  consultants, 113–114
    asset allocation, 134
    contemporary art collections,
      231
    managers of managers,
      113–114
    miscellaneous, 117
    trusts, 153, 161
  family offices, 113
  gladiatorial *vs.* collaborative
    approach, 111–112
  investment managers, 113
  lawyers, 115–116
  life insurance consultants, 116
  objective, 120
  technologists, 115
  wealth counseling, 117–118
    coordinator, 119
    mediator, 119–120
    proposer, 119
    team, 117–120
  wealth management skills,
    112–117
Firewall devices, 252
Folk Art Museum, 214
Freddie Mac (Federal Home Loan
   Mortgage Corporation), 143,
   150
Friendships, wealth and, 2–3, 4, 10,
   11, 13, 15
Funds from operations (FFO), 148
Fungibility, 148
Furniture, collecting antique, 218

Ginnie Mae (Government National
   Mortgage Association), 143,
   144, 145, 150
Goddard, Townsend, 218
Gold, 126
Governance system/structure:
  family enterprise, 76
  family offices, 183, 187
Guidestar, 67
Gun ownership, 252

Happiness, and wealth, 4, 6. *See also*
   Wealth/money, enjoying
Hedge funds, 131, 132, 133,
   175–176
Historical performance of stock,
   bond, and balanced portfolios
   (1926–2001), 129
Historical *vs.* strategic methods
   (asset allocation), 127–128
History, family (legacy
   conversations), 84
Home(s):
  alarm systems, 251–252
  furnishing with collections,
    216–218
  real estate investment, 141
  security survey, 252
  vacation, 210, 241–243, 245
Hughes, James E., Jr. (*A Reflection
   on the Role of the* Homme
   D'Affaire *in a System of Family
   Governance*), 187
Human capital management, 188

Individuals as trustees, 202
Inheritance issues:
  parenting issues (impact of
    wealth on children), 19,
    25–26
  protecting with trusts, 157–159
Initial public offerings (IPOs), 2,
   132

Institute for Private Investors (IPI), 99, 107, 108, 109

Institutional trustees/trust companies, 194, 202–203

Insurance:
  kidnapping/extortion, 254
  life (consultants), 116

International travel (private jet), 239

Investing/investment(s):
  alternative asset classes (hedge funds and private equity), 131, 132, 133, 175–176
  asset allocation, 122–139
  balancing personal/probable, 137–138
  balancing portfolio (see Asset allocation)
  classes, 126–127 (see also Asset allocation)
  diversification, 105, 127–128
  efficient frontier, 128–130
  family foundations (see Family foundations)
  family office and, 184
  fungibility, 148
  luxury items (jets/boats/second homes) as, 244–246
  portfolio problems, and trusts, 159–160
  probabilities, assessing, 137
  real estate, 143–144
    comparison of returns (1972–2001), 149
    equity REITs, 147–150
    mortgage REITs, 143, 144–145
  setting policy for family foundations, 164–178

Investment Management Consultants Association (IMCA), 104

Investment managers (on team of financial advisors), 113

Isolation, avoiding, 10–12

Jensen, Georg, 220

Jets, private, 236–241, 245–246, 255

Jewelry, 219

Johnson, Eastman, 220–221

Kidnapping/extortion insurance, 254

Kindig, Joe, Jr., 214

Krasner, Lee, 45

Lawyers:
  consulting on hiring/purchase decisions, 238–239, 256
  divorce, 38–40
  on team of financial advisors, 115–116

Legacy:
  conversations, 84
  family, 4, 81–82
  your, 4

Life insurance consultants, 116

Limited liability company (LLC), 142

Liquidity, 124, 132

Luxury(ies):
  boats, 243–244, 245
  collections, 213–222, 223–234
  enjoyment of, 209–211, 235–236, 246, 256–257
  as income source, 245–246
  as investments, 244–246
  misplaced focus on cost, 235
  "practical," 210
  private jets, 236–241
  questions to ask when considering purchase of, 236
  vacation homes, 210, 241–243, 245

Management of Institutional Funds Act (1972), 166
Markowitz, Harry, 128
Marriage, 29–41
  breakup of (*see* Divorce)
  impact of wealth on relationship with spouse/life partner, 3, 4
  keeping wealth out of marital estate, 33–35
  postnuptial agreements, 30, 35–36
  prenuptial agreements, 30, 31–33
    reasons for, 32
    relationship between investor and advisor compared to, 106
    validity of, 32–33
  second marriages and blended families, 20–21, 156–157
Merrill, Jacqueline, 13
Missile detection system, 255
Mission statement, personal, 13–15
Modern portfolio theory, 128–130
Money. *See* Wealth/money
Money managers. *See* Professional money managers
Monte Carlo Simulation, 137
Morris, Arthur, 179
Morris, Charles, 179
Morris, Victor, 179
Mortgage(s):
  collateralized mortgage obligations (CMOs), 143, 144, 150
  commercial mortgage-backed securities (CMBS), 143, 144, 145, 150
  government agencies, 143, 144, 145, 150
  REITs, 144–145
Multifamily private trust companies, 194

Museums, donating contemporary art to, 232–233

Nasdaq, 130
National Association for Corporate Art Management (NACAM), 231
National Association of Real Estate Investment Trusts (NAREIT), 147–148
National Business Aviation Association (NBAA), 237
National Center for Family Philanthropy, 67
Neuberger, Roy, 209
Neuberger & Berman, 46
Neuberger Museum of Art, 42, 47
Nonfinancial objectives of family, and trustee selection, 197, 200

Occupation, definition of, 9
Overton, Conrad, 111
Overton Worldwide Industries, 111

Paley, George, 42
Panic (Black Tuesday, October 29, 1929), 45
Panic buttons, 252
Parenting. *See* Children
Passant family, 191–196, 198, 205, 206
Personal information (keeping private), 254
Personal mission statement, 13–15
Personal/probable balance (investing), 137–138
Personal residence. *See* Home(s)
Personal security. *See* Security/safety
Philanthropy, 56–68
  capacity building, 59
  charitable lead trusts (CLTs), 64

Philanthropy *(Continued)*
  charitable remainder trusts
      (CRTs), 64, 159–160
  choosing your vehicle, 64–65
  creativity in, 59–61
  donor-advised funds, 65
  emotional satisfaction and social
      validation of, 4, 10
  family involvement, 24–25, 65–67
  family office and, 181
  finding charitable focus, 57–59
  monitoring/evaluating, 63–64
  parenting and, 24–25
  private foundations, 64–65
  rethinking current giving, 61
  sources for information, 66, 67
  "strategic" giving, 57
  "venturesome" donor, 60
Phillips, Ammi, 214
Picasso, 210
Planes, private, 236–241, 245–246,
      255
Pollock, Jackson, 45, 210
Porcelain, 217
Portfolio. *See* Investing/
      investment(s)
Postnuptial agreements, 35–36
Potter, Aaron and Ruth, 43
Prenuptial agreements, 30, 31–33
  reasons for, 32
  relationship between investor and
      advisor compared to, 106
  validity of, 32–33
Privacy of personal information, 254
Private equity funds, 131, 132, 175
Private foundations, 64–65
Private jets, 236–241, 245–246, 255
Private trust companies, 188, 194,
      203–204
Probabilities:
  assessing (in your portfolio), 137
  balancing personal objectives
      and, 137–138

Product channel trustees, 199–200,
      204–205
Professional advisors/consultants.
      See Financial advisors, team of
Professional money managers,
      99–110. *See also* Financial
      advisors, team of
  establishing expectations,
      106–107
  examining your biases/feelings
      about money, 101–102
    defining expected rate of
        return, 101
    defining risk, 101
  having more than one, 105–106
  monitoring, 107–108
  selecting, 102–104, 105, 109
Provenance, 219, 229
"Prudent" investing:
  defining, 164–165
  for family foundations, 164–178
  new look of, 166–167
Public officials (flying on private
      jets), 239–240

Qualified personal residence trust
      (QPRT), 142, 243

Real estate, 140–151
  asset allocation and, 125, 126
  direct equity ownership,
      146–147
  investment, 143–145, 147–150
  operating companies (REOCs),
      147
  options to purchase (keeping
      wealth out of marital estate),
      33–35
  personal residence (*see* Home(s))
  qualified personal residence trust
      (QPRT), 142, 243
  vacation homes, 210, 241–243,
      245

Regional Associations of Grantmakers, 67

REITs (real estate investment trusts), 143, 150
  equity, 147–150
  mortgage, 143, 144–145

Relationships. *See* Friendships, wealth and; Marriage

Remarriage, 20–21, 156–157

Reston Family Foundation, 60

Retirement, 48

Revere, Paul, 220

Revocable/irrevocable trusts, 155–156

Richman, Abe and Ida, 152

Richter, Gerhard, 223–224

Risk:
  asset allocation and, 127–128, 133, 136
  comparison of traditional portfolio mixes, and hedge funds/commodities, 133
  defining, 101
  diversification and reduction of, 127–128
  event, 144
  family office, and management of, 181
  professional money manager (selection of) and management of, 103
  real estate and, 144, 149
  sample portfolios for risk-averse investors, 136

Rituals, family, 27

Safety, personal. *See* Security/safety

Safety net, 15

Salant, Marie, 46

Second careers. *See* Career(s), changing

Second homes, 210, 241–243, 245

Second marriages and blended families, 20–21, 156–157

Security/safety, 248–258
  alarm systems, 251–252
  bodyguards, 255–256
  computer/data safeguards, 252–253
  gun ownership, 252
  home security survey, 252
  keeping personal information private, 254
  knowing your employees, 249–250
  objective (greater enjoyment of life), 256–257
  protective vehicles, 254–255
  traveling safety, 253–254

Self-selection bias, 131

Sharpe, William, 128

Sharpe Ratio, 128–129

Silver, 220

Spencer-Church, Sarah Consuelo, 219

Spouse/life partner, wealth and, 3, 4. *See also* Marriage

Staffordshire china dogs, 220

Standard Industry Fare Level (SIFL), 240–241

Stocks (and asset allocation), 126

Storr, Paul, 220

Strategic giving, 57

Strategic *vs.* historical methods (asset allocation), 127–128

Survivor bias, 131

Talking about money, 12–13, 81

Tax issues:
  asset allocation, 134–136
  deductions for donated art works, 232–233
  estate taxes and QPRT, 243
  management of taxable *vs.* tax-exempt accounts, 103

Tax issues *(Continued)*
  of private jet ownership, 239,
      240–241
  trusts, 154
  vacation home (possible benefits
      of), 242–243
Team:
  counseling, 117–120
  of financial advisors (*see* Financial
      advisors, team of)
Technologists, 115
Terrorism, threat of, 253–255. *See
    also* Security/safety
TIPS (Treasury Inflation Protection
    Securities), 125
TPI (The Philanthropic Initiative),
    63, 67
Traditional institutional trust
    companies, 194, 202–203
Travel safety, 253–254
Treasury bills, 127
Trust(s), 95, 152–163
  family foundations, 160–161
  family office and, 188
  incentives in, 158
  keeping wealth out of children's
      marital estates with, 33–35
  parenting issues and, 157–158
  private companies, 188
  professionals in, 95, 161, 188
  protecting children's inheritance
      with, 157–159
  revocable/irrevocable, 155–156
  second marriage with children,
      and, 156–157
  situs (location), 162
  solving portfolio problem with,
      159–160
  tax issues, 154
  teamwork, 162
  truth about, 154–155
  uses for, 155–159

values/goals (defining long-
    term), 161
Trustee(s)/fiduciaries, 161,
    191–208
  boutique or independent wealth
      management trust companies,
      194, 203–204
  corporate, 161, 193–194
  criteria (seven key) for
      fiduciaries, 197
    convenience/accessibility, 197
    cost control and efficiency, 197
    developing, 196–200
    loyalty and independence, 197,
        198–199
    multicompetence, 197
    privacy/security, 197
    promotion of family's
        nonfinancial objectives,
        197, 200
    responsiveness and flexibility,
        197, 198
  discovering/applying family's
      criteria, 194–195
  family fiduciary contract,
      206–207
  family unity and selection of,
      195–196
  individuals as, 202
  institutional, 194, 202–203
  multifamily private trust
      companies, 194
  perceptions of, by type, 202
  private/boutique trust
      companies, 194, 203–204
  product channel, 199–200,
      204–205
  six-step selection process,
      205–206
  strengths/weaknesses (by type),
      201–205
  types of, 193–194, 201–205

Uniform Prudent Investor Act (1997), 166
U.S. Treasury Bills, 125, 127

Vacation homes, 241–243
  estate taxes and QPRT, 243
  as investment, 245
  as "practical luxury," 210
  tax benefits, 242–243
Values:
  family:
    case illustration, 21–22
    communicating, 24–27
    defining, 22–24
  long-term (defining, for trusts), 161
Vanderbilt, Consuelo, 219
Vanderbilt, William K., 219
Van Gogh, Vincent, 44
Vehicles, protective, 254–255
Venture funds, real estate, 146
"Venturesome" donor, 60
Virus protection, 252

Wall Street crash of 1929, 45
Wealth category transition, 95–96
Wealth management, 95–98
  asset allocation, 122–139
  family foundations, prudent investing for, 164–178
  family offices, 179–190
  real estate, 140–151
  skills for, 112–117
  team of financial advisors, 111–121

trusts/trustees, 152–163, 191–208
working with professional money managers, 99–110
Wealth/money:
  dynamics of, 1–4
  emotional impact of, 1–4, 5–16
    avoiding isolation and alienation, 10–12
    making money easier to talk about, 12–13
    minimizing distortions, 7–9
    simplifying complications, 9–10
    stages of adjustment to wealth, 2
    writing personal mission statement, 13–15
  enjoying, 12, 209–211, 235–236, 246, 256–257 (see also Luxury(ies))
  family enterprises (conflicts in), 69–79
  family perspective on challenges of (see Family)
  magnifying vulnerability and suspicion, 8
  meaning of, to you, 23
  outsiders presumptions about, 2
  paradox of "money as power," 10
  social responsibility of (see Philanthropy)
  subgroups/classification, 95
Widener, Peter A. B., III, 216
Work, value of, 3–4, 42–49, 50–55

Yachts/luxury boats, 243–244, 245